Life's Highest Destiny

A Commentary on Romans

Ron Williams

Unless otherwise indicated, Scripture quotations are taken from the *New King James Version.* Copyright © 1979, 1980, 1982, 1990, 1995, Thomas Nelson Inc., Publishers.

Scriptures marked *NIV* are taken from the *Holy Bible*, *New International Version*®. *NIV* ®. Copyright © 1973, 1978, 1984 by International Bible Society. Used by permission of Zondervan Publishing House. All rights reserved.

Scriptures marked KJV are from the King James Version of the Bible.

Scripture quotation marked *RSV* are taken from the *Revised Starndard Version* of the Bible. Copyright © 1946, 1952, 1971 by the Division of Christian Education of the Nation Council of the Churches of Christ in the USA. Used by permission.

Scripture quotations marked *TM* are from *The Message*. Copyright © 1993. Used by permission of NavPress Publishing Group.

Scripture quotation marked *CEV* are taken from the *Contemporary English Version* of the Bible. Copyright © 1991, 1992, 1995 by American Bible Society. Used by permission.

Scripture quotation marked *NLT* are taken from the *Holy Bible, New Living Translation,* copyright © 1996. Used by permission of Tyndale House Publishers, Inc., Wheaton, Illinois, 60189. All rights reserved.

Book Editor: Wanda Griffith
Editorial Assistant: Tammy Hatfield
Copy Editors: Esther Metaxas
Cresta Shawver
Oreeda Burnette
Inside Layout: Mark Shuler

Library of Congress Catalog Card Number: 2002104242
ISBN: 0-87148-489-7

Cleveland, Tennessee 37311

Printed in the United States of America

DEDICATION . . .

To the memory of . . .

Dr. Leslie R. Eno,

who for 21 years was "Mr. Romans" at LIFE Bible College in Los Angeles. His passion for the Pauline Epistles, and in particular the first eight chapters of Romans, was contagious as well as challenging. He introduced me like a "blind date" to the apostle Paul and I will forever be grateful. Upon Dr. Eno's retirement, I assumed the role as the "New Mr. Romans," but never could I fill his shoes. He passed away in 1990.

To the memory of . . .

Dr. Clarence E. Hall,

the dean of LIFE Bible College for 20 years. One of the most beneficial classes I had was the Study of Ephesians, taught by this precious man of God, who at this writing is in his 90s and lives in Santa Fe Springs, California. It was Dr. Hall who showed me that there was a practicality about the epistles of Paul, that they pertained to life, not litany. He went to be with the Lord in 2002, having enjoyed a copy of the original manuscript of this book.

Dr. Ralph E. Hammon,

a professor and later, a colleague at LIFE Bible College. Dr. Hammon was an instructor at LIFE Bible College for 32 years. Upon his retirement in 1990, he requested that I assume his classes on the Holy Spirit. Throughout the years, Dr. Hammon has personified what a "man filled with the Word and the Holy Spirit" is all about. He now lives in Emmett, Idaho.

Contents

Foreword

I first met Ron Williams in 1961, when we were freshmen at LIFE Bible College in Los Angeles, California. We were classmates at our denomination's main ministerial institution.

One of the classes we shared was purposely designed to orient us into the academic side of college, which included preparing a term paper. It didn't take long for the professor to recognize Ron's obvious intelligence and ability in the area of writing. As a result, he was asked to be the professor's "TA," which included grading my term paper.

When my paper was returned, every page had red notes. I received a "B" for content and an "F" for structure, grammar and punctuation. Needless to say, it took some time to get over my relational crisis—I really didn't like Ron Williams. However, over the next four years (and now for 41 years), I have come to greatly respect, appreciate and admire this man who has become a lifelong friend and fellow minister.

One of the many things we had in common was our love for the Word of God, especially the Pauline Epistles and even more specifically, the Book of Romans. Our lives were mutually transformed by the revelation of God's grace, so wonderfully explained in that great letter. We experienced the breaking of legalism's chains as we discovered the liberating truth of justification by faith.

Dr. Leslie R. Eno, our instructor and one of those to whom this book is dedicated, was our hero. This man's passion for the first eight chapters of Romans impacted generations of students who later became pastors and leaders of our denomination. Not only was Ron one of the many who was forever changed, but now he himself has become a communicator, par excellence, of the spirit and truths found in that letter.

It was obvious God had placed His hand on this man's life and ministry. He would later use Ron as a pastor, church planter, missionary for 16 years to Hong Kong, a writer and a leader in the Foursquare denomination.

Ron's qualifications are also documented by his decade-long tenure as a college professor at his alma mater, where he was assigned to teach Romans to eager young "ministers in training." His ability as a writer has been developed through his editorship of our denomination's official voice, the *Foursquare World ADVANCE* magazine. He is also one of those upon whom our corporate leaders call when all types of communications need to be written. He truly is an exceptionally gifted writer.

There is no one in the Foursquare Church who is more respected, appreciated and sought out than Ron Williams. His wisdom, balance, insight, trustworthiness, dependability, communication skills and sense of humor are more than matched by his passion for Jesus Christ and the Word of God, accompanied by his depth of character, servant leadership and faithfulness.

The question has been raised, "Why another book on Romans?" We need a book like this because of the constant need to refresh the unparalleled presentation of God's redemptive gospel and the model of truth about life in Christ to today's generation. Also, there is a tendency for pastors to drift from presenting the "meat" of Scripture in their messages and study, opting to rely upon contemporary need-oriented illustrations that appeal to those looking for self-centered relevancy.

I enjoy the way Ron has achieved his goal of making Romans simple. The book insightfully puts Romans within reach of the common man, skillfully taking it out of the theologian's exclusive grasp and shattering the mystique that the letter is difficult to understand. Ron overwhelms us with what God has done in redeeming our lives. His style is uncomplicated, resisting the temptation of including many competing and confusing debates over the same text.

Unlike many other books, the questions Ron asks at the end of each chapter are thought-provoking, challenging, probing and usually hit spiritually sensitive nerves. I strongly recommend their use, especially as a devotional aid.

If you ever have a chance to meet Dr. Ron Williams, your initial response may be, "Why, he's just like a big teddy bear!" You will quickly recall his comments in the introduction of this book about the letter to the Romans being the same. You will immediately see the connection of the spirit of the man and the spirit of this book. He is personally what he writes about, and we are indebted for his writing "another book on Romans."

—Dr. Roger Whitlow
Senior Pastor
Valley Christian Center
Fresno, California

Introduction

"Oh no, not *another* book on Romans!" That's understandable. After all, just look in the doctrine section of any bookstore, and you will find volumes written about the longest of Paul's letters to the churches. Rightfully so! For nowhere else has the profound truth of God been condensed into 7,100 words so packed with meaning that its relevance is renewed with the rising of each day's sun.

Romans is the most powerful Christian literature of all time. While reading a passage from this letter, Augustine of Hippo was converted and Martin Luther came to grips with justification by faith alone. And look what that started! Hearing Luther's preface to this letter being read orally, John Wesley came to a living and loving relationship with Jesus. Because of the message of the Book of Romans, Karl Barth laid aside his liberalism to become one of the greatest Biblical theologians of our day.

For me, Paul's letter to the Romans has become an annual focus for verse-by-verse study for more than two decades. I count it a privilege to have taught its contents at LIFE Bible College in San Dimas, California, for nearly one of those decades. It is like a vein of precious ore that runs through the rocks of life, bringing new value to our faith and fresh motivation to our service.

"But," you ask, "why another book?" The answer is twofold: because so many of those students who studied Romans with me have pestered me unmercifully to put my understanding of the book in writing; and frankly, while being the most significant of Paul's letters, I consider the Epistle to the Romans to be the most misunderstood and misused letter in the New Testament. As I studied commentaries and treatises numerating all the theological themes that can be gleaned from it, I found four keys to understanding what the letter is all about.

First, the Book of Romans is a *letter* written to believers. It is not a theological textbook. While there are many streams of systematic theology throughout the book, it must be read as a letter. Oh yes, it is filled with God the Father, spoken of 153 times (that's once every 1.46 words). From chapters 1 to 5, we find the incarnate Christ. Who can miss the Holy Spirit in chapters 5 through 8? It deals with salvation and the sovereignty of God, the reason for the Law, and the freedom of grace. Yet, its contents are to be understood in the context of life, not liturgy; of everyday relevance, not religious philosophy or preconceived doctrinal judgments. A letter is to be read all the way through in one sitting. Try it with the Book of Romans. I'll guarantee two things: (1) it will take you approximately 57 minutes; and (2) it will change your view as to the reason for and relevance of the epistle.

Second, the Book of Romans is a letter written to reasonably *young* believers. If the letter was written around A.D. 57, and the church of Jesus Christ came into being around A.D. 33, then the most mature members in the Roman congregation had only 24 years of experience as believers and as church leaders. There seems to have been elements of syncretism in their religious worldview. They were dealing with problems in personal holiness and changing church patterns. Unlike today's Christian, these wonderful men and women did not have the Scriptures or the tomes of literature to assist them in their walk with Jesus Christ. What they did have was either Old Testament related, or orally received through the reading of letters to other believers. Paul's admonitions to them had to be clear, not confusing.

Third, the Book of Romans is a letter written to reasonably young believers, most of whom had very little education. Even in the world's premier capital city, education was limited to mainly men, in particular those males who could afford it. In understanding the early church, we must look past the learned philosophers and recognize that the bulk of the church was made up of ordinary, hardworking men and women (even slaves) who simply lived for Jesus and who lived for Jesus simply.

Fourth, like every other letter of Paul's, the Book of Romans is a letter written to reasonably young believers, most of whom had very little education, to call them to practical living, personally as individuals and corporately in relation to other believers. Paul's goal was not only to teach orthodoxy (what we believe) in creed but to encourage orthopraxy (how we are to act) in Christ. He begins with "obedience to the faith" in Romans 1:5 and ends with "obedience to the faith" in Romans 16:26. If Jesus was the obedient One (Romans 5:19; cf. 15:7), then to be Christlike was to be obedient in word and in deed.

If the above is true, then we must approach this letter through its simplicity, not its sophistication. Its message is clear, not complex. Its truth is to be demonstrated, not debated. And its principles must be proven in practice. The last half of the letter is just as important as the first. Actually, it is there you will find the letter's very purpose and rationale.

For years, I approached my study of the Book of Romans as a mountain climber, using a pick to chisel away at a theological glacier of ice. Then, one day, when I discovered the key to "making Romans simple," the ice melted and I found myself embracing the letter as a teddy bear. That's right, it became so simple, I knew I could take it to bed with me. Its softness reminded me of God's fabulous forgiveness from my past; its warmth assured me of His present provision of all I need to fulfill His plan, and its smile gave me hope for the future.

All over the Williams' living room, you will find teddy bears. No, they are not named after the epistles of Paul. But they do remind us of special places we have visited, newfound friends or how we have been touched in special ways. As you read this—another book on Romans—I trust there will be an added teddy bear to your heart's collection as well.

—Ron Williams

Chapter 1

A Date With Destiny

There are many definitions of destiny: "The right person in the right place at the right time with the right message." "You were made for this moment—for such a time as this . . . You're the right man (or woman) for the job . . . There's no one else who could do this like you do . . ." These are all phrases that bring the personality of the individual, the place of the event, a purpose greater than the immediate, and the passion of the moment into one point of time we might call "a date with destiny."

There's no more appropriate way to describe the circumstances surrounding Paul's letter to the Romans.

The Right Person

One of the most fascinating events in the Bible takes place in Acts 22, after Paul had caused an uproar among

Jews who claimed he brought Trophimus the Ephesian—a Gentile—into the Temple at Jerusalem. The Roman commander rescued the apostle from the mob's violence by bringing him back to the soldiers' barracks.

Initially asked about his identity, Paul explained, "I am a Jew from Tarsus, in Cilicia, a citizen of no mean city. . . ." He was allowed to address the crowd in Hebrew, and when he told them that Jesus had sent him to preach the good news to the Gentiles, all tumult broke loose. The commander ordered him back into the barracks. He told his men to interrogate Paul under scourging.

But as the apostle was being bound with leather thongs, Paul simply put his mouth up to the ear of a nearby centurion and innocently asked, "Is it lawful for you to scourge a man who is a Roman, and uncondemned?" (v. 25). Oops! Someone was going to pay.

The commander asked Paul how he came about the citizenship, and I can see the smile on Paul's face when he replied, "I was born a citizen" (v. 28). Things were different from then on.

But the intrigue doesn't stop there. Later, the Lord came to Paul and said, "Be of good cheer, Paul; for as you have testified for Me in Jerusalem, so you must also bear witness at Rome" (23:11). It is with this divine destiny in mind that later, when asked by Festus in Caesarea if he would be willing to face the music back in Jerusalem, Paul boldly demanded, "I stand at Caesar's judgment seat, where I ought to be judged. To the Jews I have done no wrong, as you very well know. For if I am an offender, or have committed anything deserving of death, I do not object to dying; but if there is nothing in these things of which these men accuse me, no one can deliver me to them. I appeal to Caesar" (25:10, 11).

Festus conferred with his advisers and then declared, "You have appealed to Caesar? To Caesar you shall go!" (v. 12). That was the first step to Paul's final sea voyage, which ended in disaster. But it did get him to Rome . . . finally. As a matter of record, from King Agrippa's own lips, we learn that Paul might have been set free had he not appealed to Caesar (26:32).

Writing to the church at Philippi, Paul affirmed his other side:

> If anyone else thinks he may have confidence in the flesh, I more so: circumcised the eighth day, of the stock of Israel, of the tribe of Benjamin, a Hebrew of the Hebrews; concerning the law, a Pharisee; concerning zeal, persecuting the church; concerning the righteousness which is in the law, blameless (Philippians 3:4-6).

Paul (formerly Saul) had been also born a Jew, from the lineage that had produced Saul, the first king of Israel. (Would I suggest that this man could have been named after the king, which was customary in those days?) He had been raised in the Hebrew language and religion and educated at the feet of Gamaliel (Acts 22:3) with the passionate devotion of a Pharisee! How Jewish can you get?

But the credential that impressed Paul the most was that he was "a bondservant of Jesus Christ, called to be an apostle, separated to the gospel of God" (Romans 1:1). He had met Jesus face-to-face on the road to Damascus, probably not for the first time. (Some believe Paul had been in Jerusalem and even witnessed the Crucifixion.)

When Jesus entered his life, everything changed. Paul began to fulfill the destiny that had been divinely outlined for him. Remember God's prophecy to Ananias about His plan for the new convert? "For he is a chosen vessel of Mine to bear My name before Gentiles, kings and the children of Israel. For I will show him how many things he must suffer for My name's sake" (Acts 9:15, 16).

You cannot separate the author's pen from his person, even under the inspiration of the Holy Spirit. In the same way that "out of the heart the mouth speaks," so out of the heart the hand writes. The character of the author determines the credibility of his proofs.

When Paul wrote his letter to the Roman believers, he had been a believer for nearly a quarter of a century. God had revealed the message of grace to him. He had been so fruitful in his missionary assignment, he had run out of places to preach in Asia Minor (Romans 15:19). But his vision had not paled—it had intensified. Now in his 50s, Paul was looking beyond Rome to the opening of new mission fields and was needing the Roman church's spiritual and financial support (vv. 23, 24). What a combination—the gray hair of experience coupled with the red-hot fervency of compassion for a lost and dying world.

Oh yes, I almost forgot. His destiny included suffering. Look at the list of credentials with which God had blessed him:

> In labors more abundant, in stripes above measure, in prisons more frequently, in deaths often. From the Jews five times I received forty stripes minus one. Three times I was beaten with rods; once I was stoned; three times I was shipwrecked; a night and a day I have been in the deep; in journeys often,

> in perils of waters, in perils of robbers, in perils of my own countrymen, in perils of the Gentiles, in perils in the city, in perils in the wilderness, in perils in the sea, in perils among false brethren; in weariness and toil, in sleeplessness often, in hunger and thirst, in fastings often, in cold and nakedness—besides the other things, what comes upon me daily: my deep concern for all the churches (2 Corinthians 11:23-28).

There is no shortcut that circumvents pressure and suffering on the road to eldership in the body of Christ. Still, these were not Paul's boasting points. His "crown of rejoicing" (1 Thessalonians 2:19) was the believers in the churches he had touched. The fact that they would be standing in the glorious presence of the Lord at His coming (v. 19) made his day, whether he was in chains or witnessing before rulers.

Paul was the perfect man for the job. With all the training, pedigrees and pastoral experience, he was still a man passionate in his love for Jesus and faithful to his commitment to Christ's calling upon his life. He was as much a "pray-er" as he was a preacher. Above all, he was a friend. Who cannot be moved by the reactions of the Ephesian elders who came to see Paul in Miletus during his stopover on the way to Jerusalem? Luke wrote this about Paul:

> And when he had said these things, he knelt down and prayed with them all. Then they all wept freely, and fell on Paul's neck and kissed him, sorrowing most of all for the words which he spoke, that they would see his face no more. And they accompanied him to the ship (Acts 20:36-38).

Have you ever formed an opinion about someone from hearsay, only to learn (after you had been with them for a while) that they were totally different? For years, I had always pictured Paul as a stern theologian, miracle-preacher and ecclesiastical strategist. At the risk of offending a few readers, I had pictured him about 5 feet, 4 inches tall, totally bald, with a pointed nose and piercing eyes that could send chills down your spine.

Most likely, during my first few days in heaven, after having worshiped the Lord in "the beauty of holiness," I will look around and spot a man matching that description. I will walk up to him and say, "Paul?" and he will answer, "No, my name is Charlie." Then from behind, I will hear a warm, gracious voice from a gentle giant who is 6 feet, 2 inches tall, and I will turn and meet my friend, Paul the apostle.

I don't know what Paul looked like, but I have come to know him through his writings in an intimate way. And there could be no more appropriate person through whom the Holy Spirit could reveal God's message of grace than Paul, the Hebrew, the Roman, the Christian, the church planter, the teacher, and above all, the spiritual father to those he had "begotten . . . through the gospel" (1 Corinthians 4:15). Even though we don't know the details of Paul's marital status, we do know he had an immense spiritual family.

The Right Place

The letter to the Romans was probably written between A.D. 55 and 57, while Paul was staying in Corinth. According to Acts 20:3, Paul came to Greece shortly before his return to Jerusalem. He was staying at the house of Gaius (see Romans 16:23), who was baptized by Paul during a previous visit (see 1 Corinthians 1:14). Traveling with him were Timothy, Lucius, Jason and Sosipater (Romans 16:21). In Corinth, he was entertained by Erastus, treasurer of the city, and by another spiritual brother by the name of Quartus.

The city of Corinth had become the marketplace of Asia and Europe. It was the port of commerce and with its strategic location came wealth, luxury and immorality. The center of Corinthian worship was Venus, the goddess of love or licentious passion. A temple to Venus was built on the slope of the Acrocorinthus, located above the city. Over 1,000 prostitutes served before the altar; for donations to the temple, they served the lusts of foreign merchants who arrived in the city with much, but left with little.

According to some historians, Corinth also became the most morally perverted, dissipated and corrupt city in the world. On the other hand, it was distinguished for its literature and cultural refinement.

Paul had first come to the city in A.D. 52 (see Acts 18:1). He worked as a tentmaker and preached in the synagogue every Sabbath. One of his first converts was Crispus, the ruler of the synagogue and his family. Because of a vision from the Lord, Paul remained there for 18 months, teaching the Word of God. He saw the Lord's promise come to pass, that He had "many people in this city" (v. 10).

While he was in Corinth, Paul met Priscilla and Aquila, Jewish Christians from Rome, expelled three years earlier (A.D. 49) by Claudius the Roman emperor. They too were tentmakers, and the apostle stayed and worked with them. It is interesting to note that Priscilla and Aquila accompanied Paul to Ephesus and then returned to Rome, where their house became one of the key meeting places for the church (see Romans 16:5). According to Paul's own words, sometime during the stay in Corinth or in Ephesus, an event took place where this couple literally put their necks on the line for the apostle's life (vv. 3, 4).

Unfortunately, as time passed, the corruptness of the city also entered the thinking and practices of the church. Paul wrote to correct the problems that existed. As a matter of fact, two or three letters had been dispatched. Now, just before he goes to Jerusalem, he again visits the Corinthian believers to see how they are doing, as well as to invite them to participate in an offering to assist the "mother church" in Jerusalem.

It is very natural that Paul's mind would turn to his friends and fellow tentmakers now back in Rome. Paul was deeply motivated to visit the capital of the world and see what God was doing among the believers there.

At the time of Paul's writing, much was transpiring in Rome. In A.D. 49, Claudius had expelled all Jewish people from Rome. There was a tumult over one called "Christos." Whether or not this unrest was over the gospel or simply a conflict caused in the synagogue is not certain. It is known, however, that around this time Jewish nationalism was rampant, and Palestine was a thorn in Rome's flesh.

The church in Rome was probably founded by those present in Jerusalem on the Day of Pentecost (Acts 2). They had witnessed the outpouring of the Holy Spirit and had been some of the 3,000 who believed on the Lord Jesus and were baptized in His name (v. 41). These Roman Jews returned home and founded the capital city church. We are made aware that the congregations were made up of both Jews and Gentiles and that there were, at least, four congregations that met in various homes.

As mentioned above, one of the congregations gathered in the home of Priscilla and Aquila, who had hosted Paul in Corinth. The couple also accompanied Paul on part of his second missionary journey and were very influential in the establishment of the church at Ephesus (18:18-28).

When the Jews returned to Rome during Nero's rule in A.D. 53, they found new Gentile control of the church. Dissension arose over matters of indifference; each group was defining themselves by their differences rather than their acceptance of Christ. The Jews who had originally founded the church became immediately appalled that "those Gentiles" had made massive changes in worship format and lifestyle standards. Their response was, "We never did it this way before!" And, of course, they considered themselves to be the strong in faith.

The Gentiles, who had by necessity assumed leadership in the church, had ceased "doing all those silly things demanded by the previous generation of leaders." And, of course, they considered themselves to be strong in faith, for they didn't maintain all the legalism the Jewish leaders had promoted.

There needed to be unity, not uniformity; acceptance, not accusation; deference, not dispute. Otherwise, political problems might redevelop. Thus Paul warns the believers to submit to authorities (Romans 13:1-7) and to one another (14:1—15:7).

The Right Time

Within seven years of receiving this letter, the church at Rome became the object of severe persecution by the emperor Nero, who blamed the Christians for the fire of Rome in A.D. 64. Paul had heard of the Romans' faith, which was "spoken of throughout the whole world" (Romans 1:8), and longed to see them. There was a sense of importance that both Paul and the believers in that city be "encouraged together" (v. 12) by a mutual sharing of faith. There were also some misconceptions that had appeared in the Roman congregations and needed attention.

Could it be that the apostle sensed the signs of the time? We tend to overlook the fact that during Paul's stay in Rome in the early 60s (A.D. 60, that is), there was another apostle in spiritual "Babylon"—Peter. By that time, due to increasing persecution, Jewish believers had already been "dispersed" to Pontus, Galatia, Cappadocia, Asia and Bithynia (1 Peter 1:1). The Holy Spirit moved upon Peter to write to them with a message of hope, which seems to emanate directly from the verbage and writing style that Paul uses in the letter to the Romans.

Some expositors suggest that Peter was acquainted with Paul's writings. But where could one more aptly come to appreciate another author's writings than to spend time with the author himself? I would have loved to have been a fly on the wall of Paul's house arrest as these two spiritual giants got together to compare notes and experiences. Talk about war stories . . . wow! And according to tradition, both of them died within a few years of each other by martyrdom in that great city.

Somehow, whether by human intuition or divine illumination, Paul knew his destiny would be completed in Rome. Oh yes, he had the vision to travel on to Spain (see Romans 15:19-24). To do so he would need their support, spiritually and financially. It is doubtful whether Paul ever reached Spain. In A.D. 60, he arrived in Rome as a prisoner; for the next two years, he remained in Rome, kept under guard in his private home with permission to receive visitors and to share the gospel (Acts 28:16-31).

By the way, those who have a heart for missions find a way to share the gospel wherever they are. As one of my good friends, Dr. Don McGregor, used to say, "If you know how to use your dining room table and your front room sofa, you'll never lack the opportunity for evangelism."

However, with his sense of destiny came another sense . . . one of urgency. Before Paul could visit Rome, he had to make a trip to Jerusalem. The Holy City where it all began was now in political upheaval. Peril loomed on the horizon. There was the rise of nationalism, assassins, zealots and economic chaos. All of this would come to a climax with the fall of Jerusalem in A.D. 70, when the Roman general, Titus, would march through the city leaving no stone unturned.

The "mother church" was in trouble, and Paul felt a moral obligation toward that congregation. The believers in Greece and Achaia had given an offering to assist the Jerusalem church, and Paul felt compelled to take the funds to them. It was more than an obligation, it was a *debt* and a *duty* (Romans 15:27) that far exceeded the provision of money.

But every time Paul had revisited the church in Jerusalem he seemed to get on their blacklist. Now, with this very solemn task, he asks the church in Rome to pray with him that he would be delivered from his old cronies—the unbelievers in that city—and that the church would graciously receive this act of love and reconciliation (vv. 30, 31). Only then could he come to Rome having "sealed" (v. 28) his relationship with his fellow countrymen. A final gesture was being made. It was no ordinary trip to visit friends and family back home!

Seeing the importance of the times, knowing the shortness of the hour and recognizing an urgency to settle all personal accounts, Paul did end up in Rome and while in prison testified, "I have fought the good fight, I have finished the race, I have kept the faith" (2 Timothy 4:7). Sometime between A.D. 63 and 65, the apostle was led out of the city of Rome and beheaded.

By the way, whose greatness has lasted the passing of time, Paul's or Nero's? People today name their sons Paul and their dogs Nero. Think about it!

LESSONS ANYONE?

1. Can you remember a time when you were the right person at the right place? Share it with a family member or a friend today.
2. Relate a time when other people showed up in your life at just the right place and the right time.
3. Looking back over your life, how has God prepared you for this moment or season in your life?
4. Prayerfully write out the purpose for which God has placed you where you are today.

Chapter 2

The Right Message

I shall never forget the night of June 10, 1997, and the opportunity I had to speak at the National Convention of our Foursquare Church in Hong Kong and Macao. My wife, Carole, and I had served 16 glorious years in that British Crown Colony, from 1969 to 1985, and had come to love the Chinese brothers and sisters immensely. We had seen the various congregations planted and matured, and the final service of that convention became a satisfying experience, remembering the victories and the challenges that had been confronted and overcome.

As I stood on the platform, I thought back to years before, when we first learned that Hong Kong would come under the sovereignty of the People's Republic of China on July 1, 1997. There had been the initial shock of the announcement, followed by years of strategic and deliberate preparation for whatever that date would mean for the believers under our shepherding. The concept of home cell groups, discipleship and the ministry of the laity had been carefully and prayerfully taught. Now, after several years, I was to bring one of the concluding messages before the changeover would occur.

The wastebasket in my office was filled with paper where I had tried to gather my thoughts, but had failed. This was not to be an ordinary service, but one which could have extensive, even eternal significance. Being one of their spiritual fathers, my words would be recalled and repeated, possibly during times of great persecution and duress. During times of discouragement and even facing the eventuality of death, what I was about to share could mean the difference between men and women remaining faithful or recanting the faith. Last words are usually the first to be remembered.

Finally, after much struggle, the message came. Six months later, in December following the changeover, Carole and I were able once again to visit Hong Kong, China, and discover that what many had feared had not, nor has it, come to pass. The church in Hong Kong is alive and well, and we are praying that the preaching of the gospel will continue to have free course.

What was my message on that first week of June 1997? It was all about hope, one of the major "brushstrokes" Paul included in his letter to the Roman believers. Seven years following the writing of this letter (A.D. 64), fire would destroy major portions of the city of Rome; Nero would blame this fire on the Christian community. Persecution resulted, and all of us remember the horror stories of the catacombs, the lighting of the city streets by burning believers (literally), and the excitement of the gladiator games where skins of animals would be wrapped around the Christians to be attacked by wild animals.

Whether or not the apostle was fully aware of what lay before the believers in that city is not certain. But the Holy Spirit was, and there was a sense of urgency as well as unction about the message He brought through Paul to prepare them for that time.

The "golden brushstrokes" of hope are painted throughout the entire letter. In Romans 4:18, there is an explanation of hope. The promise of hope given to Abraham, that he would be the "father of many nations," was totally contrary to what the patriarch could perceive, but he based his hope on the integrity and surety of God's person (see v. 21).

There is the experience of hope expressed in Romans 5:2, 4, 5, resulting from the process of pressure that leads to consistency and character. It is fully based on the "love of God [which] has been poured out in our hearts by the Holy Spirit who was given to us" (v. 5) and will never disappoint us. That's why we can rejoice "in the hope of the glory of God" (v. 2), the possibility of fulfilling all He has created and now recreated us to be.

Hope also brings expectation (8:20, 24, 28). Paul uses the terminology of the maternity ward and the concept of labor pains. Those challenges we experience, in particular the problems, are to be birth pangs rather than death throes, catapulting us into new levels of maturity and spiritual life.

Such hope elicits emotion (12:12). In the *New English Bible*, this verse is translated "Let hope keep you joyful." In the same way the "joy of the Lord is your strength" (Nehemiah 8:10), so the joy of the Lord comes from understanding the hope that lies before us.

Finally, hope is to be extended to others (Romans 15:4, 13). Whereas the Scriptures written before had come through patience and comfort so we might have hope, now we must encourage one another that "the God of hope fill you with all joy and peace in believing" (v. 13).

Add to this the red brushstrokes of the death and resurrection of Jesus, the ivory hues of righteousness, the browns of human sin and weakness, the blues of divine processing, the greens of mercy and grace, and the overarching brilliance of "obedience to the faith" (1:5; 16:26); and the mural of our destiny becomes explicit with splendor and majesty.

In addition to the overarching brushstrokes, the apostle addresses numerous important subjects, such as the truth of original sin, justification by faith, the relationship of Israel and the Law to the gospel of grace, the definition and description of a living sacrifice, the relation of the believer to the state, and living in the light of the return of Christ. There is the delineation of spiritual gifts and natural abilities (talents), both of which are supernatural and come from God. And the list continues.

But the key to unlocking the letter is found toward its end, when Paul addresses the matter of the weak and the strong (14:1—15:7). Dissension had presented its ugly face over the way the church, now under Gentile leadership, was conducting itself. No longer did it follow the legalism of the Law, which the Jewish leadership had imposed on it from its founding 24 years earlier. At the same time, the new leadership was not being sensitive to the negative impact that change without graciousness had upon the weaker believers. Paul writes to remind them that even though they were free in Christ, they were still debtors to those who were weaker in the faith. Thus, they were to consider themselves so free that they wouldn't have to demand all their own rights, in order to bring unity to the church.

Paul's Approach

The apostle accomplishes this purpose in the systematic format of a lawyer, proving that whether you are Jew or Gentile, adhering to the law of Moses or the law of the land, all have equally received the mercy and grace of the Lord Jesus.

In Romans 1:1-7, Paul states that the gospel of God that was promised through the prophets, provided through Jesus Christ, was to be for "obedience to the faith among all nations" (v. 5). In verses 14-16, he describes himself as a debtor to both Greeks and barbarians, because the gospel is the power of God both for the Jew and for the Greek.

Verses 18-32 inform us of the guilt of the irreligious Gentiles, followed in chapter 2 about those religious Jews, who through their religiosity defamed God, because they sought praise from men and failed to realize that obedience to God is of the heart, not through legislation. Thus, according to 3:1-20, the whole world is guilty before God.

Now comes the good news: "Now the righteousness of God . . . which is through faith to all and on all who believe . . . has been revealed" (see 3:21, 22—4:25). Abraham is not only the father of the Jews, but he is the father of the faithful, even us Gentiles. All of us have been justified on the same basis, not of our worth, but of Jesus' work on the cross.

By the way, if you and I are equally guilty, yet equally justified, not because of anything we have done, then how dare we put up boundaries as to who are our brothers and sisters? It confronts our prejudice and self-righteousness. It is all because of God's mercy, isn't it?

Having peace with God, we then read that there is "much more" in our Christianity: it is to be a life of obedience that can only be realized as the Holy Spirit does His work in and through us (see Romans 5—8). We do not have to yield to sin because we have changed masters, and the master we now serve is much better than the old (ch. 6). We serve, not out of necessity, but of willingness (ch. 7) and through the power of God's processing Spirit within us (ch. 8). We have been saved by God's love and nothing will separate us from it. We are His people.

The principle is the same for the nation of Israel. Throughout its history, God's mercy sovereignly sustained Israel (ch. 9). Even though they are disobedient, divine mercy is still outstretched toward them (ch. 10). And in the future, God has an amazing mercy that will bring them back to the purpose for which they were originally called (ch. 11).

Ouch! Since God does not see us simply as we are, why should we feel such toward one another? We are all still in the process of becoming! What matters is not how we get there, but what we will look like when we finish. It will not be by anything we accomplish for Him, but what He accomplishes in us. Mercy requires that we do not demand from others what Christ does not demand from us!

Who are living sacrifices? Those who rest on the mercy of God (which the first part of the letter has explained), and those who are merciful (which the rest of the letter will explain). From chapter 12, we learn that in all of us, the fruit of the Spirit will give credibility to our giftedness.

Chapter 13 instructs us to walk with respect for authority, responsibly loving and in light of the Lord's return.

Then Paul really hits home. In light of the mercy and grace God has bestowed upon us, if we think we are the ones who are spiritually strong (mature), then we have just lined ourselves up for accountability. Rather than judging those whom we think are still unspiritual, we are to be the ones who must take the responsibility of nurturing them. It becomes a matter of acceptance rather than accusation. Moreover, they will be answering to God, not us; and we will be answering to God for our attitude toward them. Remember, the kingdom of God is not cultural adherence or preference, but righteousness of character, peace of mind and joy in service. Thus, rather than criticism, let us pursue those things that bring unity.

Does this mean that I am so free in Christ that I would not do certain things simply because of their possible impact on others? Am I their servant? That's exactly what Christ did (15:1-7).

To be a saint of God demands that we be servants of others. In the rest of chapter 15, Paul shares his personal testimony. And in chapter 16, he talks about those in Rome who are role models of what he has been trying to describe. All of them were servants.

He then concludes: "Now I urge you . . . be wise in what is good, and simple concerning evil. . . . Now to Him who is able to establish you according to my gospel . . . made known to all nations . . . for obedience to the faith—to God, alone wise, be glory through Jesus Christ forever" (vv. 17, 19, 25-27).

During a recent visit to China, I had the opportunity of interacting with officials in a major northern city of 100,000 inhabitants. In today's China, there are less than 30 million members of the Communist Party. It appears that with increased contact with the Western world and its values, lifestyle and luxuries, China's youth have now rejected the party for the partying—the commercialism and hedonism of Western culture. They have turned from the Mao-jackets to Levis, from the red bandannas to gold chains around their necks and gold pins in their ears and noses. Government officials are sacrificing the "Red Book" for English-language textbooks, so their professionals and businesspersons can compete on the world market.

In today's China, there are more than 70 million believers in Jesus Christ, some worshiping in the official government church and others in unregistered home meetings throughout the nation.

If this is true, in today's China, there are more than twice as many believers in Jesus Christ than those who hold to the party line. One leader, himself a member of the party who grew up through the educational systems established during the cultural revolution, admitted, "The greatest need of Chinese youth today is to find something to believe in." When asked what that should be, he responded, "I don't know, and neither do they." Later, during our time together, I had the opportunity to share the message of Jesus Christ with him.

What was it that caused the church in China to grow from less than 2 million in 1949 to more than 70 million in 1999? Remember, their pastors were imprisoned and church buildings confiscated.

According to Chinese church leaders who endured that era, it was the fact that Chinese believers recognized that the basis of Christianity was a relationship with Jesus Christ, which resulted in a relationship with one another. The strength of the church was not the proclamation from the pulpit, but the mutual support of the saints who cared for one another. Again, their communities reiterated the words of the Caesars who watched the martyrs die: "My, how they love one another!" They came to salvation through Jesus because of the sincere compassion and unity of those who shared His name and message through love and life.

Our society and the times in which we are living are beginning to look more like A.D. 57! Whether in China or California, Damascus or Denver, Calcutta or Chicago, Rome or Reno, the church of Jesus Christ will only be renewed as Biblical relationships are restored. The believer in Jesus Christ will only mature as the church begins to experience cross-generational understanding and servanthood. The world will only respond to arms that are open, not opinionated.

I love to call Christian writing the "Ministry of the Second Look." It is different from oral speech. Whereas oral speech is to be applied within the context of the original setting in which it was spoken, written speech can also be applied within the context of the present setting in which it is read. Each time you read the content, you can glean fresh nuances and insights. In addition, it can be received for years, decades—even centuries—following. The "Ministry of the Second Look" has the privilege of combining history with prophecy.

There is no greater example than Paul's letter to the Romans. For as we open its pages, we discover the *right* message for the *right* time. It is written to all who have been declared *right* in the grace of our Lord.

LESSONS ANYONE?

1. Read through the letter to the Romans in one sitting. As you do, list at least eight "brushstrokes," or themes, that seem to reappear throughout the letter.
2. Why are those "brushstrokes" especially important for you today?
3. How is hope maintained? Why is it important for a person to maintain hope for today? For tomorrow?
4. Where do you stand on your "hope chart" at this moment? What factors are impacting your feelings?

Chapter 3

God's Design—Our Destiny

Romans 1:1-17

In 1975, when the renowned author, Aleksandr Solzhenitsyn, visited the United States, he told about his imprisonment in Russia. One of the hardest things to endure was the silence of the jailers. Prisoners were forbidden to speak.

A fellow prisoner noticed the effect it had on Solzhenitsyn. With each succeeding day, Aleksandr became weaker and more depressed. Finally, without saying a word, this man took a stick and drew a cross in the dust.

Solzhenitsyn looked. Immediately, he remembered his destiny. Because of the tremendous price his triune God had paid at Calvary, he had everlasting life and an eternal inheritance. The silence between his soul and God was broken. He realized once again that even in his imprisonment, God wanted him to make it.

That's the very first point the apostle Paul wanted to impress on the believers in Rome.

Paul—the Servant

As he begins his letter, Paul identifies himself with descriptions that are of the highest value to him. Above all, he is a servant of Jesus Christ.

As Dunn suggests: "Paul, with deliberate emphasis, introduces himself to the capital of the empire not as a citizen proud of his freedom, but as the slave of a crucified Jewish messiah"[1]

Paul can neither fathom nor forget the difference Jesus has made in his life. Since that day on the road to Damascus, his Savior has been the central theme in Paul's thoughts and endeavors. In these first seven verses, the name of Jesus Christ appears four times. To Paul, Jesus is the master, the fulfillment of every Old Testament promise; the Son of God—the very expression of divine intervention in the history of humankind; and in particular, the One who set him on the road to a redeemed destiny. Like a king issuing the invitation to come to a meal, Paul has been called to a place of great honor and dignity.

To be a servant of Jesus Christ carries two implications: great authority and intimate relationship. It is a unique but demanding role. The phrase is parallel to the appellation "Servant of Jehovah," a phrase used only in connection with the prophets in the Old Testament. On the other hand, the acceptance of that role is motivated by love and choice. The bond servant in the Scriptures had been a slave who had been released to do as he wished, yet still chose to serve his master. To Paul, simply serving Jesus is the highest credential any person could have.

Paul—the Apostle/Pharisee

The invitation King Jesus had issued the writer of this letter has a divine purpose. The price of Paul's feasting on the Lord's table carries with it a price. To Paul, being one sent with a commission implies that his responsibility is to the One who sent him—God (see Galatians 1:10).

I especially enjoy the inference when Paul states he is "separated to the gospel of God" (Romans 1:1). The root of the verb *separated* indicates that in the same way he had been a zealous Pharisee in the past, he is still a Pharisee—this time with an even greater zeal for the good news of Jesus, the fulfillment of all the holy promises, prophecies and pictures that had been part of God's revelation from the very beginning of time.

Jesus was the Son of God—divine; Jesus was of the lineage of David according to human genealogy—a royal prince. The writer to the Hebrews says it well:

> God, who at various times and in various ways spoke in time past to the fathers by the prophets, has in these last days spoken to us by His Son, whom He has appointed heir of all things, through whom also He made the worlds; who being the brightness of His glory and the express image of His person, and upholding all things by the word of His power, when He had by Himself purged our sins, sat down at the right hand of the Majesty on high (Hebrews 1:1-3).

During His earthly ministry, Jesus said, "Believe Me because of the works that I do" (see John 10:38; 14:11). He lived a life that could only be possible by a divine and holy nature. But what proved beyond a doubt that Jesus had been appointed and defined as the Son of God was His resurrection from the dead. Whereas, on the cross,

Jesus declared "It is finished" in relation to His mission, it was in the garden of the Resurrection, early that Easter morning that God declared, "It is finished" in relation to our redemption, satisfying all that was demanded by His righteousness and justice.

Paul—the Recipient of Grace

It is also through Jesus Christ, God's Son, that Paul received the wherewithal (grace) to be obedient to the faith. Through Jesus Christ, God's Son, Paul received an assignment in making others obedient to the faith, even from all nations (*ethne*). Character and ministry can never be separated; ministry and vision will always emanate from what we are, rather than what we do.

As a matter of fact, the believers in Rome shared this same heritage and assignment. They too had been called to the banqueting table of commission, were divinely and intimately loved by God, and were on the road to becoming *saints*—as set apart in practice as they were in their spiritual position before God. It should be noted that in the New Testament, the word *saints* is never used in the singular, but always in the plural form. When individuals come to know Jesus, they are never saved in isolation, they are saved in relation to all who have made the same confession of Christ. They have become part of a community set apart for God. Independence in spirit has no place in the dictionary or vocabulary of the redeemed.

Paul—the Friend

Romans 1:8-16 is filled with a relational vocabulary. Paul's feelings are stated in such terms as *thank* (v. 8);

mention (v. 9); *long* (v. 11); *comforted* (v. 12, KJV); *purposed* (v. 13, KJV); *want you to know* (v. 13, *NLT*); *debtor* (v. 14); and *not ashamed* (v. 16). Not only is Paul's connection with the Roman church through his friends, Aquila and Priscilla, but also through his friend, Jesus. In every letter except one, Paul commended the believers for all or some of three qualities: faith, hope and love. When he wrote to the believers in Galatia, he was absolutely stunned that many were abandoning their faith.

In the case of the Romans, he was thankful to God for His work in them—that faith had resulted; and for His work through them—that their faith was spoken about throughout the then-known world. Like Paul, they too had received grace and apostleship.

Paul prays for the Romans. This is not an appendage to Paul's apostleship, it is an integral part of it. In this letter, he prays for the recipients without ceasing. In another letter, he thanks God that the Corinthians were blessed with abundant gifting (1 Corinthians 1:4-7). He prays that the eyes of the Ephesian believers would be enlightened (1:16-23). He prays for God to strengthen those same people in their inner life (3:14-19). He prays that the love of the Philippian believers would abound, and that they would have greater spiritual discernment (1:9-11). He continually prays for the believers in Colossae, that they would know God's will through wisdom and spiritual understanding (1:9-12).

In his first letter to the church at Thessalonica, Paul intercedes on behalf of the pressures they were experiencing (1:2-7). He prays that he might see them and provide understanding that is lacking in their faith (3:9, 10). In his second letter to the Thessalonians, the apostle prays they would become a people of hope; that God would fulfill His goodness in them and that a work of faith with power would be their portion (1:11).

He encourages Timothy to make supplications, prayers, intercessions and thanks for all men, including kings and those in authority, that the believers might lead a quiet and peaceable life in godliness and dignity (1 Timothy 2:1, 2). Even in the very last letter Paul writes to his son in the faith, there is the reminder that the apostle remembers Timothy in prayer day and night (see 2 Timothy 1:3-5).

Without doubt, what made Paul the great expositor and miracle-worker in his public preaching was his praying in private. God's integral work within Paul was prayer; Paul's outward ministry resulted in the testimony of others. By the way, wasn't that the pattern our Lord followed?

Paul prays that he would be able to come to Rome by the will of God (Romans 15:32). The purpose of his visit seems to be threefold: he wanted to make a spiritual deposit in their lives; he needed to be encouraged by their faith; and, according to verse 24, he sought their support for his journey to Spain.

I like the words of John Calvin, who wrote, "Note how modestly Paul expresses what he feels by not refusing to seek strengthening from inexperienced beginners."[2] I am reminded of the discussion between John the Baptist and Jesus. When John first heard Jesus' request to be baptized of him, he refused, stating that it should be the other way around. Jesus rebuked him, saying, "This is the right thing to do" (see Matthew 3:13-17).

The greatness in a man or woman of God will never be in their exploits or their press releases. The authenticity of their spiritual authority and giftedness will always be understood in their interdependency on and cooperation with others. Paul clearly understood the mutuality of faith.

Paul—the Debtor

Romans 1:14 begins a series which some have called the "I Ams" of Paul. Because of the grace and mission God had placed in his life, he writes . . .

- "I am a debtor" (v. 14).
- "I am ready to preach" (v. 15).
- "I am not ashamed of the gospel" (v. 16).

To be a debtor leaves no room for feelings or choice. A debt is what someone owes, morally and by obligation. Throughout this letter, Paul reminds us that one of the fruits of being a recipient of grace is that we become debtors. First of all, we become debtors to the world around us (v. 14). Because of the work of the Holy Spirit, we are indebted to God to live righteously by the divine power within us (8:12). And because of the impartation of grace which we have received through others, we are obligated to support them in time of need (15:27).

If we were to tell the church of today that it is indebted to the world, we'd probably hear many say, "I don't think so!" In the attitude and actions of many believers, the world should be indebted to us! Too often, our being salt and light in a sick and fallen world has deteriorated to demanding our rights. We expect the world to make room for us and heed to standards that fallen men and women can neither comprehend nor keep. In some cases, we turn to civil disobedience (an oxymoron, for civil disobedience can neither be civil nor obedient), and when arrested, demand our rights. We recoil in anger when the world calls us intolerant. We so conveniently forget the heart of Stephen as he was being stoned: "Lord, do not charge them with this sin" (Acts 7:60). Sounds like another morning when the Son of God prayed, "Father, forgive them, for they do not know what they do" (Luke 23:34).

It is of no small significance that standing there consenting to young Stephen's death was the apostle himself when he was known as Saul. Most likely, one of the key events that led to Saul's later conversion was Stephen's attitude. Twenty-four years later, Paul stated that those who have received forgiveness are those who should most strongly feel indebted to all people—Greeks or barbarians (all nationalities), wise or unwise (all levels of society).

The acceptance of obligation created within Paul an eagerness to preach the gospel in Rome. It should also motivate us to share the gospel among those with whom we come in contact.

Paul—the Destined

Having been called, set aside, graced, commissioned, gifted and motivated, the apostle declared his pride in the power of the gospel. "Not being ashamed" is a theme that recurs throughout the letter. In 1:16, he is not ashamed of the gospel of Christ; in 5:5, hope that stems from the love of God will never make us ashamed or fail us. In 10:11, he who believes on Christ will never be put to shame.

William Barclay makes this comment: "Paul was imprisoned at Philippi; chased out of Thessalonica; smuggled out of Berea; laughed out of Athens; foolish at Corinth, yet not ashamed."[3] Just the opposite, he boasted or bragged about it. He was proud of it and had a positive conviction of its value and truth.

The gospel of Jesus Christ will never disappoint or fail us. It is the dynamite of God—dynamic power that has been part of God's plan from before time began. It is capable of overcoming any obstacles that stand in the way, and will effect great change in all those who believe. It includes deliverance from the past—the penalty of sin; it provides victory over the present—the power of sin; and one day, we will be released from sin's very presence. It includes all a person receives through faith in Jesus, from the moment he is declared righteous until he experiences in heaven all that he is anticipating by faith here on earth.

In the Old Testament, those who wished to make a sin offering brought a spotless lamb to be slain. As they presented the sacrifice to the priest, they placed their hands and weight on the animal as an expression of reliance, for the offering took on the burden of the offerer. In the Greek language, the word *believe* is always followed by the preposition *into,* implying a transition to the center of gravity—that of placing the weight of our future on the divine offering, Jesus himself. It requires taking a chance on God and then realizing that the chance was in reality a certainty.

Dunn writes: "It was not a matter of blind trust that such a power must be operative whatever the appearances, but rather a matter of actual experience marked by a visible and marked alteration in a current condition that could not be attributed to human causation."[4]

Paul takes this opportunity to establish a point of understanding. He reminds everyone that the gospel had come to the Jew first and then to the Gentile (Greek). This has to do with chronology, and it indicates a special relationship that God has preserved for the Jew.

God's righteous way of making man righteous is revealed in the gospel. He makes known His plan for acquitting men and women from their sin and admitting them to His gracious favor. Beginning and ending with God, His favor would never be known had God not shown it to us.

That delineates the difference between religion and revelation. Religion is man seeking God, determining the qualities the object of their search must possess. Revelation is God seeking man, and the divine Creator taking responsibility to bring that destiny to its fullness. Its origination is in the faithfulness of God and its culmination dependent on the faithfulness of God—from "faith to faith." It is us taking God at "face value" as well as at "faith value."

The writer then draws from history to put an exclamation point to this portion. Late in the seventh century B.C., the prophet Habakkuk demanded a frank answer from the Lord: "How long shall I cry, and You will not hear? . . . plundering and violence are before me; there is strife, and contention arises. Therefore the law is powerless, and justice never goes forth. For the wicked surround the righteous" (1:2-4).

Jehovah answered, "Look . . . be utterly astounded! For I will work a work in your days which you would not believe, though it were told you" (1:5). He then assured the prophet that wickedness would not prevail. Righteousness and those who are righteous would ultimately be vindicated. "The earth will be filled with the knowledge of the glory of the Lord, as the waters cover the sea" (2:14).

In the middle of His response, Jehovah called the prophet's attention to the fact that it would be those who are just that will make it, not the proud or the perverse. Just as the glory of the Lord would triumph, those who are righteous would declare, "I will rejoice in the Lord, I will joy in the God of my salvation. The Lord God is my strength; He will make my feet like deer's feet, and He will make me walk on my high hills" (3:18, 19).

Someone said, "Christianity is the only subject where the student is given a passing grade at the beginning of the course rather than the end." The emphasis of Romans 1:17 is not on the word *faith*, nor on the *just*. It is on the fact that we will make it. It is the delightful and divine destiny God has outlined for us!

John 3:16

One dark night in the city of Chicago, a blizzard set in. A little boy was selling newspapers on the corner while all others were out of the cold. The little boy walked up to a policeman and said, "Mister, you wouldn't happen to know where a poor boy could find a warm place to sleep tonight, would you? I sleep in a box around the corner and down the alley. It would be nice to have a warm place to stay."

The policeman responded, "You go down the street to that big white house and knock on the door. When they come to the door, simply say 'John 3:16.'" The little boy did as he was told, and a lady at the house said, "Come in, Son." She sat him down in a split bottom rocker in front of a huge fireplace and left the room. The little boy sat there for a while and then thought to himself, *John 3:16 . . . I don't understand it, but it sure makes a cold boy warm.*

The lady returned. "Are you hungry?" she asked. "Well, I sure could stand a little bit of food," the boy answered. The lady took him into the kitchen and sat him down at the table. He ate until he couldn't eat anymore. He thought, *John 3:16 . . . I don't understand it, but it sure makes a hungry boy full.*

The lady then took him upstairs to a bathroom where there was a huge tub filled with warm water. He soaked for a while, then thought, *John 3:16 . . . I don't understand it, but it sure makes a dirty boy clean. I've never had a real bath in all my life.*

The lad was then taken into a warm room and tucked into a big old feather bed. After pulling covers up around his neck, he was kissed goodnight. As he laid in the darkness and looked out the window at the snow falling, he thought to himself, *John 3:16 . . . I don't understand it, but it sure makes a tired boy rested.*

The next morning, following breakfast, the lady took out a Bible and asked, "Do you understand John 3:16?" The boy said, "No, ma'am, the first time I ever heard it was last night when the policeman told me to use it." Right there he gave his heart to Jesus and thought, *John 3:16 . . . I don't understand it, but it sure makes a lost boy feel safe.*

I don't understand it either, how God would be willing to make such a great sacrifice. But it sure does give life a fresh start . . . and a promised destiny.

LESSONS ANYONE?

1. State five words that describe your walk and/or service with the Lord.
2. What does each of the above descriptions imply? What obligations do they carry?
3. Describe the place prayer has in your "grace and apostleship." What priority does prayer have in your discipleship?
4. In your present experience as a believer or witness for Christ, state three "I ams" as a personal statement of commitment.

Chapter 4

Destiny Rejected

Romans 1:18-32

Some time ago, I heard the following story from a friend:

> I was flying from San Francisco to Los Angeles. By the time we took off, there had been a 45-minute delay. Unexpectedly, we stopped in Sacramento on the way. The flight attendant explained that there would be another 45-minute delay, and if we wanted to get off the aircraft, we would reboard in 30 minutes.
>
> Everybody got off the plane except one gentleman who was blind. I noticed him as I walked by and could tell he had flown before because his seeing-eye dog lay quietly underneath the seats in front of him throughout the entire flight. I could also tell he had flown this very flight before,

> because the pilot approached him and, calling him by name, said, "Keith, we're in Sacramento for almost an hour. Would you like to get off and stretch your legs?"
>
> Keith replied, "No thanks, but maybe my dog would like to stretch his legs."
>
> Picture this: All the people in the gate area came to a completely quiet standstill when they looked up and saw the pilot walk off the plane on the back end of the leash led by a seeing-eye dog! The pilot was even wearing sunglasses. People scattered. They not only tried to change planes, they were also trying to change airlines!

We laugh at this, but it is a perfect picture of humankind since the time of Adam. In Romans 1:17, we read that God's righteous way of making man righteous has been revealed from heaven. Now, we discover from verse 18 that there is a second aspect to that revelation; it is the wrath of God. In other words, we are either under the redemption of God because of our trust in Him, or we are under His wrath because of our guilt. Ernst Kaseman makes this observation:

> The nature of the world before Christ and outside Him is to stand in lostness, bondage, and rejection. . . . This is disclosed, not by two different revelations, but in one and the same act of revelation.[1]

Because it is revealed, it cannot humanly be discerned. It is ludicrous to expect the world to be the standard bearers of right conduct. Just the opposite; the world is totally incapable of establishing righteousness or even recognizing it. To rely on society or human goodness to make that change is like flying on an airplane with a blind pilot!

James D.G. Dunn adds: "Wrath is not something for which God is merely responsible, nor merely an attitude of God, but something God does."[2] It is the response of a holy God to the rebellion of sinful man. It is neither revenge nor hate, but a divine opposition to everything that is evil. God loves all His creation, but His holy nature cannot tolerate unrighteousness. He actually and actively opposes it; it is "against all ungodliness and unrighteousness of men" (v. 18).

C.E.B. Cranfield sums it up: "[God's] wrath is an expression of His love. Because He loves us truly, seriously and faithfully, He is wroth with us in our sinfulness."[3] If the great command is to "love the Lord your God with all your heart" (Matthew 22:37), then turning against Him becomes a violation of all His commands. There can be nothing more vile or vicious . . . and eternally disastrous.

How could humankind fall so far from their original destiny? It wasn't God's fault! While some expositors feel that Paul remembers the Genesis account, this scenario is being repeated in the life of every human being, even today. The fall of humanity was hard; it was real; and the extent of its toll multiplied in stages.

Suppression of the Truth (vv. 18 - 20)

The truth of God was surely clear. Note the verbs used in these three short verses: *revealed* (v. 18); *manifest*—making known that which had heretofore been present, yet not visible (v. 19); *shown*—making one capable of investigating His person and works; *clearly seen*—not only capable but actual; *being understood*—reason and conscience (v. 20); *known*—experienced (vv. 19, 21).

According to verse 20, the truth of God was His existence (invisible attributes); His eternal power; and His Godhead—His glory, majesty, supremacy and role as Creator. Looking at Romans 1:32, we become aware that they understood His justice (righteous judgment), including the penalty of the same.

There was no need for anything else. Plummer explains: "The reason why a miracle was never wrought to prove the existence and power of God was that creation fully evidenced both. If men will not believe the things that are made, they would not believe the things God might do."[4] For Adam and Eve, there was naivete, but there was no excuse. God had given them complete reign, rule and delight of the Garden, except for one tree. The serpent came along and immediately brought into question the truth of God's pronouncement ("You will not surely die," Genesis 3:4) and the integrity of His person ("For God knows . . . ," v. 5).

We often joke about the fact that when God caught Adam hiding in the Garden, the man said, "The woman made me do it!" The woman said, "The serpent made me do it." And the serpent didn't have a leg to stand on. But the fact of the matter is that all the serpent did was put up the advertising sign, and Adam and Eve together and equally bought the farm. It was called Sin and Death.

They not only hindered the truth; they rejected it. They willfully chose death and rejected life, in spite of all they knew to be true. Thus, they were without excuse. There need be no apology on God's part in punishing sin; nor can there be any apology on man's part for his ignorance and rejection.

Separation From the Light (vv. 21-23)

In making their choice, Adam and Eve immediately experienced the entrance of a new dimension in their lives. "Good" had already been there, but now the textbook for living included "Evil." They became acutely aware of everything they originally had not been destined to know.

The Fall was not simply "oops," it was deliberately opening the door for darkness to enter. Though they knew God, they did not give Him appropriate respect of reverence. They changed the center of deity to themselves rather than honor the One who was truly divine. They became unthankful and willfully refused to acknowledge God for the life and blessings they daily had received at His hands.

Paul also states that humanity became "futile in its thoughts." The word he used was far beyond his time. In today's vocabulary, *futile* could be translated "without focus." Rather than having their eyes and understanding sharply focused on that which was real, they turned clarity (v. 20) into speculation. The result was that their hearts became "foolish" and they wandered through life without clear focus of who they were, why they were there and to whom they were responsible. We will never get in touch with our inner self if we do not get in touch with the divine Savior.

How much of blind piloting do you want? When you already have the flight plan, you rip it up, ignoring the very principles of navigation. You tell the control towers you don't need them, then cover up the windows of the cockpit. You turn off the compass and rely on your instincts. The result is the plight of today's humanity!

Universalism says all religion is a road that leads to the same divine address. Paul stakes his claim to the contrary.

Rather than the worship of corruptible images concocted by human passion as a "discovery channel" to find God, it is humanity objectively and deliberately trying to establish a "family channel" to worship itself. It is absolute folly.

In the Wisdom of Solomon 13:11-14, the author writes:

> For health he [humanity] appeals to a thing that is weak; for life he prays to a thing that is dead; for aid he entreats a thing utterly inexperienced; for a prosperous journey, a thing that cannot take a step.

Plummer quotes Chrysostom:

> The first change is, that they did not find God; the second, that they failed to do so, although favored with the best and most manifest opportunities; the third, that they failed though calling themselves wise, and the fourth, that they merely did not find him, but degraded his worship to demons and stones.[5]

Much is being said about intolerant Christians. No, the most intolerant act is for the creation to turn such a jaundiced eye to the One who created it. The result of rebellion in the Garden was just the opposite of what the serpent said would happen. The result of rebellion in today's world will be just the opposite of what those wise fools are proposing. What makes it even more intolerable is that they boast about their reason (or should I say, chosen darkness).

Substitution for the Real (vv. 24-28)

The scary consequence was that "God gave them up" (see vv. 24, 26, 28). Adam and Eve, as well as every man, woman and child afterward, had been destined to have dominion over all of God's creation. But now, they become the dominated.

The phrase "gave them up" must be understood as God simply lifting His hands of restraint from them. He no longer protects them from themselves or from the consequences of their actions. The wisest man on earth once wrote, "Rejoice, O young man in your youth, and let your heart cheer you in the days of your youth; walk in the ways of your heart, and in the sight of your eyes; but know that for all these God will bring you into judgment" (Ecclesiastes 11:9).

When God's hand of restraint is removed, hell's fury unleashes its hand of rage against all those who are now left naked and vulnerable, at their own request.

A few years ago, I was asked to write an article for a New Age, left-wing magazine in Los Angeles. They wanted to know why a loving God would allow human beings to suffer with AIDS. At first, I thought about refusing the invitation, but then reconsidered. My response was that a loving God had done all He could to protect humanity from sin's consequences. But man asked Him to remove His hand and "shot himself in the foot." Suffering and AIDS were not God's choice; it was man's. The problem was not with a loving God, it was with a ludicrous humanity.

The term "God also gave them up" occurs three times in these five verses. In verse 24, God gave them up to uncleanness, to follow the lusts of their hearts and to dishonor their bodies among themselves. Because they had taken the truth back to the store and exchanged it for a lie, they became self-worshipers with no accountability. No longer was there a Creator to be worshiped or obeyed, just the evolution of natural selection.

The problem with the theory of evolution was not scientific discovery as opposed to the study of creationism; it was the fact that if today's humanity is only the result of a biological process, there is no source of accountability other than to humanity itself. Humanity has no hope in assuming the role as moral guides.

Because humanity no longer was accountable (v. 26), God lifted His hand and in came vile passions. Bodies and emotions that, like nature, were to reflect the glory of God, were turned into disgraceful receptacles of animal life forms, such as lesbianism, homosexuality, and all the other devices that degrade beauty into bestiality, loveliness into lust, and delight into degrading of all that is decent and proper. When there is no discipline, the result is disease and despair.

Isn't it amazing that when the mind becomes darkened, the immediate result is that the body becomes sinful? Those who believe an alternative lifestyle can coexist with the Spirit-filled lifestyle have no foundation for their reason, nor for their future. In verse 27, such a lifestyle is not based on a tendency but on the acts, and whatever naturally results from such abuse of what was designed to be the temple of God will be a penalty, or "fitting wage" (*NEB*).

When the spirit and soul of man are corrupt, where there is no accountability nor discipline, there can be no absolutes. The mind becomes destitute of distinguishing right and wrong. It becomes totally incapable of bringing order to our lives or even our community. Those who are without God will always have to settle for a lousy substitute for reality.

Submission to Total Depravity (vv. 29-32)

We could, and should, become depressed over the list that follows: *unrighteousness*—injustice; *sexual immorality*—including fornication and adultery; *wickedness*—evil action; *covetousness*—the desire to obtain that which belongs to others or to get what we think is due us; *maliciousness*—violence or the desire to inflict injury upon others; *envy*—discontent by another's success; *murder*—including hate, strife, contention or debate; *deceit*—fraud, as a fellow or as a felony; *evil-mindedness*—the disposition of making the worst out of everything; *whisperers*—slanderers or gossipers; *backbiters*—speaking against others in their absence; *violent*—those who are insolent, stiff-necked; *proud*—self-conceited; *boasters*—those who give themselves accolades that they do not deserve; *inventors of evil things*—developers of sin, vice and evil; *disobedient to parents*—dysfunctional homes and relationships; *undiscerning*—no moral insight; *untrustworthy*—covenant breakers; *unloving*—lack of affection toward children or others; *unforgiving*—irreconcilable; and *unmerciful*—without compassion.

Paul then declared that all who practice these things—in other words, all of us—are worthy of death (v. 32). We also participate in giving approval to those who do these things. The court systems of our day affirm the apostle's insight. Even many churches are conspicuously silent to such practices by their members.

Dunn nails it well when he writes, "It was not simply a case of humans being distracted by something else and losing sight of God; they gave God their consideration and concluded that God was unnecessary for their living."[6]

But look what could have been. Instead of injustice, there could have been the reign and role of God.

- Physical intimacy could have been enjoyable and pure; all action could have been full of goodness.
- There would be the helping of one another rather than hurt; there would have been the sharing of wealth and goods.
- Love, not hate, would rule the day.
- There would be harmonious living.
- There would be transparency.
- We would be optimistic.
- Our words would be the same in person or in absence.
- We would have peace, not violence.
- There would be others-centered living in humility and creativity of that which is good.
- Homes would be functional with considerate and loyal people.
- There would be expression of affection in an appropriate manner with reconciliation and mercy.

Littleton, Colorado, is a model community of 35,000, a suburb of Denver, with educated families with above-average incomes. On Tuesday, April 20, 1999, two teenage boys stormed into the Columbine High School at lunchtime with guns and explosives. They killed 12 students and one teacher, and wounded at least 20 others.

Littleton is also the location of the Living Way Foursquare Fellowship, pastored by Al and Alona Eastland. During the shooting rampage, some of the youth from their congregation barricaded themselves in a music room with nearly 60 other students to escape the assailants. For four hours, while more than 100 police and SWAT teams tried to capture the two gunmen and evacuate wounded students who were then treated by paramedics, these youth bunkered down, even praying for others in danger.

Though Al and Alona's children are grown and married, these pastors immediately drove to the school to be with parents as they waited for news about their sons and daughters. Throughout the afternoon they offered counsel and comfort during this time of chaos. The shooting in Littleton was reported to be the worst of its kind to date in American history. Following the tragedy, their church held a citywide prayer service and has begun ministering to countless students whose lives have been altered by this tragedy.

Some of the stories told by students were mind-boggling. One student shared, "There was a girl crouched beneath a desk in the library. One guy came over and said, 'Peekaboo,' and shot her in the neck." Another teenage boy stated, "Then they pointed at us . . . bullets were bouncing everywhere. Two guys next to me got hit."

In the weeks that followed, there was tremendous speculation as to why something like this would happen. Why would two young men join a cultish group called the "Trenchcoat Mafia" and in the end take their own lives? Blame is being laid at the feet of everyone—those who possess guns in their homes, those who exploit violence in the media, dysfunction in the home and even those who simply didn't open their arms to embrace two disenfranchised youth.

During a visit to that city a few weeks afterward, my wife, Carole, and I were shocked to learn that just the weekend before the shooting, one of the young assailants had been in an evangelistic service where the minister stopped his message, pointed in his direction and stated that there was a young person planning to kill others. He admonished the youth, whoever he was, to forgo his plans and turn to Jesus Christ. That night, the young man walked away from God and the rest is history.

That young man could have had a great destiny, but he rejected it. What a tragedy and what an editorial on the lostness of humankind.

LESSONS ANYONE?

1. In your own words, briefly state the importance of Christianity being a revelation rather than a religion.

2. What is your reaction to Cranfield's statement that "[God's] wrath is an expression of His love"? How is His wrath related to His justice?

3. List the various consequences of Adam and Eve's sin. What was the one underlying cause of their disobedience?

4. How are believers tolerant, yet maintain without compromise their conviction that Jesus is the only Way, in today's society toward those of other religions?

Chapter 5

Surely Not Me

Romans 2:1-16

That is fine for those pagan Gentiles, but as a Jew I have a unique relationship with the Judge. Thus, what has been said surely isn't talking about me!" The continual references in Jewish writings and thought regarding the heathenism of the Gentiles make it certain that as some would hear the first part of Paul's letter, a response such as this one would occur. On the other side of the coin, there's a bit of the Pharisee in all of us, even we sanctimonious Gentiles who would pass judgment on horrible sinners of any race.

While the discussion will continue as to whether Paul was addressing the Jews or Gentiles or both, there is no question as to what he was talking about. In the first five verses of this chapter, Paul used the word *judge* or *judgment* seven times. There seems to be a comparison between our judging and God's judgment. Those who judge others are in actuality judging themselves, because they practice the same things.

The indictment is immediately established. In the same way that those who suppressed the truth are without excuse (1:20), so those who have sought to obtain security through moralism are equally as inexcusable (2:1). The self-righteousness of men is totally indefensible, because they sin against clear light. There is no reasonable defense when sinful man stands before the holy Judge.

God's Judgment—Full of Integrity (vv. 2-5)

By judging others, those who are self-righteous feel they will escape the judgment of God. The source of this is a hardness of attitude. But Paul responds that the judgment of God will be full of integrity—it will be "according to truth" (v. 2). It most surely will take place.

According to truth means that God truly knows what we are like—there is no putting something over on Him. It also means God knows truly—He understands the real nature of the conduct.

Another truth of the matter is that God's just judgment is closely related to His mercy. There is no greater description of the mercy of God than by the words penned in verse 4: "the riches of His goodness, forbearance, and longsuffering."

Goodness has to do with God's purposes and plans for us. Even while the nation of Israel was in Babylonian captivity because of its spiritual adulterous state, fully deserving to be judged, God expressed His feelings about them: "For I know the thoughts that I think toward you, says the Lord, thoughts of peace [wholeness, goodness, wellness] and not of evil, to give you a future and a hope"

(Jeremiah 29:11). For even the vilest sinner, God's desire is to give them a merciful destiny. As Charles Hodge states: "The goodness of God has both the design and tendency to lead men to repentance. If it fails, the fault must be their own, not God's."[1]

Forbearance is God's restraint in not immediately responding to humanity's sinfulness. Unfortunately, from mankind's perspective, that patience is often misunderstood as being a peace treaty, rather than a temporary truce. But as forbearing as God is in not immediately responding to such unholy acts, our hard and impenitent hearts continue to practice and accumulate those unholy acts (Romans 2:5—"treasuring up," *NKJV*; "storing up," *NIV*) until His judgment and wrath fall. Eternal interest daily accrues to our temporary loan on God's patience.

Longsuffering is God's patience and slowness in executing that horrible judgment. From God's perspective, His restraint is always to give us another chance to return to Him. Peter stated it this way: "The Lord is not slack concerning His promise, as some count slackness, but is longsuffering toward us, not willing that any should perish but that all should come to repentance" (2 Peter 3:9).

The moment will arrive when the "day of wrath and revelation" (Romans 2:5) occurs. Whereas those who have turned in repentance to a gracious God will receive "the riches of His goodness" (v. 4), those with insensitive and impenitent hearts will receive the total accumulation of His wrath.

The real story will be told. What a contrast! How foolish it would be to store up an inheritance of wrath and woe. In the words with which Paul began this portion, it is totally inexcusable . . . and may I add, irrational.

God's Judgment—Reasonable (vv. 6-10)

For centuries, the Jews had sung this song: "Also to You, O Lord, belongs mercy; for You render [recompense, reward] to each one according to his work" (Psalm 62:12). The psalmist's son wrote, "Every way of a man is right in his own eyes, but the Lord weighs the hearts. To do righteousness and justice is more acceptable to the Lord than sacrifice. . . . If you say, 'Surely we did not know this,' does not He who weighs the hearts consider it? He who keeps your soul, does He not know it? And will He not render to each man according to his deeds?" (Proverbs 21:2, 3; 24:12).

Perspective makes all the difference. Whereas Paul contrasted the riches of God's goodness with the treasury of wrath in Romans 2:4, 5, here he contrasts the recompense of eternal life to those who obey the truth with the reward of indignation, wrath, tribulation and anguish to those who do evil. It makes no difference whether the person is a Jew or a Greek. As the power of God is for the Jew first and then for the Greek (1:16), so is the judgment of God (2:9).

For many years, I saw only the negative side of this: *God's indignation*—His anger; *God's wrath*—deliberate plan of punishment; *God's tribulation*—pressure and afflicted pain; *God's anguish*—anxiety and distress of mind, which one experiences when pressed in from all sides by afflictions, trials, wants and, above all, the demands of God's justice.

Then, as if I was reading this portion for the first time, I was overwhelmed with the positive aspect of God's judgment: *His glory*—His delight in us, the dignity He gives us; *His honor*—rewarding us with beauty and splendor; *His gift of immortality*—instilling in us eternal perspectives and values.

In verse 10, he substituted the word *peace* for immortality. And when you do the math, glory plus honor plus immortality/peace equals eternal life. As the songwriter penned, "Who could ask for anything more?" God's goodness is designed to lead all to make the right choice. How inexcusable could man be, to reject all the above by continuing to obey unrighteousness?

God's Judgment—Impartial (vv. 11-16)

There is no running from the responsibility for sinfulness, whether it be the Gentiles—whether they know the Law or not—or the Jews, whose knowledge of the Law will literally punish them unless they keep it in its entirety.

William Barclay states: "A man will be judged by his fidelity to the highest that it was possible for him to know."[2]

Hodge adds: "Men are to be judged by the light they have severally enjoyed. The ground of judgment is their works; the standard of judgment, their knowledge."[3]

The Gentiles, who are without the written or supernaturally revealed Law, are guilty because they possess a conscience that bears witness to an internal law within themselves, either endorsing their action or bringing guilt. Even the social orders that seem to be prevalent among tribal groups, who had never heard the gospel, testify to the innate knowledge of right and wrong. Their conscience bears witness when they fall short of even their own standard, not to speak of God's.

During Paul's day, a sense of a moral conscience was well established in Greek philosophy. While not determining the legitimacy of a right action or illegitimacy of a wrong action, it does serve as a reference. When an action falls above the moral standard within an individual, it brings reward; when that action falls below the standard, it brings reprimand. As Plummer writes: "If a man knows enough to judge others and rightfully condemn them, he knows enough to condemn himself for doing the same or like things."[4]

There was no question about the Jews' responsibility. They not only had the moral law written in their conscience, they had the written law published in the Canon. No one was excused from judgment.

1. The Law's very design was as a mirror or plumb line to show how short they came to God's demand (3:20).

2. Human flesh could not keep it (8:3).

3. Its goal was to bring everyone to Christ (10:4, 5).

We must never forget the impact the above would have had on those in Rome. They were professionals at judging, whether it be in the church or personal character practices. Paul is reminding them that they have no foundation, right or privilege to pass judgment on anything, since each party, Jew or Gentile, is equally inexcusable.

To judge is lethal. To judge is to demand that the penalty of divine justice be carried out on another. While we require that the execution be carried out, we forget that we are requesting God to carry out the same judgment upon us.

God's Judgment—According to the Gospel (v. 16)

The Jew will also be judged according to the person of Jesus Christ and the purpose for which He came. They would also discover that it was the same message Paul had found and was now proclaiming. In their rejection of Him, they were not only rebellious but were also missing the good news they had been designated to portray.

Since being unveiled in 1541, Michelangelo's *Last Judgment* has been revered for its towering spiritual strength and enduring symbolism. It was so overpowering that upon first seeing it, Pope Paul II sank to his knees and murmured, "Lord, charge me, not with my sins when thou shalt come on the Day of Judgment." The 40- by 45-foot fresco on the west altar wall of the Sistine Chapel, on which Michelangelo labored for five years, is one of the most unique and amazing works of art in the history of the world.

The *Last Judgment* is a swirl of more than 300 figures. As Christ majestically takes a step forward at the center, saints, angels, the redeemed and the damned gesticulate, struggle and cringe in the shared moment of cataclysm. The seven angels of the Apocalypse trumpet vigorously, exhibiting two books to the figures on the lower levels: the enormous book that lists the names of the hell-bound and a small one telling the names of those who merit salvation.

It is interesting to note that after completing his masterpiece, Michelangelo lived 23 years, dying in 1564 at the age of 89. In his last, dying confession, he lamented, "I regret I have not done enough for the salvation of my soul." Here was a man who had, with his heart and his art, tried to find salvation in his magnificent deeds. He made it so hard, he forgot his destiny. All he found was sadness and frustration.

What he had forgotten was that Jesus Christ had come to save humanity from the very subject he was painting. "[God is] not willing that any should perish [experience

His wrath and judgment] but that all should come to repentance [salvation, joy and faith]" (2 Peter 3:9).

LESSONS ANYONE?

1. In your opinion, what is the underlying root of self-righteousness?
2. Contrast the negative (His treasury of wrath) and the positive (recompense of eternal life) aspects of God's judgment. How did this chapter change your perspective on God's judgment?
3. Can one truly say, "Let your conscience be your guide"? How should your conscience relate to God's standards?
4. Taking the truths of Romans 1 and 2, are the heathen really lost? What should this say about our view of missions and evangelism?

Chapter 6

Will the Real "Jew" Please Stand Up

Romans 2:17—3:8

After Paul established that all are without excuse—those heathen Gentiles who willfully left God out of the equation, and those who criticized others to try to cover up their own guilt and to escape the judgment of God—he now deals with three perceptions among the Jewish sector, both in the church and in the community.

1. The name Jew indicated that the person belonged to a race chosen by God. They were to represent the name of Jehovah before the rest of the world.

2. The Jew was to be a separated person, set aside to be graced by divine covenant with the blessings of God.

3. If the above two relationships were valid, then for God to place the Jew on the same plane as the guilty Gentile was actually in contradiction with God's original promise.

After all, rather than leaving God behind, they had brought God with them. Instead of imitating the heathen in irreverence before God, they were extremely religious.

In Name Only (2:17-24)

Several things suggested that the Jew had a superior privilege. The name *Jew* originated in the tribe of Judah, the lineage from which the blessed Messiah would come. Following the time of the Maccabees, the name *Jewish* or *Jew* replaced the term *Israelite* or *Hebrew*. It was a name to be proud of, as can be seen by the attitude expressed in the apocryphal writings of Baruch:

> In you we have put our trust, because, behold, your Law is with us, and we know that we do not fall as long as we keep your statutes. We shall always be blessed; at least, we did not mingle with the nations. For we are all a people of the Name; we, who received one Law from the One. And that Law which is among us will help us, and that excellent wisdom which is in us will support us.[1]

The great Jewish historian, Josephus, declared, "I might boldly affirm that we Jews are originators in respect of most things and the best for all others."[2] Kaseman also quotes Wisdom 18:4: "Who [we Jews] point out the way of life to all mortals." To capture the Jews' feeling of superiority, we look at the four verbs and four nouns that appear in Romans 2:17-20.

1. *Rest*—to put one's weight on; to rely; carries with it the idea of the leaning of the supplicant as he presents his offering to the priest in the Temple. His entire future is based on having been a recipient of God's revealed Law.

2. *Boast*—a legitimate pride of being part of a privileged people who know God. It is more clearly defined in Jeremiah 9:23, 24: "Thus says the Lord: 'Let not the wise man glory in his wisdom, let not the mighty man glory in his might, nor let the rich man glory in his riches; but let him who glories glory in this, that he understands and knows Me.'"

3. *Know*—to know God's will heightened the privilege, for "He declares His word to Jacob, His statutes and His judgments to Israel. He has not dealt thus with any nation; and as for His judgments, they have not *known* them" (Psalm 147:19, ital. mine).

4. *Approve*—to encourage and even embrace those things that are of the highest value in moral judgments. (By the way, the Jews' problem was never with their moral judgments, but with their immoral conduct.)

Now the nouns. The Jews considered themselves to be "a guide to the blind" (Romans 2:19); they were going to instruct the heathen world. The only problem was that instead of becoming guides to the world in their search for returning to God, they brought dishonor to His name (v. 23). This resulted in the world despising a religion that seemed to be powerless. I cannot get over the words of Jesus in rebuking the Pharisees: "Let them alone. They are blind leaders of the blind. And if the blind leads the blind, both will fall into a ditch" (Matthew 15:14). Later, He also said, "Woe to you, scribes and Pharisees, hypocrites! For you travel land and sea to win one proselyte, and when he is won, you make him twice as much a son of hell as yourselves" (23:15).

They also professed to be "a light to those who are in darkness" (Romans 2:19). Truth was to be their torch.

They were the ones to whom truth was revealed. But what did they do with it? Listen to the Gospel of John:

> In Him [the Word—Jesus] was life, and the life was the light of men. And the light shines in the darkness, and the darkness did not comprehend it. . . . He [John the Baptist] was not that Light, but was sent to bear witness of that Light. That was the true Light which gives light to every man coming into the world. . . . He came to His own, and His own did not receive Him (1:4, 5, 8, 9, 11).

The result was idolatry. Malachi 1:7, 8, 12, 13 is very graphic:

> "You offer defiled food on My altar, but say, 'In what way have we defiled You?' By saying, 'The table of the Lord is contemptible.' And when you offer the blind as a sacrifice, is it not evil? And when you offer the lame and sick, is it not evil? Offer it then to your governor! Would he be pleased with you? . . . But you profane [the Lord's name], in that you say, 'The table of the Lord is defiled; and its fruit, its food, is contemptible.' You also say, 'Oh, what a weariness!' And you sneer at it."

Finally, the Jews were to be "an instructor of the foolish" and "a teacher of babes" (Romans 2:20). But what did the teachers do? According to Paul, they didn't listen to their own lessons. They taught against one thing and as soon as class was over, they practiced it. The rabbis were accustomed to give the names *foolish* and *babes* to the ignorant proselytes, but Jesus observed the following: "The scribes and the Pharisees sit in Moses' seat. Therefore whatever they tell you to observe, that observe and do, but do not do according to their works; for they say, and do not do" (Matthew 23:2, 3).

The bottom line was that they were Jews in name only. They proclaimed the dignity of their religion, but defamed it by being powerless, pointless and "principle-less."

In Flesh Only (vv. 25-29)

For the Jew, the cutting off of the foreskin was of extreme importance. It was the sign of superior position.

At age 99, Abraham once again heard the covenant of God: "I will make you exceedingly fruitful; and I will make nations of you, and kings shall come from you. And I will establish My covenant between Me and you and your descendants after you in their generations, for an everlasting covenant, to be God to you and your descendants after you" (Genesis 17:6, 7). God then stated, "Every male child among you shall be circumcised; and you shall be circumcised in the flesh of your foreskins, and it shall be a sign of the covenant between Me and you" (vv. 10, 11).

Every male child was to be circumcised on the eighth day of their lives. The father usually performed the rite, and the child was named. According to Exodus 4:25, a woman could also perform the ritual. Later, a Hebrew surgeon was called in. The rite marked the admission of the child to God's covenant relationship.

In my study for writing this chapter, I ran across a statement by Rabbi Akedath Jizehak, who wrote: "Abraham sits before the gate of Hell and does not allow any circumcised Israelite to enter there."

But circumcision was to be more than physical. The outward sign was to be symbolic of an inward work of the heart. Deuteronomy 30:6 states this: "And the Lord your God will circumcise your heart and the heart of your descendants, to love the Lord your God with all your heart and with all your soul, that you may live." And later, Jeremiah lamented: "All the house of Israel are uncircumcised in the heart" (9:26).

Paul states that "circumcision of the heart" is that which validates "circumcision of the flesh" (see Romans 2:28, 29). And the physically uncircumcised Gentile who keeps the law of God in his heart will act as judge over those who have the physical sign but lack it in their heart.

The question comes down to this: Just who is the real Jew in this case? In verse 29, Paul makes a play on words. The word *Jew* means "the one who praises." In return, the qualifying of a true believer does not come from other men or women, but from God, who knows the heart.

There are so many lessons that could be stated at this point. What makes up a true believer can never be measured in physical, visible or ritual terms. Christianity is something invisible, hidden in the heart and energized by the Spirit of God. It is not inherited, but conditional; it is not external, but internal; and not physical or political, but spiritual and relational.

If you'd like to study further, in Romans 2, circumcision is inward; in chapter 3, it is by faith; and in chapter 4, it is to all who "walk in the steps of the faith which our father Abraham had . . ." (v. 12).

But God Wouldn't Dare... (3:1-8)

Immediately, that brings up the question, "Then what benefit did the Jew have?" What is interesting about this portion is that Paul continues to remind the Jews of the benefits they have received from God, rather than their good deeds. This is very consistent with Paul's premise that "the goodness of God leads [one] to repentance" (2:4). Even today, the world will not be drawn to God's way by a word of condemnation, but by the testimony of His mercy.

Paul is also using a Hebrew form of debate—stating a principle, forecasting the response and then providing the logical conclusion.

The greatest benefit of circumcision and belonging to God's covenant people was that "to them were committed the oracles of God" (3:2). I like Dunn's explanation:

> For a Gentile readership the word 'oracle' would evoke the thought of inspired utterances preserved from the past, often mysterious and puzzling in character, awaiting some key to unlock their meaning (see chapter 1:19)—their stewardship was a commissioning to make these revelations known to the wider world.[3]

The Jews were to be stewards. Instead, the oracles became systems: "For indeed the gospel was preached to us as well as to them [the Jews]; but the word which they heard did not profit them, not being mixed with faith in those who heard it" (Hebrews 4:2). How descriptive of so much of today's Christianity. Often it becomes more a culture than a conversion.

The debate begins. Even if one doesn't keep his end of the bargain, God still has to be faithful to His promise (Romans 3:3, 4). Justin Martyr said, "They suppose that to them universally who are of the seed of Abraham, no matter how sinful and disobedient to God they may be, the eternal kingdom shall be given."

This attitude was prevalent during our Lord's day. "They answered Him, 'We are Abraham's descendants, and have never been in bondage to anyone. How can you say, 'You will be made free?' Jesus answered them, 'Most assuredly, I say to you, whoever commits sin is a slave of sin. . . . You seek to kill Me, because My word has no place in you'" (John 8:33, 34, 37).

Used often in the letter to the Romans, Paul's answer is simple: "Certainly not!" To the contrary, though the people have violated their end of the covenant, God is still maintaining His side of the agreement. While every man is a liar, God is still true to His word. God had remained faithful to Israel in the past, despite her unfaithfulness. He will remain faithful now and in the future, despite her continuing unfaithfulness. God is always consistent.

To show this, the apostle quotes from Psalm 51:4: "That You may be justified in Your words, and may overcome [prevail] when You are judged [placed on the stand]" (Romans 3:4).

In 2 Samuel 11 and 12, we read of David's sins against God, Uriah and Bathsheba. The result of David and Bathsheba's adultery was that the child born of their sin died. David went before the Lord in sorrow and instead of blaming God, he used the picture of a divine courtroom and stated that if God himself were put on trial for the way He punished David and Bathsheba, the verdict would be "Not Guilty!" Not only was God's judgment consistent with His integrity, His punishment of sin was correct.

The second part of the debate follows this line of reasoning: Since the Jews' unrighteousness by contrast highlights God's righteousness, He ought to be grateful and excuse them. He would be unjust to do otherwise. (Today, the argument goes, "How could a loving God ever send anyone to hell?")

Here's that answer again: "Certainly not." God will not go against His nature. On the surface, the Jews' rationalizing may seem ridiculous, but as Plummer notes:

> If sin ceases to be sin and cannot be punished because God overrules it, and makes it the occasion of glorifying Him, and showing forth His excellent nature and providence; then no sin can be punished, and so there is nothing to be condemned, and of course there is not and will not be any judgment of God on human conduct.[4]

Now, for the third and final try: "God ought to encourage us in doing wrong, because look at the good that has come out of it for everyone else" (see Romans 3:7, 8). Paul's conclusion is final. "Their condemnation is just" (v. 8). In the same way God's gospel is to the Jew first and then to the Gentile, so God's wrath in certainty is to the Jew first and then to the Gentile. If they had all these benefits, then they are even more inexcusable.

Some time ago, a church near Charlotte, North Carolina, decided it was time to "ask the customer!" Of its 700 members, 80 percent were formerly unchurched, finding Jesus through the ministry of this congregation.

Before this church was started, a survey of the area was conducted, posing the question "Why don't you go to church?" Two of the responses were very revealing.

Seventy-four percent said, "There is no value in attending." While recognizing their need for God, the vast majority felt they could experience Him just as easily on the golf course as they could in the average worship service. The verdict would be similar to McDonald's discovering that people wanted hamburgers, but didn't think McDonald's was a place to get one. Does this imply that the church has become more a ritual than it is relevant?

Eighty-one percent felt, "Churches have too many problems." One response in the survey said, "I have enough problems in my life. Why would I go to church and get more?" Is there really a difference between the believer and the unbeliever? Can God really solve our greatest need? Does the world see that change in our lives?

You and I are the only gospels the world reads. The question is, "How are they perceiving what they read?" If it's "in name only," or "in flesh only," God will hold us responsible for them. It is a matter of our stewardship as God's covenant people, and the destiny and salvation of those around us.

LESSONS ANYONE?

1. Consider what it means for believers to be true "guides, lights, instructors and teachers" in today's society.
2. Why does your Christianity often deteriorate into outward acts of habit or ritual rather than inward reality?
3. In your own words, describe what it means to be "circumcised in the heart."
4. As the people of God, the Jews had certain benefits. What benefits do God's people (you) have today?

Chapter 7

The Bottom Line—"All"

Romans 3:9-20

"What then?" (v. 9) brings us to the bottom line of the first section of the letter. We could say, "In light of all that has been said, what else is there we human beings have to put forward as a defense in the divine courtroom before God our judge?"

Note Paul's inclusiveness:

- "All under sin" (v. 9)
- "None righteous, no, not one" (v. 10)
- "None who understands . . . none who seeks" (v. 11)
- "All turned aside . . . together become unprofitable . . . none who does good, no, not one" (v. 12)
- "Every mouth may be stopped . . . all . . . become guilty" (v. 19)
- "No flesh will be justified" (v. 20).

Again, I turn to Dunn:

> Man experiences (consciously or unconsciously) a power which works in him to bind him wholly to his mortality and corruptibility, to render impotent any knowledge of God or concern to do God's will, to provoke his merely animal appetites in forgetfulness, that he is a creature of God—and that power Paul calls "sin."[1]

Paul builds a chain-link fence around the entire matter by quoting seven Old Testament passages describing humanity's relationship with God, its character and deeds.

Relationship With God (vv. 10-12)

Psalm 14 begins with these words:

> The fool has said in his heart, "There is no God." They are corrupt, they have done abominable works, there is none who does good. The Lord looks down from heaven upon the children of men, to see if there are any who understand, who seek God. They have all turned aside, they have together become corrupt; there is none who does good, no, not one (vv. 1-3).

Remember the progression of Romans 1:18-23? Suppression of the truth will always lead to willful ignorance—"There is none who understands" (3:11). Separation from the Light will result in active neglect—"There is none who seeks after God" (v. 11). Substituting the real with a lousy substitute gives approval to rebellion—"They have all turned aside" (v. 12). Submitting to the "fitting wage" of sin always makes one depraved—"They have together become unprofitable [Hebrew: corrupt]" (v. 12).

To be spiritually depraved simply means that every worldview of humanity that leaves God out will naturally dissipate into actions that not only will question His veracity but also His very existence.

Earlier in this book, I spoke of the April 20, 1999, Columbine massacre in Littleton, Colorado. Shortly thereafter, I received a cartoon in the mail from a friend depicting two students standing outside the school. One of the students asked the other, "Where was God last Tuesday?" His friend replied, "Don't you know? God isn't allowed in school anymore."

Throughout the weeks that followed the horrible tragedy, every news service in America interviewed psychologists, sociologists and clergy asking why such an event would happen. I almost threw my shoe through the television set when I heard a clergyman respond, "Well, it just means we have to learn to love each other more." On the other hand, as I listened to a sermon by my Foursquare colleague, Pastor Al Eastland, I realized that God truly was there, preventing nearly 60 other bombs planted in the building from going off and killing hundreds of faculty and students. There was more to the news, but the media didn't want to address such a sensitive issue. Finally, two youth stood before the microphone and reminded the entire world on Fox News Network that the bottom line was humanity's willful neglect of God's presence in their world. Man has usurped the role of the Creator.

Far too often we have tried to make the message of redemption "seeker-sensitive." We have also endeavored to make it "socially relevant." We will never right the wrongs of society or reestablish moral righteousness in our nation's practices until we recognize the source of the cancer that has spread throughout our system—spiritually, mentally, emotionally and physically. It's a three-letter word pronounced *sin*. And it is first directed against God!

Humanity's Character (vv. 13, 14)

I am amazed at the graphic word pictures the apostle used to describe the character of humanity that begins from the inside out. Paul quotes Psalm 5:9: "For there is no faithfulness in their mouth; their inward part is destruction; their throat is an open tomb; they flatter with their tongue. Pronounce them guilty, O God!" The image of a tomb suggests there are offensive and pestilential vapors emanating—not just bad breath, but lethal breath. The mouth also becomes a garbage receptacle of all that has been devoured and is putrid. It shouldn't surprise us that the "f" word fills our movies and our vocabularies.

Proverbs 18:21 reminds us, "Death and life are in the power of the tongue, and those who love it will eat its fruit." Paul applies it this way: "With their tongues they have practiced deceit" (Romans 3:13). It has been said that power corrupts. Paul takes it even deeper and lets us know our speech is never transparent and genuine, but it is smooth and full of flattery, just like a flytrap. Manipulation and control have become the motives behind our discussion.

The next description is taken from Psalm 140:3: "They sharpen their tongues like a serpent; the poison of asps is under their lips." Can you just picture a person trying to sharpen his tongue on a whetstone? It takes planning and a totally debased heart. We call it being socially and politically astute.

At first glance, the words "whose mouth is full of cursing and bitterness" (Romans 3:14) seems pretty plain. But looking at Psalm 10, we find a much deeper significance. It has to do with motives and stubbornness:

For the wicked boasts of his heart's desire; he blesses the greedy and renounces the Lord. The wicked in his proud countenance does not seek God; God is in none of his thoughts. His ways are always prospering; Your judgments are far above, out of his sight; as for all his enemies, he sneers at them. He has said in his heart, "I shall not be moved; I shall never be in adversity." His mouth is full of cursing and deceit and oppression; under his tongue is trouble and iniquity (Psalm 10:3-7).

Humanity's Actions (vv. 15-20)

If you are not already convinced of humanity's depravity, read Isaiah 59, from which the next phrase is taken:

> For your hands are defiled with blood, and your fingers with iniquity; your lips have spoken lies, your tongue has muttered perversity. No one calls for justice, nor does any plead for truth. They trust in empty words and speak lies; they conceive evil and bring forth iniquity. They hatch vipers' eggs and weave the spider's web; he who eats of their eggs dies, and from that which is crushed a viper breaks out. Their webs will not become garments, nor will they cover themselves with their works; their works are works of iniquity, and the act of violence is in their hands. Their feet run to evil and they make haste to shed innocent blood; their thoughts are thoughts of iniquity; wasting and destruction are in their paths (vv. 3-7).

Finally, from Psalm 36 we read, "There is no fear of God before his eyes" (v. 1). Immediately following that statement, the psalmist continues: "For he flatters himself in his own eyes, when he finds out his iniquity and when he hates. The words of his mouth are wickedness and deceit; he has ceased to be wise and to do good. He devises wickedness on his bed; he sets himself in a way that is not good; he does not abhor evil" (36:2-4).

Sounds like today's headlines, doesn't it? When we talk about Adam and Eve's fall in the Garden, it wasn't simply "Everybody out of the pool—you're grounded!" It was the most disastrous and lethal decision and has infected every man, woman and child of every generation and genealogy.

Paul concludes: "Whether you are a Jew under the law, or the rest of the world, there's only one defense you can present to the righteous Judge—none. There's only one verdict—guilty." He lists the first of several reasons the Law was given: "By the law is the knowledge of sin" (Romans 3:20).

For four wonderful years (1965-1969), Carole and I planted and pastored a church in Surrey, British Columbia. We began the church in a building that in 1965 was already at least 30 years old. It literally sat at the top of a hill overlooking the entire region, and one corner of the building rested on a huge boulder that later had to be dynamited.

Believe it or not, we were able to purchase that 5.5 acres of land for $5,200. Years later, it was cleared out, subdivided and sold, making it possible for the congregation, under another pastor, to build a new sanctuary, family-life building and parking lot. Today the church, spiritually and physically, stands as a lighthouse for the gospel in one of the fastest-growing communities of Canada.

One day, a close friend who, with his family, had helped us begin the church scheduled an appointment to meet me on the property. When I pulled into the parking lot, I noticed he had attached a string to a steel weight that was hanging from one corner of the roof. That day I learned the lesson of the "plumb line." As it revealed what was straight in natural forces, it also revealed just how crooked the walls of that old building had become. It was Wallace Stelting's way of informing me that we had to put steel rods across the inside of the building to brace the walls so they would be safe for people to enter and worship the Lord.

The law of God was the divine plumb line to show us two things: just how crooked humanity's hearts (that's us) had become; and just how important it was that immediate action be taken to rectify the danger. Whereas we could use our own initiative to fix the building, there was no way humanity could save itself. As a matter of fact, it doesn't need self-help—it needs divine help for a divine destiny.

LESSONS ANYONE?

1. Why don't individuals want to confront the issue of sin in their lives? What makes them try to find other answers to today's social problems?
2. Can unbelievers truly understand the root of their problem before they accept the gospel?
3. How has God's law served as a "plumb line" in your own life—before and after your conversion?
4. Discuss the fine line between the church being "seeker-sensitive" and "seeker-saving." Can it accomplish both purposes?

Chapter 8

But Now!

Romans 3:21-31

One thing about being at the bottom is that there's no way but up! No one can escape the bottom line, because we are sinners and thus worthy of death. We are literally naked before God. We come to Him telling of our good deeds, and He responds with something about filthy rags (see Isaiah 64:6). We try to earn His favor and He repeats what Paul has just said: "There is none righteous, no, not one" (Romans 3:10). We cry out for mercy and He responds, "But now . . ."

There are certain high marks throughout the letter to the Romans. Dr. Richard Mouw has likened it to the Golden Gate Bridge, which connects San Francisco with Northern California. On either end are the words "obedience to the faith" (Romans 1:5; 16:26), and there are the supporting spans at 1:16, 17; 3:21-26; 5:1-5; 8; 12:1, 2; and 14:1. If you memorize these portions of Scripture, you'll understand what Paul is trying to say in this letter.

It was also at this point in the letter to the Romans that revelation came to Martin Luther:

> I greatly longed to understand Paul's epistle to the Romans and nothing stood in the way but that one expression, "the Righteousness of God," because I took it to mean whereby God is righteous and deals righteously in punishing the unrighteous. . . . Night and day I pondered until . . . I grasped the truth that the righteousness whereby, through grace and sheer mercy, He justifies us by faith. Thereupon I felt myself to be reborn and to have gone through open doors into paradise. The whole of scripture took on a new meaning, and whereas before, the righteousness of God had filled me with hate, now it became to me inexpressibly sweet in greater love.[1]

"But now" makes all the difference in the world . . . and in eternity!

It is almost as if Paul reaches back to Romans 1:17 and drags the cursor over to chapter 3, bringing the words *righteousness* (vv. 21, 22, 25, 26) and *faith* (vv. 22, 25-28, 30, 31) with it. Furthermore, it is important to recognize the word *revealed* in verse 21—remember 1:17. Recall the meaning of the term—that which was previously in existence but now is made visible and known. In other words, we are declared righteous not *because* we believe, but *when* we believe.

The Righteousness of God—Revealed (vv. 21, 22)

It is imperative to understand the words *righteous* or *righteousness* from the Biblical perspective. The phrase "righteousness of God" is used 428 times in Scripture. In the Old Testament, we constantly see a righteous God responding to the supplicant (especially David in the Psalms), in defending or giving credibility to the "good guy's" cause against his enemies. It is the deliverance from opponents who seek someone's head simply on the basis that the one has obeyed the law of God.

In the New Testament, however, the phrase includes just judgment, just guidance, approval of right action, acceptable conduct and a lifestyle that corresponds to faith. The source of this righteousness is God, who is and who expresses that righteousness:

> He shall judge the world in righteousness, and He shall administer judgment for the peoples in uprightness (Psalm 9:8).
>
> "For the Lord is righteous, He loves righteousness; His countenance beholds the upright" (11:7).
>
> The fear of the Lord is clean, enduring forever; the judgments of the Lord are true and righteous altogether (19:9).
>
> My mouth shall tell of Your righteousness and Your salvation all the day, for I do not know their limits (71:15).
>
> The Lord has made known His salvation; His righteousness He has revealed in the sight of the nations (98:2).
>
> Wealth and riches will be in his house, and his righteousness endures forever. Unto the upright there arises light in the darkness; He is gracious, and full of compassion, and righteous (112:3, 4).
>
> Righteousness shall be the belt of His loins, and faithfulness the belt of His waist (Isaiah 11:5).

> "Let righteousness spring up together. I, the Lord, have created it" (45:8).

> "And you shall swear, 'The Lord lives,' in truth, in judgment, and in righteousness" (Jeremiah 4:2).

The Old Testament prophecies regarding the Messiah and the testimony regarding Jesus describe Him as righteous:

> By His knowledge My righteous Servant shall justify many, for He shall bear their iniquities (Isaiah 53:11).

> "Behold, the days are coming," says the Lord, "That I will raise to David a Branch of righteousness; a King shall reign and prosper, and execute judgment and righteousness in the earth. In His days Judah will be saved, and Israel will dwell safely; now this is His name by which He will be called: the Lord our Righteousness" (Jeremiah 23:5, 6, see also 33:15, 16).

> For Christ is the end of the law for righteousness to everyone who believes (Romans 10:4).

> But of Him you are in Christ Jesus, who became for us wisdom from God—and righteousness and sanctification and redemption (1 Corinthians 1:30).

> And be found in Him, not having my own righteousness, which is from the law, but that which is through faith in Christ, the righteousness which is from God by faith (Philippians 3:9).

> Simon Peter, a bondservant and apostle of Jesus Christ, To those who have obtained like precious faith with us

> by the righteousness of our God and Savior Jesus Christ (2 Peter 1:1).
>
> And if anyone sins, we have an Advocate with the Father, Jesus Christ the righteous (1 John 2:1).

In other words, it was "witnessed by the Law and the Prophets" (Romans 3:21). It is also "apart from the law" in that discovery was not possible by human search. It was made possible totally because of the faithfulness of Jesus Christ (v. 22, literal meaning). It was the Lord's willingness to be considered as the Son of God and as our Savior that provided our eternal redemption (John 1:12; 3:15, 16; 8:24; Romans 9:33; 10:14; Galatians 2:16, 20; 3:24; Ephesians 3:12). His "robe of righteousness" (Isaiah 61:10) has now replaced our "filthy rags" (64:6).

Here's that word *all* again—"to all who believe" (Romans 3:22)! There is no difference in Jew or Gentile. Jesus Christ, who put a face on God for us, also clothed Himself in our human (not sinful) nature and, acting before God on our behalf, suffered and died on the cross, completing all that was necessary to restore us in right relationship with the divine Creator, whom we had previously scorned.

The Righteousness of God—Described (vv. 23-26)

As stated before, I love to make the statement "God pronounces believers righteous at the beginning of their course, not at the end of it." Moreover, because we have the tendency to only quote Romans 3:23 when we witness to others, we miss the beauty of Paul's sentence structure.

Take a fresh look at the words: "For all have sinned and fall short of the glory of God, being justified freely by His grace. . . ." We had all "come short"—like an archer's arrow that failed to reach the target, or the runner who fails just before the finish line. We had failed to honor God, secure His approval, realize His destiny and were actually in opposition to Him. Still He found a way not only to make up the difference, but to provide everything from beginning to finish. There's the depth of guilt and the height of redemption!

We were never rehabilitated, for rehabilitation only restores us to where we were before. We were redeemed! Paul describes this redemption through three scenarios: the courtroom, the slave market and the mercy seat.

We are "justified freely by His grace." Immediately, we find ourselves standing in the courtroom before God the Judge. Just as the pronouncement of our guilt and penalty is about to be made, our advocate, Jesus Christ, states the terms of His blood covenant on the cross and we are declared "not guilty." Frankly speaking, it is not just as if we had never sinned, for that would permit God to excuse our sin. Forgiveness has nothing to do with excusing sin and its horror. But God declares us righteous in spite of our sin. The mercy of God means that those who place their trust in the death and resurrection of our Lord are spared from receiving what they deserve. Moreover, God's grace gives them everything they don't deserve!

Such grace is experienced through the "redemption that is in Christ Jesus" (v. 24). Here we have the image of the slave market. The word *redemption* is not used much in the Bible, but it was well-known in Jewish literature. It was the ransom paid to acquire a captive or free a prisoner of war. Paul uses this picture of God being the redeemer of His people Israel, especially when He delivered them from slavery in Egypt. There is now freedom from bondage and a new hope and destiny. All who place their trust in the death and resurrection of Jesus Christ are now free to live!

It was Jesus whom God set forth to be a "propitiation by His blood" (v. 25). Whereas *justification* brought forgiveness and *redemption* brought freedom, this phrase brings favor. The description here is of the mercy seat in the Tabernacle and later in the Temple, where God communed personally and intimately with the high priest. It included the sprinkling of the blood, as Dunn so eloquently describes: "As the sinner's sin was transferred to the spotless sacrifice, so the spotless life of the sacrifice was transferred to the sinner."[2]

Paul once again picks up the picture of the night of Israel's departure from Egypt. He states that in His forbearance, God "passed over" their sins. (Remember the statement in Romans 2:4?)

We have been placed in a new relationship with God, no longer as sinners, but as sons! Because God has *revealed* (3:21), *set forth* (v. 25) and *demonstrated* (vv. 25, 26) His righteous way of making men righteous (see 1:16), He punished sin (*was just*) and continues to accept the sinner (*the justified*) when we believe.

No Boasting, Just Thanksgiving (vv. 27-31)

Then what was the relationship of the law to God's redemptive plan? First of all, Paul states we can never earn or deserve what God has given us. It is by believing that such righteousness is imputed to us. Moreover, salvation is for everyone, the circumcised and the uncircumcised (believing Jew and Gentile).

We must also remember that in no way is the Law left out or discounted. Paul writes, "On the contrary, we establish [fulfill, complete the aim or purpose of] the law" (v. 31, definitions mine). I am grateful when I think about my "falling short" in verse 23 and God's "filling in" in verse 31.

But there is another aspect that is even more thrilling. When God first gave the Law, He also established a covenant with His people Israel.

> "Then it shall come to pass, because you listen to these judgments, and keep and do them, that the Lord your God will keep with you the covenant and the mercy which He swore to your fathers. And He will love you and bless you and multiply you; He will also bless the fruit of your womb and the fruit of your land, your grain and your new wine and your oil, the increase of your cattle and the offspring of your flock, in the land of which He swore to your fathers to give you. You shall be blessed above all peoples" (Deuteronomy 7:12-14).

It suddenly dawns on me that all the promises God gives to the righteous in the old covenant are part of His new covenant with all of us on this side of the Cross. As you link these promises together, they become a chain of destiny, hope and rejoicing to all who call upon the name of the Lord:

> "Therefore the Lord has recompensed me according to my righteousness, according to my cleanness in His eyes" (2 Samuel 22:25).

"I put on righteousness, and it clothed me; my justice was like a robe and a turban" (Job 29:14).

For You, O Lord, will bless the righteous; with favor You will surround him as with a shield (Psalm 5:12).

"For the Lord is righteous, He loves righteousness; His countenance beholds the upright" (11:7).

"As for me, I will see Your face in righteousness; I shall be satisfied when I awake in Your likeness" (17:15).

He restores my soul; He leads me in the paths of righteousness for His name's sake" (23:3).

"He shall receive blessing from the Lord, and righteousness from the God of his salvation" (24:5).

"The eyes of the Lord are on the righteous, and His ears are open to their cry. . . . The righteous cry out, and the Lord hears, and delivers them out of all their troubles" (34:15, 17).

"Oh, continue Your lovingkindness to those who know You, and Your righteousness to the upright in heart" (36:10).

"For the arms of the wicked shall be broken, but the Lord upholds the righteous" (37:17).

"I have not seen the righteous forsaken, nor his descendants begging bread" (37:25).

"The righteous shall be glad in the Lord, and trust in Him. And all the upright in heart shall glory" (64:10).

"Righteousness will go before Him, and shall make His footsteps our pathway" (85:13).

Surely the righteous shall give thanks to Your name; the upright shall dwell in Your presence (140:13).

The name of the Lord is a strong tower; the righteous run to it and are safe (Proverbs 18:10).

"To console those who mourn in Zion, to give them beauty for ashes, the oil of joy for mourning, the garment of praise for the spirit of heaviness; that they may be called trees of righteousness, the planting of the Lord, that He may be glorified" (Isaiah 61:3).

"Those who are wise shall shine like the brightness of the firmament, and those who turn many to righteousness like the stars forever and ever" (Daniel 12:3).

"But now . . ." What a destiny!

LESSONS ANYONE?

1. Looking back over your life, trace the "But Now's" from God in your life. How has He made a difference?
2. How was God's gift in Jesus Christ just judgment—just guidance and just action?
3. Respond in your own words what this means: "God pronounces believers righteous at the beginning of the course, not at the end of it."
4. In your own words, define these terms: *justification*, *redemption* and *propitiation*.

Chapter 9

Now, About Faith

Romans 4:1-25

In the preceding passage, Paul wrote eloquently about righteousness. He alluded to the fact that it was according to the faithfulness of Jesus, and accepted through the faith of all who believe. He also stated that faith in Christ fulfills the very aim of the Old Testament law. To the Jew, this brought understanding regarding the purpose of all those regulations. To the Gentile, it informed them of the beautiful covenant God had made with all who would believe, even them. The Law and the old covenant were never to be discounted; their focus was to bring people to God's promise of destiny, deliverance and delight.

Paul continues in the same vein to focus on faith, using Abraham as the prime example. Of all the fathers in Israel, none was compared with "Father Abraham." To the Jew, Abraham was the father of their nation; to the Gentile, he was the first—the father—of their faith.

Paul is a man of few words, but he uses them over and over again. By watching for repetitive words or phrases, the apostle leaves no question as to his focus.

We are immediately confronted with the word *boast.* In Romans 1:22, the Gentiles professed (boasted) to be wise; in 2:17, the Jews boasted in their relationship with God; in 3:27, there is no boasting about our worthiness; and now in 4:2, there is no boasting in our works. The only things we can boast of is found in 5:2, 3, where we rejoice (boast) in the hope of the glory (destiny) of God and in the process that brings us to that place (boast in tribulations, perseverance, character and hope). But that's a topic for another study.

Another key to understanding this passage is the word *accounted* or *imputed* (4:3-7, 9, 10, 22, 24). Still another is *promise* (vv. 13, 14, 16, 20, 21).

Faith—Nothing to Boast About (vv. 2-8)

In Genesis 15, immediately after Abraham rescued his nephew, Lot, God came to Abraham in a vision, stating, "Do not be afraid, Abram. I am your shield, your exceeding great reward" (v. 1). Abraham responded with the cry of urgency in his heart, "Look, You have given me no offspring; indeed one born in my house is my heir!" (v. 3).

God then promised that there would be one who would come from Abraham's own body that would be the heir. God then brought him outside and said, "Look now toward heaven, and count the stars if you are able to number them. . . . So shall your descendants be" (v. 5).

Abraham accepted God's promise as fact, and God "accounted it to him for righteousness" (v. 6). There had been no merit, no action, no searching or expectancy; God promised and Abraham believed it. If there were to be any bragging rights, it would have to be on the side of God, not the patriarch.

If it had been because of the endeavors of Abraham, Sarah's womb would not have had to be miraculously opened, and Ishmael would have been God's choice as the heir. Abraham's actions would have made God his divine debtor, not his divine deliverer.

Today, much of the faith teaching in the church focuses on making God our debtor. We have faith in our faith (actually determinate self-centeredness) and simply by making a statement, we place an obligation for God to perform. God becomes a puppet on the string of our lust and greed. It makes us the creator and God our servant. In essence, it is idolatry, following the same pattern as Romans 1.

True faith teaching is the bringing of men and women into the knowledge of their rightful place in Christ, His promises to them and their acceptance that what He has promised and provided will indeed come to pass. It is based on His person, not our perception; His integrity, not our interests; His desires, not our demands. We simply embrace His will and it takes place. It is nothing for us to brag about or post on billboards.

In contrast to Abraham, the one who never did anything wrong (oops, at least in the Jews' memory, see Genesis 12:10-20), we see David. How would you like to be the ungodly part of the illustration, written for all to see? God not only imputed righteousness to David, but He covered up his unrighteousness.

In Romans 4:7, 8, Paul quotes David's lyrics from Psalm 32:1-5:

> Blessed is he whose transgression is forgiven, whose sin is covered. Blessed is the man to whom the Lord does not impute iniquity, and in whose spirit there is no deceit. When I kept silent, my bones grew old through my groaning all the day long. For day and night Your hand was heavy upon me; my vitality was turned into the drought of summer. Selah. I acknowledged my sin to You, and my iniquity I have not hidden. I said, "I will confess my transgressions to the Lord," and You forgave the iniquity of my sin.

Plummer, in his commentary, quotes Owen in describing what this imputation of righteousness is:

> This imputation is an act of God, of his mere love and grace, whereby on the consideration of the mediation of Christ, he makes an effectual grant and, donation of a true, real, perfect righteousness, even that of Christ himself unto all that do believe and accounting it as theirs, on his own gracious act both absolves them from sin and grants them right and title until eternal life.[1]

In application, isn't it amazing that we usually approach God by reminding Him of all the wonderful reasons we deserve an answer and the great things we have done for Him? He then reminds us what He has done for us, and proceeds to do what is best on our account.

Faith—Before... (vv. 9-15)

Looking at the chronology of events, we discover that when God accounted righteousness to Abraham in Genesis 15:6, it was nearly 29 Jewish years before he himself was circumcised (17:24), as well as Ishmael, the son of his own doing. According to the Scriptures, Ishmael was born when Abraham was 86 years of age; the circumcisions took place when Abraham was 99 and his son 13. Thus, circumcision was a response to the righteousness of faith—the result of it, not its cause.

According to Romans 4:11, circumcision was the "seal" of righteousness. In the Oriental culture, a seal unique to the parties of an agreement was dipped in ink and then pressed on the document, as well as upon the wax that sealed the envelope or skin portfolio preserving the document. The agreement was valid as long as the wax was not broken. It signified God's willingness to bless and Abraham's willingness to obey.

Paul continues to address the giving of the Law. The promise of having many heirs took place 430 years before the law of Moses (see Galatians 3:17) was established. Paul more completely defines the promise in Galatians 4:22-26, 28:

> For it is written that Abraham had two sons: the one by a bondwoman, the other by a freewoman. But he who was of the bondwoman was born according to the flesh, and he of the freewoman through promise, which things are symbolic. For these are the two covenants: the one from Mount Sinai which gives birth to bondage, which is Hagar—for this Hagar is Mount Sinai in Arabia, and corresponds to Jerusalem which now is, and is in bondage with her children—but the Jerusalem above is free, which is the mother of us all. . . . Now we, brethren, as Isaac was, are children of promise.

The divine promise was to take place by faith—by God

opening Sarah's womb. There had to be divine intervention. But Abraham had followed human understanding, and instead of trusting God, he took the matter in his own efforts. The result was that Ishmael and his mother, Hagar, had to be expelled. And, by the way, Ishmael was to be blessed; and today, we have the Palestinians and the Israelites still contending for their birthrights.

In addition to not being the way God planned, the Law was not designed to bring salvation for one simple reason: its very demands were too stringent—it was impossible for man to completely obey. As an exclamation point to his reasoning, Paul uses a Roman maxim: "Where there is no law there is no transgression" (Romans 4:15). But there was a law, and man continually transgressed it.

What lessons would this portion serve the church at Rome? Both the Jewish leaders and the Gentile leaders were debating form and lifestyle, whether the matters of the Law should be followed or considered foolish. To the Jew, Paul reinforces the priority of faith—that form follows faith, not determines it. To the Gentile, on the other hand, faith without form is only hearsay, not holy living. There is no need to "throw the baby out with the dishwater," just to prove your point.

Faith—Contrary to… (vv. 16-22)

Paul's conclusion is that the promise is guaranteed to all the seed, both Jew and Gentile. This is the third time Paul states our common ancestry in Abraham (vv. 1, 11, 12, 16-18). You'd think we'd get the point.

First of all, the promise given to Abraham was contrary to logic. To see the promise fulfilled, there would have to be a creative act (v. 17). By this time, Abraham was 100 years old, and Sarah was 90. When God changed her name from *Sarai* to *Sarah*, the Bible says, "Abraham fell on his face and laughed" (Genesis 17:17). And when the three men (angels) informed Sarah of the future, she laughed within herself. The Lord asked, "Is anything too hard for the Lord? At the appointed time I will return to you, according to the time of life, and Sarah shall have a son" (18:14). Later, they named their son Isaac, which means "laughter."

The promise was also contrary to circumstances. Paul states that Abraham, "contrary to hope, in hope believed" (Romans 4:18). Against all human hope and rational expectation, Abraham confidently believed. Where verse 17 had Abraham looking at Sarah, the present, verse 18 has Abraham looking at the end of history. It was not a wish on Abraham's part; it was a firm confidence in the integrity of the One who had promised.

Third, the promise was contrary to feelings. Though there were times when Abraham had doubts, he did not allow his doubts to carry the weight of the day. I like the words of John Calvin, who made the following observation:

> The mind is never so enlightened that there are no remains of ignorance, nor the heart so established that there are no misgivings. With these evils of our nature, faith maintains a perpetual conflict, in which it is often sorely shaken and put to great stress; but it still conquers.[2]

Instead, Abraham was strengthened in faith, giving glory to God.

Romans 4:21 gives the greatest definition of faith in the

Bible: "being fully convinced that what [God] had promised He was also able to perform." Our faith is based on the person of God, and His right and ability to do what He says.

"Ron, you've had a phone call," was the way Carole and I were greeted as we arrived at Camp Cedar Crest that Friday afternoon in the spring of 1988 to speak at a students retreat at LIFE Bible College. Looking at the note, we recognized the number as the home of our oldest son, Scott, and his wife, Dana.

Weeks earlier, we had been delighted to hear that Dana was pregnant with our first grandchild. Finding a telephone and dialing the number, I discovered that Dana had been sitting anxiously waiting for our call.

The news was not good. Through her sobs, Dana informed us that due to the unusual shape of her reproductive organs, the doctors had suggested that for her own welfare, maybe the pregnancy ought to be aborted. She questioned me, "Dad, what do I do?" There was no desire on her part to cut short the blessed event; yet wisely, she was seeking confirmation.

To those who always have pat answers for everything, I would like to say, "Get real!" At this point, my daughter-in-law didn't need a cliché, she needed counsel. With my emotions responding wildly, I asked her when the decision needed to be made. She said she had the weekend to decide. I prayed with her and told her, if it was OK, I'd get back to her the next morning.

I will never forget the restless night I spent wrestling with all that was going through my mind. All our family had been strongly convinced of the pro-life stance; but this had to do also with my daughter-in-law's health. Carole and I would sleep awhile, get up, cry and pray, and then go back to bed. Fortunately, I didn't have to speak to the students until mid-Saturday morning.

About 4 a.m., after five or six cycles of sleep, crying and praying, I felt led to turn to the section of Romans I had just taught a few days before in class. Between tears, I read Romans 4. Questioning the Lord as to the value of this, suddenly I read verses 17-24, phrases like "God, who gives life to the dead and calls those things which do not exist as though they did . . . contrary to hope, in hope believed . . . being fully convinced that what He had promised He was also able to perform . . . Now it was not written for his sake alone . . . but also for us."

I could hardly wait for 8 a.m. to arrive. Dana answered the phone and I simply said, "Honey, we will support whatever decision you make. But I want to read you what the Lord has placed on my heart." There was no hype or heroism. We could only depend on God's Word.

The decision was to continue with the pregnancy. During the months that followed, the doctors again expressed concern. But I will never forget the morning of November 23, 1988, when I looked at my grandson, Kyle, through the glass in the hospital nursery and later held him in my arms. There's never a time that I read this portion without remembering the goodness of God in giving me my first grandson.

Three years later, Grandma and I took Kyle back to the hospital nursery. Lifting Kyle up to see his newborn sister, Hannah, I decided to give him a lesson on family history. I said, "Kyle, that's where you met Grandpa for the first time." Then I decided to push the envelope a bit further, "Do you remember that?"

The answer was unexpected: "Yeah, and it was scary!"

All Because ... (vv. 23-25)

The death of Jesus completely paid the price for our sins. Listen to the words of Isaiah 53:5, 6:

> But He was wounded for our transgressions, He was bruised for our iniquities; the chastisement for our peace was upon Him, and by His stripes we are healed. All we like sheep have gone astray; we have turned, every one, to his own way; and the Lord has laid on Him the iniquity of us all.

The following poem were written by an unknown author:

His holy fingers formed the bough
Where grew the thorns that crowned His brow.
The nails that pierced the hands were mined
In secret places He designed.

He made the forests whence there sprung
The tree on which His holy body hung.
He died upon a cross of wood
Yet made the hill upon which it stood.

The sun which hid from Him its face
By His decree was poised in space.
The sky which darkened o'er His head
By Him above the earth was spread.

The spear that spilt His precious blood
Was tempered in the fires of God.
The grave in which His form was laid
Was hewn in rocks His hands had made.

The resurrection of Jesus was God's way of letting us know all that would ever be required for our redemption had been fully paid. It was the Father's turn to say, "It is finished!"

When our relation to God is changed, our relation to the future is also changed. It now becomes, "Christ in you, the hope of glory" (Colossians 1:27). The fulfilling of God's original design for us is once again possible, whether we are Jew or Gentile.

LESSONS ANYONE?

1. What is the difference in our being justified "when" we believe, rather than "because" we believe?
2. Provide your own definition of Biblical faith. Now compare that definition with where your faith is focused at this moment.
3. Take a few moments and compare this chapter with the Book of James. What is the relationship of faith and works?
4. Consider times when you have used "cute clichés" that sounded "spiritual," but were in fact not even Biblical.

Chapter 10

It's How You Look at It

Romans 5:1-11

The Williams family served in Hong Kong almost 16 years. Hong Kong is one of the most crowded places on the face of the earth, but it is also one of the most beautiful. Just following nightfall, when all the lights were being turned on, one of our favorite pastimes was to drive to the top of Victoria Peak. From this vista, the homes of 6.5 million inhabitants looked like sparkling diamonds. You could look below and see the financial capital of Asia, or across the bay to Kowloon, the City of Nine Dragons. The word Hong Kong means "Fragrant Harbor," and the serenity you could feel from that high point silenced the hustle and bustle of the multitudes below. Somehow, it brought the troubles of the day into perspective and made you feel like the most privileged person in the world to experience the moment.

Having dealt with humanity's inhumanity against God, and then the definition and discussion of justification by faith, it is as though Paul ascends to "Victory Peak" and with a breath of fresh rejoicing, inhales the blessings of being justified by faith.

The View From the Peak (vv. 1, 2)

He begins, "Therefore, having been justified by faith, we have peace with God through our Lord Jesus Christ" (v. 1). In the mind of the Greek (Gentile), peace was the absence of war; in the mind of the Jew, it was the establishment of a right relationship. In the case of the gospel, both are true. No longer are we at war against the Creator, but we have returned to look at Him face-to-face, with a brand-new relationship. Unlike Adam, we no longer hide because of our spiritual nakedness, but we stand firmly and fully clothed in God's righteousness.

Not only has peace been established, but we have an open door through Christ into a stance of grace. *Access* (v. 2) has the imagery of being introduced into the royal room to be presented to the king or queen. When your name is called out, the entire court bows and you are granted a royal audience. Another analogy that was often used in Paul's day was the moment experienced by a tired mariner who finally made a safe landing on solid shore following a violent storm. Our access into the life of grace carries a little bit of both. "Wow!" and "Whew!" seem to flow out of our heart simultaneously.

We also rejoice in the "hope of the glory of God" (v. 2). I like the observation of Plummer, who made the following suggestion: "If peace with God tells us of friendship with God, access points to a covenant relation in which all needed grace is pledged and supplied."[1]

Suddenly the "glory of God" is a possibility. Kaseman's words are so appropriate here: "*Elpis* (hope) is no longer the prospect of what might happen, but the prospect of what is already guaranteed."[2]

We were originally created to fulfill a divinely ordained destiny. We were formed in God's image and made to complete the beauty God designed for us. Look at Psalm 139:13-16:

> For You formed my inward parts; You have covered [knitted] me in my mother's womb. I will praise You, for I am fearfully and wonderfully made; marvelous are Your works, and that my soul knows very well. My frame was not hidden from You, when I was made [embroidered] in secret, and skillfully wrought [adorned, decorated] in the lowest parts of the earth. Your eyes saw my substance, being yet unformed. And in Your book they all were written, the days fashioned [purposed and put on display] for me, when as yet there were none of them.

But all had sinned and fallen short of God's glory—His original design. Now, being justified by faith, the hope of realizing that potential—God's glory—is once again before us. Each day we are being changed "from glory to glory" (2 Corinthians 3:18), from one degree of His plan to another. Accepting our position immediately initiates within us a process.

The View on the Pavement (vv. 3-5)

It is one thing to rejoice in the hope before us, but it is entirely another thing to rejoice (boast) in that which will produce the experience of hope within us. Now, leaving the peak of rejoicing, the apostle returns to the pavement of reality.

"We also glory in tribulations [pressure], knowing that tribulation produces perseverance [constancy and endurance]; and perseverance, character [evidence, maturity]; and character, hope" (Romans 5:3, 4). Hope is not a gift that is given to us, it is a grace that is produced in us. You see, God is more interested in what we become than what we do or get.

You know how it works! You ask for love, and God sends someone very unlovely into your life. You ask for patience, and problems arise. You ask for joy, and sorrow comes knocking at your door. You ask for self-control and end up with the short end of the stick, making you want to blow your top.

The key word in this passage is *produces,* which means "to harvest." It is the verb form of the word used for the "fruit" or "harvest" of the Spirit. You don't get more love, you just become more loving; you don't get patience, you just develop more of it; you are never given a basketful of joy, you simply become more joyful. And the harvest goes on.

Notice the result: "Hope does not disappoint [make ashamed]" (v. 5). For a clearer understanding of the depth of this, we must look at Psalm 22:4, 5: "Our fathers trusted in You; they trusted, and You delivered them. They cried unto You, and were delivered; they trusted in You, and were not ashamed." As a friend of mine, who has gone through tremendous trials with her children, wrote, "When you can't see God's hand at work, you still can trust His heart."

Why is such trust possible? "Because the love of God has been poured out in our hearts by the Holy Spirit who was given to us" (Romans 5:5). We have just reached the third span of the bridge that ties the letter to the Romans together. It ties up the previous section (3:21—4:25) and introduces us to the next (5:1—8:39). In chapter 5, we begin with the love of God being "flooded over our hearts" (Moffatt's translation) and in chapter 8, we end with nothing being able to separate us from the love of God. The verses in between, focus on God loving us.

When God's love has seized us so totally and centrally, we no longer belong to ourselves; a change of existence has taken place. Secondly, since the Holy Spirit is a down payment, we have an "objective" pledge that our hope will not be confounded. Finally, when the Holy Spirit makes us constantly sure of His love, we can praise God in the midst of earthly affliction. No longer left to ourselves and the world, we are set in the kingdom of freedom, which is no other than the openness of access to God and the peace granted therein.[3]

The View of His Love (vv. 6-11)

If you ever doubt God's love, return to Romans 5:6-11 to rediscover it. The gift of Jesus Christ to die on the cross on our behalf was the most magnificent exhibition ever hosted by God. It was the highest expression and conceivable proof that "God so loved the world . . ." (John 3:16). John later wrote, "By this we know love, because He laid down His life for us" (1 John 3:16). Once again, "In this the love of God was manifested toward us, that God has sent His only begotten Son into the world, that we might live through Him. In this is love, not that we loved God, but that

He loved us and sent His Son to be the propitiation for our sins" (4:9, 10).

In my introduction, I alluded to the impact of this letter on Karl Barth. A group of students at Harvard asked Dr. Barth what he thought was the greatest theological truth he had ever learned. Not wasting a second, this great interpreter of the truths of the Bible responded, "Jesus loves me, this I know."

Note Paul's repetitive phrase in Romans 5:6-11: "Christ died . . . Christ died . . . justified by His blood . . . death of His Son. . . ." Among those whom the Holy Spirit inspired to author the New Testament, not a one of them ever became nonchalant about the fact that Jesus had died for them.

Paul describes a downhill slide regarding our state. We were "still without strength"— destitute and unable to do anything spiritually good. Moreover, we were "ungodly"— everything that God wasn't. Couple that with the word *sinners* (v. 8) and you make our state even worse. But the real "kicker" is when he states we were *enemies* (v. 10). Now, you'd expect someone to die for a good or righteous man. But for someone with the above reputation, you've got to be kidding! Fortunately, God wasn't kidding and now, having been justified by His blood, we are saved from His wrath (v. 9), reconciled and restored to His favor (v. 10), and we now are of one mind with His purposes and design (v. 11).

Boasting Anyone?

Forty miles to the east, across the mouth of the Pearl River from Hong Kong, is the Isthmus of Macao, which returned to Chinese sovereignty at the end of 1999. This 20-square-mile piece of mainland and two islands is now populated by nearly 1.5 million people. For all the 16 years Carole and I served as Foursquare missionaries in Hong Kong and Macao, part of our supervision was the operation of the Macao Foursquare Gospel Children's Home. Administrative trips to Macao by jet were necessary at least three days each month.

Loving the children who had come from such horrendous family backgrounds was draining; at times, I found myself heading for the fortress that overlooked the entire isthmus. Built in 1628, it had been the last port for the East Indies trading ships before they sailed up the river into South China. You can still walk up the uneven pavement into the fort, deliberately designed to allow the horses rapid entry. Cannons were positioned on the walls, ensuring the safety on all sides of the fort, and to remind tourists of the battles fought over the strategic location of the city/state. In one battle, the Portuguese prevailed over the Spanish, drowning more than 3,500 soldiers in the bay that divided the fort from the country of China. Today, trees dot the landscape of the fortress. It is about the only retreat from the cacophony of sound of cars and buses, all trying to beat the other to wherever they are going.

Just below the east wall of the fortress is the Cathedral of Saint Paul. Today, the only thing standing is the elegantly carved marble and cement front of the cathedral with a huge cross dotting its top. The back of the church had been built out of wood and its insides were lit by candles. According to the story, the cathedral caught fire during a severe typhoon, and all but the front facade was completely destroyed. Sir John Bowring, then governor of the British Crown Colony of Hong Kong, was on a ship at sea during this typhoon. Winds swept their ship off course, and the clouds cut visibility to a minimum. Hopeless and helpless, the mariners and the governor thought they were going to lose their lives.

Suddenly, there was a shout. As Sir John looked up, he saw the fire at the church. Standing above the blaze was the cross. The captain headed his vessel toward the cross and the fire, arriving safely on land. Their lives had been spared.

This experience led the governor to pen these lyrics:

In the cross of Christ I glory,
Towering o'er the wrecks of time;
All the light of sacred story
Gathers round its head sublime.

When the woes of life o'er-take me,
Hopes deceive, and fears annoy,
Never shall the cross forsake me:
Lo! It glows with peace and joy.

When the sun of bliss is beaming
Light and love upon my way,
From the cross the radiance streaming
Adds more luster to the day.

Bane and blessing, pain and pleasure,
By the cross are sanctified;
Peace is there that knows no measure,
Joys that thro' all time abide.

No wonder Paul uses phrases such as "Much more then . . . And not only that . . ." when referring to life's highest destiny.

LESSONS ANYONE?

1. Do a short word study on the word *glory* both in its noun and verb forms. What does this say regarding the destiny God has designed for you?

2. Respond to the statement "God is more interested in what we become than what we do." Do you agree or disagree? Why?

3. Scanning the Letter to the Romans, find other passages which use the words "do not disappoint" or "not make ashamed." What does this say to you about God allowing us to go through pressure because He loves us?

4. Take a few moments and, from one of the Gospels, read again about the day Christ died for you. Then respond by writing a prayer to Him.

Chapter 11

Much More!

Romans 5:12-21

To fully understand Paul's explanation of these verses, we must recognize that it was a common practice for the Jewish rabbis to use a vocabulary of "light" versus "heavy" when they emphasized a particular truth. Jesus also used this method in Matthew 6:30: "Now if God so clothes the grass of the field, which today is, and tomorrow is thrown into the oven, will He not much more clothe you, O you of little faith?" In discussing the need for all the members of the body, Paul states that the eye cannot discount the hand, and then continues, "No, much rather, those members of the body which seem to be weaker are necessary" (1 Corinthians 12:22).

This same trend of discussion can be noted in 2 Corinthians 3:9, 11: "For if the ministry of condemnation had glory, the ministry of righteousness exceeds much more in glory . . . For if what is passing away was glorious, what remains is much more glorious."

The classic use of this style of argument is also found in Hebrews 9:13, 14: "For if the blood of bulls and goats and the ashes of a heifer, sprinkling the unclean, sanctifies for the purifying of the flesh, how much more shall the blood of Christ, who through the eternal Spirit offered Himself without spot to God, cleanse your conscience from dead works to serve the living God?"

In today's language, the words would go something like this: "If you think that is significant, you ain't seen nothin' yet!"

Paul used this superlative comparison in Romans 5:9, 10, when he stated that if we think being justified by Christ's blood was wonderful, it can't compare with being "saved from wrath . . . saved by His life." Paul teaches *much more* than simply justification by faith. He talks about being empowered by all Christ provided through His matchless life while here on earth.

The Priority of Life (vv. 12, 18-21)

Many have stated that Romans 5:12-21 is the most difficult passage in the Bible to understand. Paul begins his argument in verse 12, then throws in a parenthesis through verse 17. He picks up his thought in verse 18 and continues to the end of the chapter.

> Therefore, just as through one man sin entered the world, and death through sin, and thus death spread to all men, because all sinned . . . therefore, as through one man's offense judgment came to all men, resulting in condemnation, even so through one Man's righteous act the free gift

came to all men, resulting in justification of life. . . . Moreover the law entered that the offense might abound. But where sin abounded, grace abounded much more, so that as sin reigned in death, even so grace might reign through righteousness to eternal life through Jesus Christ our Lord (vv. 12, 18-21).

First, the likeness: Adam's choice was deliberate (v. 12), just as Christ's choice was deliberate. And that's as far as the similarity goes.

Then the contrasts: Through one man's offense—Adam's act—sin, death and judgment came to mankind; but through one man's righteous act—Christ's offering—justification, life and grace (the free gift) were even more evident. Remember, we have been *much more* saved from wrath (v. 9). Grace broke the *penalty* of sin.

By one man's disobedience—Adam's—many were made sinners; but by one man's obedience—Christ's—many will be made righteous. We have *much more* been saved by His life (v. 10). In other words, whereas the Law simply showed how horrible sin was, the grace of God abounded in that it broke the power of sin.

Sin reigned supreme only until grace showed up, and now a life of righteous living reigns. Grace is designed to overcome even the preeminence of sin. Life is to flow from our position—not in Adam, but in Christ. *Not only that*, we rejoice because we are in agreement with God (v. 11). There's some living to be done.

To show how superlative our hope in Christ is to our hopelessness in Adam, we only need to look at Isaiah 14:12-15, which describes the fall of Lucifer, now known as the devil.

> How you are fallen from heaven, O Lucifer, son of the morning! How you are cut down to the ground, you who weakened the nations! For you have said in your heart: "I will ascend into heaven, I will exalt my throne above the stars of God; I will also sit on the mount of the congregation on the farthest sides of the north; I will ascend above the heights of the clouds, I will be like the Most High." Yet you shall be brought down to Sheol, to the lowest depths of the Pit.

Putting the above portion of Scripture under the microscope of God's grace, we discover a truth that makes us marvel. Do you realize that by grace, you and I will enjoy all Lucifer tried to usurp by force? Look with me at these passages:

He said, "I will ascend into heaven." Jesus promised, "I go to prepare a place for you. And if I go and prepare a place for you, I will come again and receive you to Myself; that where I am, there you may be also" (John 14:2, 3).

He said, "I will exalt my throne above the stars of God." Paul wrote: "But God who is rich in mercy, because of His great love with which He loved us, even when we were dead in trespasses, made us alive together with Christ (by grace you have been saved), and raised us up together, and made us sit together in the heavenly places in Christ Jesus" (Ephesians 2:4-6).

He said, "I will sit on the mount of the congregation on the farthest sides of the north." The psalmists sang: "Great is the Lord, and greatly to be praised in the city of our God, in His holy mountain. Beautiful in elevation, the joy of the whole earth, is Mount Zion on the sides of the north, the city of the great King. . . . He shall call to the heavens from above, and to the earth, that He may judge His people: 'Gather My saints together to Me, those who have made a covenant with Me by sacrifice.' Let the heavens declare His righteousness" (Psalms 48:1, 2; 50:4-6).

He said, "I will ascend above the height of the clouds." We look forward to the day that "the Lord Himself will descend from heaven with a shout, with the voice of an archangel, and with the trumpet of God. And the dead in Christ will rise first. Then we who are alive and remain shall be caught up together with them in the clouds to meet the Lord in the air. And thus we shall always be with the Lord" (1 Thessalonians 4:16, 17).

He said, "I will be like the Most High." John writes: "Beloved, now we are children of God; and it has not yet been revealed what we shall be, but . . . we shall be like Him, for we shall see Him as He is" (1 John 3:2).

No wonder God said to the serpent, "And I will put enmity between you and the woman, and between your seed and her Seed; He shall bruise your head, and you shall bruise His heel" (Genesis 3:15).

That's what I call *much more*!

The Parenthesis (vv. 13-17)

There is a great deal of discussion whether this section of Romans is a true parenthesis. However, it certainly is an expanded explanation of verse 12. Paul states that even though there was no law to make sin apparent, it most definitely existed; as a matter of fact, the Law reigned between Adam and Moses, even over those who did not yet have any stated prohibition as Adam did. On the heels of sin came death—physical, spiritual and eternal.

The sin that rushed in like a storm sweeping across the coast remains to this day, ripping apart every ounce of resistance. By Adam's offense, many died; all were condemned and were dominated by death's presence. By the way, that's exactly the state you and I were in before we came to Jesus. We call it the old nature . . . and it is still with us.

On the other side of the coin, *much more* did the grace of God and the gift of Jesus Christ abound to man—bringing life, justification and the reign of righteous living with it. It is called the new nature . . . and it also is within us.

This is the reason we struggle as believers. Before we were saved, we were great sinners. We only had one master to follow and we went our own (at times, merry) way. There was no other dynamic crying for attention in our lives.

Then we heard the message that if we would accept Christ, all our problems would be over. The truth was, after we accepted Christ, our problems began. We became lousy sinners; no longer could we enjoy it. There was a new dimension to our lives now clamoring for more and more space in our hearts. The old does not want to leave, and the new is here to abide with us forever! Even though the grace of God is *much more* powerful, we seem to take pity (or dare I call it pleasure) on the underdog and find ourselves listening and obeying the old. In doing so, we settle for *much less*!

The story is told of ancient church fathers who came to St. Anthony, seeking the direct line to perfection, so that a man could shun the snares of Satan. Responding, St. Anthony asked them to speak their opinion. The first said, "Sobriety [seriousness] and watching [alertness]." The second shared, "Fasting and discipline." A third said,

"Humble prayer," and another said, "Poverty and obedience." Still another suggested, "Piety and works of mercy."

When everyone had spoken, St. Anthony answered, "All these are excellent graces indeed, but discretion is chief of them all." Discretion is the ability or power to decide responsibly, the freedom to act or judge on our own.

St. Anthony was right! The quickest way to turn back the traps of Satan is resident in our will—in our choice as to whose voice we will obey.

Will it be *more* or *less*?

LESSONS ANYONE?

1. From your understanding of Scripture, why is the devil such an enemy of the believer? Is his battle with God, with us or both? According to Scripture, how should we respond to his hate and accusations?

2. Take a few moments to consider what I call "The Smores" of God (much mores). Why do we often settle for less than what God has designed for us?

3. Compare the first and last Adams. Why is Christ called the "last" Adam, not the "second" Adam?

4. Define the word *discretion*. How is it to be a part of your Christian experience?

Chapter 12

A Fresh Look at Home Improvement

Romans 6:1-14

Josh Billings said, "If a man should happen to reach perfection in this world, he would have to die immediately to enjoy himself."[1]

But if you feel that only reaching 99.9 percent is good enough, read these statistics:

- Two million documents will be lost by the Internal Revenue Service this year.
- Over 810,000 faulty rolls of 35 mm film will be loaded into cameras this year.
- In the next 60 minutes, there will be 22,000 checks deducted from the wrong bank account.
- Twelve babies will be given to the wrong parents each day.

- Nearly 2.5 million books will be shipped over the next 12 months with the wrong cover.
- More than 18,000 pieces of mail will be mishandled in the next hour.
- In the next 12 months, 20,000 incorrect drug prescriptions will be written, and 107 incorrect medical procedures will be performed by the end of today.
- Can you believe that 291 pacemaker operations will be performed incorrectly this year?
- And in case you are a sports fan, each day of the year nearly $10,000 is spent on defective, often unsafe sporting equipment.
- During the coming year 104,000 income tax returns will be processed incorrectly.

One of the brush strokes we find throughout the Book of Romans is the reality that the Christian life is truly a "body religion." Our faith is lived out in human flesh. In Romans 1:18—3:20, we discovered that sin in people is expressed bodily. The physical death and the shedding of Christ's blood for our salvation was real, not virtual reality (3:21-26, esp. v. 25). The promise to Abraham, as well as Abraham's faith, flowed through his body (4:19). Moreover, in the passage we are about to study, we are not to allow sin to "reign in our mortal bodies" (6:12). Rather, we are to yield our bodies as "instruments of righteousness" (v. 13). For us, the redemption of our bodies is the culmination of our faith here on earth (Romans 8), and in 12:1, 2, we are to present our bodies as "living sacrifices."

Simultaneously, we must realize that, according to 12:2, such actions are not the *conforming* or aping of another's actions that only occur on the surface. They should be the expression of transformation—that which grows out of an inward condition. Above all, in the same way the mind was darkened and the body became sinful (see Romans 1), when the mind is transformed (undergone metamorphosis), the body becomes a living sacrifice.

Lenski put it this way:

> The renewed mind is ever bent on finding out and following God's will, what God wants of us; it has utterly ceased its old disregard of God's will, its old folly of contenting itself with its own will.[2]

This opens an arena of great challenge the apostle introduced in the "parenthesis" of Romans 5 and continues in chapters 6-8. When we come to Christ, our sinful nature is not done away with, but it enters a new dimension of understanding and divine empowerment.

It is easy to follow the major headings of Romans 6 and 7, simply by following the signs that read, "What shall we say then" and "Do you not know?" (6:1, 3, 15, 16; 7:1, 7). There are four things we must know as we go through the process that will ultimately bring us to dependency on the Holy Spirit (see ch. 8).

- We must know that our relation to the old nature has changed (6:1-14).
- We must know that we have changed masters (vv. 15-23).
- We must know that we have been freed to relate to a higher law (7:1-6).
- We must know that it's going to be a battle (vv. 7-25).

Speaking in Funeral Terms (vv. 1-14)

You cannot read this portion of Scripture without noticing the recurring word pictures Paul presents: *died* (v. 2); *death* (v. 3); *buried/baptism/death/dead* (v. 4); *united/death* (v. 5); *crucified* (v. 6); *died* (v. 7); *died* (v. 8); *dead/death* (v. 9); *death/died* (v. 10); *dead* (v. 11); and *dead* (v. 13). These are funeral terms, which simply mean that when someone dies, that which surrounds them need no longer exert any influence on them.

Paul again uses the rabbinical form of forecasting an argument, then answering it. If it is true that "where sin abounded, grace abounded much more" (5:20), then would it be better if we continued to sin so that people could more readily see God's grace? Paul had a few favorite responses to stupid questions, and one of those was "Certainly not" (6:2, 15; 7:7).

In 6:2, he gives the principle: "How shall we who died [past perfect tense—once for all] to sin live any longer in it?" Note that it was not sin, but the sinner who died. We no longer live under sin's domination. Why?

The apostle begins with an illustration of baptism. The term depicts people drowning and ships sinking. Leon Morris makes this observation: "To 'baptize' evoked association with violence . . . Josephus used it metaphorically of crowds who flooded into Jerusalem and 'wrecked the city.' When it is applied to Christian initiation we ought not to think in terms of gentleness and inspiration; it means death, death to a whole way of life."[3]

When we experienced water baptism, the act of being immersed into the water was linked to Christ's death, becoming our expiation of sin. In addition, as we came out of the water, we were linked to His resurrection, which imparts His life to our beings. Second Corinthians 4:10, 11 gives further understanding:

[Paul and his entourage are] always carrying about in the body the dying of the Lord Jesus, that the life of Jesus also may be manifested in our body. For we who live are always delivered to death for Jesus' sake, that the life of Jesus also may be manifest in our mortal flesh.

Also remember Galatians 2:20:

> I have been crucified with Christ; it is no longer I who live, but Christ lives in me; and the life which I now live in the flesh I live by faith in the Son of God, who loved me and gave Himself for me.

Not only were we baptized into Christ, we were *planted*—a name given to a field of grain where the seeds were sown at the same time and then harvested together. Linkage is the thought here: "What the believer has been 'fused/knit together with' is the reality of Christ's epoch-ending, sin's domination-breaking death, in its outworking in the here and now."[4]

I like Plummer's quote of Brown:

> This life, which believers in Christ have gotten through quickening influence from Him, is not idle, fruitless life, without fruits of holiness, but an active, stirring principle, setting folk on work constantly, and in this life believers can never win to perfection, but are still advancing and growing in grace.[5]

In Romans 6:6, Paul adds another word picture—*crucified*, which means literally to be "fenced off." Sin has been rendered inoperative, powerless, unless we reopen the gate. In 7:2, 6, sin has been taken out of the sphere of influence. The Biblical use of the word also means to "lose power" (1 Corinthians 2:6; 13:8-10); "set aside" (v. 11); "fade" (2 Corinthians 3:7, 11, 13); "remove a veil" (Galatians 5:4); and "remove or end" (v. 11).

In other words, sin has no title to rule us, no claim upon us, nor any demand to which we are obligated. In addition, having been fenced off from such dominion, we are now free to enjoy the life God has provided through the spirit of the risen Christ.

Know...Reckon...Present

The verbs in Romans 6:1-4 follow a process. *Know* (vv. 3, 6, 9) has to do with the mind. Many believers sincerely try to follow God. Yet, they are still living according to the flesh, because they simply have never known they didn't have to. That is the reason for all the above word pictures. Paul is indelibly stamping the fact in our minds.

Reckon (v. 11) is an accounting term and has to do with the will. It means that once we know it to be true, we choose to act accordingly. This is where the rubber meets the road. *Dying to sin* (v. 11) simply means that when sin tries to raise its claim on your mind and body, you remember you do not have to yield to it. Yes, it is possible not to sin, but the problem with living sacrifices is that, too often, they'd prefer to crawl off the altar. The old nature will only reign in your body as you allow it.

Present (v. 13) is the same term we will study in Romans 12:1. It has to do with making an offering, such as in presenting a substitute lamb for one's sin. There is an element of dedication, such as Mary presenting Jesus to the Lord following her days of purification (Luke 2:22). It has the idea of being "put at the disposal of" another.

In this case, our bodies became "instruments"—channels through which our Christianity is expressed. The word was used in Greek as a tool in the hands of an artisan, as well as weapons or arms.

Verse 14 is a promised conclusion—not a hopeless struggle the believer is engaged in, but one in which victory is certain. Lietzmann agrees:

"This is not a fictitious or pretend event, but a settled determination to live in the light of Christ's death and in the strength of a power which has already defeated sin's reign in death."

My Final Lesson From "Pop" Williams

My dad, Henry Lawrence Williams, was a railroader. He was born in 1902 to the son of an English immigrant. As a young boy being raised in central Illinois, "Bus" (as he was nicknamed by his friends) fell in love with baseball. For the first 12 years of his railroad career, he worked for the Illinois Terminal System, an interurban train system running between Chicago and St. Louis. We always teased him, because he was paid for being a catcher on the company's baseball team.

During those days, there were no minor leagues and the major league's schedule was short. Thus, many of the stars from the majors would continue into the fall by playing in what was then called "The Industrial Leagues." My dad caught for Dutch Leonard for 11 seasons, played with the Dean Brothers, Leo Durocher and many others. He would sit for hours, pointing his fingers (all 10 of which were broken, having played with spitballs, Emory balls and all kinds of substance being legal) and telling about his baseball days. He also had a split lip from being hit in the face with a foul ball, which scarred his mouth for over six decades of his life. Of course, one of his favorite memories was being in Wrigley Field in Chicago, Illinois on the day Babe Ruth supposedly pointed to the center field bleachers and then drove the ball out of the park at that exact spot.

After his baseball days, and having married my mother, Dad continued to work for the railroad as an electrician, later specializing in air-conditioning in the coaches. Even after we moved from Illinois to California in the winter of 1949-50, Dad continued with railroads, working until 1967 as an electrician with the Southern Pacific Railroad.

One of my fondest memories of my father was his love of trains. We could be going to a very important appointment, but if Pop Williams heard a train whistle, we'd chase it down. To do what? To count the number of cars behind the engine, of course! The rest of the world could wait until that caboose went by.

Pop died on February 9, 1980. We buried him at Rose Hills in the San Gabriel Valley of Los Angeles County. At the internment, as Dr. Paul Risser, pastor, a family friend and presently the president of the International Church of the Foursquare Gospel, was saying "dust to dust, ashes to ashes . . . ," off in the distance, a train blew its whistle. Everyone around smiled and thought, *That's fitting for the occasion.* I should say, everyone but me.

My immediate reaction was to stare intently at the casket, thinking that Pop would fling open the lid, come out and say, "Hang on, Lord, I've got a train to chase!"

But he didn't. Something was different. The train was still there . . . the sun was still shining . . . his friends were still around . . . but Pop was dead. He had been transformed into another dimension, and all the reality he had previously experienced had not vanished. But because he had died, this world's reality no longer controlled or dominated him.

Likewise, Paul states that we too have died. Our relationship to our previous lifestyle has changed. The old nature is still there, but it no longer controls or dominates us. Second Corinthians 5:17 states: "Therefore, if anyone is in Christ, he is a new creation; old things have passed away; behold, all things have become new."

That is, unless we lift up the lid and let the old things back in.

LESSONS ANYONE?

1. What is the difference between the believer dying to sin or the sin nature dying to the believer? Which is the Biblical perspective? Why is this important to you in your daily experience?

2. Define the difference between temptation and sin.

3. What areas in your life do you find to be the most difficult to overcome? How can the words *know*, *reckon* and *present* assist you?

4. Discuss what is meant by the author's claim that Christianity is a body religion.

Chapter 13

It's All About the Owner

Romans 6:15-23

There is a paradox about the Christian life. About the time you're told you're free, you are told you're still a slave. Yet, that's the beauty of it! You see, the word *slavery* expresses the total "belonging-ness," the total and willful obligation and accountability that characterizes life under grace. There is a vigor and vividness no other image can equal. The rewards are enormous!

Having informed the believers in Rome that their relation to the old sin nature has now been changed, Paul answers for the third time (3:19; 6:1, 15-23) the question about license to sin, since we are no longer under the law. He again uses that famous reply: "Certainly not! Do you not know . . .?" (vv. 15, 16).

The Option (vv. 16-18)

What words recur here? There are but two: *slaves*

(vv. 16, 17, 18, 19, 20, 22); and the concept of *obedience*—(*obey*/*obedience*, v. 16; *obeyed*, v. 17; *presented*, v. 19; *fruit*/*holiness*, vv. 21, 22). Slavery and obedience are twins. As Morris so aptly puts it:

> For the slave, obedience is the only option; as the chattel of his master he has no other function. Conversely, the reality of mastery is indicated by the practical expression of everyday submission. The function of a slave is to do what he is told. There is a change of owner, but still obedience.[1]

Plummer agrees: "Freedom from the law is not freedom from moral obligation. Whoever so charges slanders the gospel and perverts the grace of God."[2]

Another interesting look at the passage shows Paul communicating through antithetical pairs. In verse 15, he shows there is a difference between obedience under law, and obedience under grace. In verses 16-19, Paul informs us that the object of our obedience will either bring sin, death and frustration, or it will bring righteousness, holiness, and in the end, "everlasting life" (v. 22). There is an option and we are the ones who have to make that choice.

The apostle deliberately chooses to use the word *present.* We found it earlier in the chapter, and defined it as being the willful choice of the offerer as they brought their sacrifice to the Temple to be placed on the altar of God. This sounds like the same terminology Paul uses later in Romans 12:1.

Paul praises God that the obedience of a believer is from the heart, whereas their slavery to sin was involuntary. The difference is that before, we obeyed not by choice, but now from the heart, voluntarily and with sincerity. Paul does not praise them for what they have done, but he thanks God for what He has done in them.

The Obligation (vv. 19-22)

Leon Morris states:

> If our religion does not conquer our strongest evil inclination, it is worthless. A sound conversion conquers the strongest sinful inclination, and gives scope to the noblest principles and motions."[3]

Paul reminds the believers of their responsibility. If they have been freed from sin and now belong to another, it is degrading to the new master if the slave commits their loyalty to the previous owner. While what we were should always be a guidepost to our future, it should never become a hitching-post. Too often while testifying, believers spend more time and give more attention to what they were than what they are now, with a better master. Quite frankly, if the old masters were as bad as the Bible says they were (uncleanness and lawlessness; see Romans 1:18-32), then who would even want to remember or rehearse any of it?

I find it amazing that what Paul looks for in the new converts is exactly what the Law was looking for in the first place. Note the goals in the Old Testament:

- "Be holy" (Leviticus 11:44, 45)
- "Be holy" (19:2)
- "Be holy . . . separated . . . that you should be Mine" (20:26)
- "A holy people . . . for Himself [Jehovah], a special treasure" (Deuteronomy 7:6)
- "A holy people . . . a special treasure" (14:2)

- "Which He has made in praise, in name, and in honor . . . a holy people" (26:19)
- "A holy people" (28:9).

The goal of the Law was holiness, but Paul recognized that holiness was to be the end result of the process, rather than a means.

I am not a gardener. It probably is fortunate that Carole and I live in an apartment that demands no yard work. However, there was one time I got the urge to grow some flowers on our front veranda. Because of previous experiences (or dare I say, failures), my wife laughed when I told her my plan.

I went to the store and purchased the bulbs. The salesperson told me to make sure the soil was nurtured with light and water. I returned home, planted the bulbs and each morning checked on the progress of the plants.

Although I watered the soil every day, there was a long period of time when I saw no signs of growth. It was tempting to dig up the bulbs and see what was taking place underneath the soil. My better judgment assured me that doing so would kill any progress, so I decided to patiently follow the instructions and keep watering. Weeks later I was rewarded with sprouts, then stems and finally a whole flower pot of blooms.

What was the key to my success as a gardener? I patiently maintained the soil with light and water. In time, if we keep the soil right, the blooms burst forth.

Holiness is the result of, not the requirement for, our relating to our new Master. We are obligated to acknowledge His lordship; He is obligated to activate His lordship in our lives.

Kasemann writes:

> Belonging to God should find earthly manifestation. Sanctification means that the world sees . . . God reflected in one's bodily (social) expressions of life, as a mirror, and it thus catches a glimpse of the God who looks on His creature. The world is thus confronted by its true Lord through his servants.[4]

The Owner (v. 23)

It all comes down to the integrity of the owner. What is the difference between the old master and our new one? The distinction is found in these words: *wages* and *gift*. *Wages* were the rations or subsistence paid that the Roman soldier received while on the field of battle. In other words, the only thing that serving the old master will bring is lawlessness and uncleanness (v. 19); death, frustration and failure (vv. 16, 21, 23); and shame (v. 21).

Gift has to do with the donation of land the king gave to his victorious soldiers, which provided them sovereign dominion. For all who faithfully obey and serve the new Master, God's gift will bring forth righteousness (vv. 16, 18); holiness (vv. 19, 22); and life (vv. 22, 23).

In today's vernacular, this would be like choosing between mere existence as opposed to finding abundant enablement and enjoyment.

In my book, *Life's Highest Delight*, I shared the story of an immigrant family who saved every dime to move to the new land of America. Because of the cost of the tickets, the family had no extra money to purchase food. All they could afford was peanuts, dry bread and water. It would be demanding and somewhat degrading, as they were cramped into steerage among hundreds of others. Still they were willing to make the necessary sacrifice. During the voyage, while other passengers enjoyed the ship's cuisine, the mother and father gathered the children into a corner in the lower deck to feed them their daily rations.

The ocean liner docked at the pier in New York two weeks later. Glad that their ordeal was over, the family gathered their belongings to disembark. As they walked down the gangplank, the captain stopped them and inquired where they had been for the past 14 days . . . why they had not taken advantage of the facilities of his ship.

The captain was aghast when the father, filled with embarrassment, spoke about the family's poverty, yet their determination to make it to the new country. He responded, "My good man, didn't you know when you bought the tickets that all the meals on the ship were included? Didn't you read the brochure or the back of your tickets that explained all the amenities you could freely enjoy? This ship is the world's most modern sailing vessel and all its facilities were at your service! All your family's meals were included in the price of the ticket!"

Too many of us, like the family in the story, are willing to live out our Christian life in agonizing frugality of faith and "fruitless-ness." We continue to run back to the old master, who is not only the enemy of our souls but who dishes out failure and frustration.

Paul writes, not in derision or ridicule, but in loving encouragement, "Do you not know that you are now the servant of a new Master—One who has bought you with a price, One who has provided all things that pertain to life and godliness?" It is more than just a nice spiritual concept. It is a practical reality and life's highest destiny. Since we are already His anyway, why not enjoy it? It only stands to reason.

LESSONS ANYONE?

1. How do you respond to those who consider their position in Christ as their total sufficiency, but who leave obedience out of the equation?
2. What is the Biblical definition of holiness? In your own experience, how often is holiness a matter of consideration or discussion?
3. Why do people settle for a mere Christianity rather than an abundant experience?
4. In the author's illustration of the immigrants, what was the biggest misperception the father had? Why was he not aware of the available abundance? Apply this to your experience today.

Chapter 14

And There's One More Thing

Romans 7:1-6

Herb Schneidau is a gentle giant of a man. His 6-foot, 8-inch frame is only exceeded by the size of his hands—the largest I have ever seen—and the size of his heart, for he is the most godly man I have ever met. For several years, Herb served as the chief administrative officer and corporate secretary of the International Church of the Foursquare Gospel, overseeing all property transactions, approval of loans and administrative matters of our Foursquare congregations across the United States. He was responsible for presenting these matters for approval each week to the Executive Staff Committee of our denomination.

Almost without exception, after we had considered his printed agenda, he would comment, "And there's one more thing . . ."—presenting us with some emergency or expedient matter that needs to be considered.

In Romans 5, Paul began the section on the process of Christian growth by telling us that God has much more in store for us than simply being saved. In chapter 6, he tells us that our relationship to the old sin nature has changed; we have a new master. That new master will bring us to the place of reigning in holiness and fresh relationship, which we call "everlasting life." If this is not enough, as he begins chapter 7 (which is our division of the text, not his), he sounds like Herb Schneidau: "And there's one more thing!"

That "thing" has to do with the role of Jewish law in relation to living a holy life. Paul had discussed what we have been delivered from:

- We have died to sin (6:2).
- We were justified from sin (v. 7).
- We are free from sin (v. 18).
- We walk in newness of life.

Now, it is the apostle's aim to speak to the Jewish believers regarding the truth that likewise . . .

- We have died to the law (7:4).
- We were justified (delivered) from the law (v. 6).
- We have been freed from the legalism of the law (v. 3).
- We walk in the newness of the Holy Spirit, not the oldness of some formal code of conduct.

It has to do with "life" not "letter."

The Integrity of the Law (v. 1)

Paul brings in a new analogy. Immediately, he gets in

trouble. Barclay comments: "Seldom did Paul write so difficult and so complicated a passage."[1] Dodd agrees: "Paul's illustration is confused from the outset. . . ." But Lenski disagrees and writes, "Paul's words are perfectly chosen, just as he wanted."[2] I guess it's just how you look at it.

The confusion lies in how we look at this passage. Remember, the context is about reigning in righteousness, not a treatise on marriage and divorce. Paul is not dealing with adultery, he is describing living abundantly by the power of the Holy Spirit who lives in each of us.

I especially like the observation of Joyce A. Little, who is quoted by Leon Morris:

> "First, Paul is concerned with demonstrating that the law played a necessary role prior to the coming of Christ (hence the validity of the law governing the first marriage). Second, Paul wishes to use verses 2 and 3 as an analogy demonstrating that death can change one's relationship to the law. Third, Paul wishes to use the analogy structurally as a means by which to develop his view that our death to the law takes place for a specific purpose, in order that we might 'serve in the new life of the Spirit.'"[3]

First of all, whether the law of the Lord or the law of the land, there is a legal order to which citizens of the capital are subject. Writing to the Galatians, Paul describes the purpose of the law: "But before faith came, we were *kept under guard* by the law, kept for the faith which would afterward be revealed. Therefore, the law was our *tutor* to bring us to Christ, that we might be justified by faith. But after faith has come, we are no longer under a tutor" (3:23-25). The law of the Lord served as a guardian and a teacher.

Sounds like parenthood to me. As our three sons were growing, and even after they had become young adults still at home, there was a set of rules and a lifestyle they were expected to follow.

It might be interesting to let you in on some of the rules around the Williams household as the boys were growing up. No major decision was made before we held a "family meeting." Mom was always there when the boys came home from school. At least 30 minutes were spent at supper, and a time of devotion or family activity held precedence over everything. Every Saturday morning was "workday" at the house. Each boy was required to help before participating in any play or activity.

When leaving the house, the child told us where he was going, whom he was going with and his time of return. Lateness required a telephone call. The penalty for not adhering was being grounded for two weeks. Likewise, the boys always knew our whereabouts, and the rules regarding telephoning applied to Mom and Dad as well.

Above all, there would be no sassing of their mother or using the Lord's name in vain. By the way, they also ate what was on the table—at home and everywhere else.

While we were serving overseas, the boys (and the parents) were never allowed to refer to the nationals as "them." We discouraged the use of any phrase that put the missionary in a separate category from the national. Activities and special celebrations in the national church were required for all of the family. After we returned to the U.S., while the circumstances changed, many of the rules remained in effect.

The purpose was not to thwart their freedom, but to protect and instill within them a set of values that would benefit them when they finally got on their own. I am not suggesting that you establish the same set of rules; if you focus on minutiae, you will miss the message of the illustrations, both Paul's and mine. The establishment of boundaries is necessary in God's kingdom (the church), human society and in the home. Unfortunately, most Christians have established for themselves a new type of ACLU—Anything-goes Christian Liberties Union.

An Intruder Into the Marriage (vv. 2-4)

Note the change in the subject here. Both in the Jewish law and the Gentile order of the day, the woman is bound to her husband as long as he lives. According to Deuteronomy 24:1, since only the man could initiate the right of divorce, if she marries another man, she breaks the divine covenant and the decree of the land. She is called an adulteress.

However, should her husband die, no matter what, the woman is *released* from the laws by which she had been bound. She is free to marry another. By the way, it is important to note that it wasn't the law that died; it was the husband.

Paul now sums it up. We who have identified with Christ through faith have "become dead" so that we might be married to another, even better husband—"Him who was raised from the dead" (v. 4). We will then be able to "bear fruit" to God. That fruit has already been identified in 6:22 as holiness.

Evans writes: "The great end of our marriage to Christ is our fruitfulness in love, and grace and every good work." Hosea prophesied this: "'And it shall be, in that day,' says the Lord, 'that you will call Me "My Husband," and no longer call Me "My Master" . . . I will betroth you to Me forever; yes, I will betroth you to Me in righteousness and justice, in lovingkindness and mercy; I will betroth you to Me in faithfulness, and you shall know the Lord'" (2:16, 19, 20).

Not only do we have a better Master, but now a better Husband: "As the bridegroom rejoices over the bride, so shall your God rejoice over you" (Isaiah 62:5).

"I Do" Takes on a New Meaning (vv. 5, 6)

When we tried to live according to the demands of external rites, ceremonies and legalistic commands, our evil affections and corrupt desires were only *aroused* (awakened). We came to the conclusion that we could never be able to make the "ole man" happy. Frustration resulted and we quit trying.

But then death occurred and we were *delivered* (Greek: *katargeo*) from that which bound our feelings and our actions. Actually, this term was never used in common Greek conversation or literature. Paul uses it in 7:2 (*released*), here in verse 6, and also in Galatians 5:4, where the idea of invalidating one's relationship with God is stated.

That release has made it possible for us to now serve willingly, not out of obligation. And it provides the wherewithal, as well as the willingness. We now serve by our own choice and by the power of the Holy Spirit, who has come to reside within us.

Plummer suggests the following:

> God's regenerated servants have a new apprehension of truth and of duty, of privilege and of obligation; new dispositions towards God and man, towards God's Word and

> people, His laws and His promises, new qualities of heart, loving what they once hated, hating what they once loved, fearing and hoping as they never did before; faith displacing unbelief, love superseding enmity and penitence taking the place of hardness of heart. And all this is done with a freshness of spirit, a vigor and an earnestness.[4]

The story is told about a husband who was a perfectionist and demanded the same from his wife. For many decades, no matter what his wife did for him, it never seemed to be enough. At the beginning of each day, the husband would make out his list of chores for the wife to do. At the end of each day, he would scrutinize the list just to be sure that she did all she was supposed to do. The best compliment she ever received was a disinterested grunt if she had finished everything. She grew to hate her husband. When he died unexpectedly, she was embarrassed to admit to herself that she was relieved.

Within a year of her husband's death, she met a warm and loving man who was everything her former husband was not. They fell deeply in love with each other and were married. Every day they spent together seemed better than the day before.

One afternoon, as she was cleaning out boxes in the attic, a crumpled piece of paper caught her eye. It was one of the old chore lists her first husband used to make out for her. In spite of her chagrin, she couldn't keep from reading it again. To her shock and amazement she discovered that, without even thinking about it, she was now doing for her new husband all the things she used to hate to do for her old husband. Her new husband had never once suggested that she do any of those things; she was doing them because she loved him. Work that had been naked drudgery had been clothed in love and transformed into joyful service.

Our love for God clothes our service to Him in joy. When we worship God, we respond to His love for us by expressing our love for Him in song, prayer and thanksgiving. God wants to impress His love upon us so that we are transformed, little by little, into His lovers. When that happens, our motive for service will be changed into a labor of love.

Someone once said, "Duty makes us do things well; but love makes us do them beautifully." The Scriptures say: "For this is the love of God, that we keep His commandments. And His commandments are not burdensome" (1 John 5:3). Allow God to give you a fresh start in your obedience and service to Him by understanding that His law is not a list of burdensome chores, it is His gracious promises for your destiny.

Wasn't that the purpose of the Law in the first place? Wasn't it to bring us to a knowledge of our sinfulness and a reliance on His sinlessness? This "one more thing" makes all the difference in our service!

LESSONS ANYONE?

1. Having considered the various difference of opinions of commentators, why do you think Paul wrote this passage as he did? Was he confused or was there a particular "reason to his madness"?

2. Contrast obeying and serving God out of freedom, and obeying and serving Him out of obligation. Does this free believers to do as they wish?

3. In past generations, the church set standards of acceptable lifestyle for the Christian. Should it still set and expect such standards? Why?

4. Where does holy living fit into witnessing to the society?

Chapter 15

The Real Battleground

Romans 7:7-25

Some months ago I was talking with a beloved sister in the Lord. She was excited about a new fervency she had experienced about the effectiveness of prayer for other nations. She said, "You know, this 'spiritual warfare' thing is beginning to become fun! I am taking dominion over powers that control Argentina; over demons that bind India . . ." and the list went on.

I was aghast. Either I had totally misunderstood what she was trying to convey, or she had totally missed the very essence of what spiritual warfare is all about. Warfare is never pretty; it leaves scars and wounds, and it is furious and unrelenting. It never brings about peace accords, for we are never innocent victims—we are targets of the one who is the "enemy of our souls."

Moreover, while I do believe in destroying demonic strongholds around our world through powerful and anointed intercession, combating the demonic strongholds over places on the map is easy compared to combating the demonic strongholds over problems in our own lives. You see, once we have prayed for overseas battlegrounds, we can relieve ourselves of any responsibility to act. But when the battle rages within our stubborn ego, we discover the battleground actually is within us. The responsibility to act is now ours. That's warfare—spiritual warfare!

The Benefits of the Law (vv. 7-13)

As he has previously done, the apostle now presupposes some of the questions that will be asked. Since the "passions of sin" were awakened by the Law, does it mean that the Law in itself was evil? Paul's favorite words: "Certainly not! On the contrary . . ."

First of all, we would not have recognized our own sin if it weren't for the presence of the Law (vv. 7-9). Knowledge and guilt came with the publication of the divine design. While God's "word is a lamp to my feet and a light to my path" (Psalm 119:105) and guides my steps, it also reveals flaws in my steps and in my character. After having been away for several days, have you ever turned on the light in a messy room?

Actually that was the very design of the Law. As God was revealing His coming punishment upon Israel's spiritual rebellion, the Lord told the prophet Amos that He was "setting a plumb line in the midst of [His] people Israel" (Amos 7:8). The concept of the plumb line or straight edge has already been stated in Romans 3:20.

The Law only discovered sin—it did not originate it! Every morning when I look into the bathroom mirror, I come face-to-face with this principle. The mirror is only reflecting the mug peering into it, flaws and all!

Recently, I discovered that a growth on my forehead had suddenly enlarged and changed colors. At first I passed it off as not important, but after three other people asked me about it in the same day, I decided to see a doctor. Fortunately, a small medical procedure took care of something which, if ignored, could have become very serious.

The real problem with my nonconformance to the Law is not with the standards God has set forth, but with the sin that already exists within me. As someone has said, "The fault lies not in the ideal, but in the man who reacts against it."

Paul describes the assault of our sin nature as "taking opportunity by the commandment" (Romans 7:8). His metaphor is a military one—the act of an army invading territory and setting up a base camp for its operations. After taking areas of our lives captive, it literally "killed the happy sinner."

By the way, I find it amazing that Paul would refer to the 10th commandment ("You shall not covet," v. 7) rather than one of the other more vivid ones. Could it be that this was the very essence of the problem between the Jewish and Gentile believers in Rome? Both were at fault. Their problem was neither social nor generational—it was with sin that had set up camp in both of their hearts!

Second, the Law itself was to bring forth life (vv. 10-12). The Law was holy, because it came from God. It was just because it was fair and accurate (we call it objective), and it was good in that its purpose was to promote right living.

Paul's imagery sounds just like Genesis 3:13, when Eve responded to God, "The serpent deceived me, and I ate." We cry "Foul! Seduced!" but fail to realize the words of James when he wrote the following:

> Let no one say when he is tempted, "I am tempted by God"; for God cannot be tempted by evil, nor does He Himself tempt anyone. But each one is tempted when he is drawn away by his own desires and enticed. Then, when desire has conceived, it gives birth to sin; and sin, when it is full-grown, it brings forth death. Do not be deceived, my beloved brethren (1:13-16).

Our enemy is not the commandments of God; our enemy is sin.

Third, the Law highlighted the seriousness of our sin and our desperate attempt to rely on our own ability to overcome it (Romans 7:13). The phrase "sin, that it might appear sin," is used deliberately by Paul. The verb connotation *appear* is of being "unmasked, identified, made apparent." In other words, the Law showed sin for what it truly is. Then, because the Law's role was to inform, not energize us to righteousness, sin seized the opportunity. We recognized how helpless we were; in fact, it inflamed the situation and our sinning became deadly.

The Battle Within (vv. 14-25)

Within the next 12 verses, note that the word *I* appears 25 times. There are several reasons why we are led to believe that these verses describe Paul's experience *after* his conversion.

Note Paul's use of the present tense, as opposed to the past tense in which he has just finished writing. His view of the unbeliever's experience is much different (Romans 1—3) than what he expresses here—the unbeliever reveled in his sin, not hated it (7:15). As a matter of fact, the unbeliever was adept in performing what was evil (v. 19) and in no way tried to find out how to perform what was good (v. 18). There was only one principle or nature resident in the unbeliever. Here there are two: the inward delighting in the law of God (v. 22) and "another law" (v. 23), warring against and taking Paul captive as a prisoner of war (POW) to be sold as a slave. Finally, Paul confesses that only through Jesus Christ can he be rescued from the corrupt and evil propensities of his flesh (v. 25).

Keeping this in context with the entire letter, Paul deals with what takes place in the believer, both Jew and Gentile, when the "doubtful things"—foods, days, customs and prejudices of Romans 14 and 15—become the criteria for our relationship to God and to one another. It not only causes war within, but it also causes a skirmish among His people.

All of us identify with the words "For what I will to do, that I do not practice; but what I hate, that I do" (v. 15) and the verses that follow. There's not a believer who has not fallen prey to the attack of the flesh. We don't understand it . . . we hate it . . . we feel helpless. Sin demands sovereignty; it is an unwanted guest and a hostile witness to God's purpose in us. Even on our bumper stickers, we express our frustration: "Be patient with me; God's not finished with me yet," or "I'm not perfect, just forgiven."

While it is normal to experience this struggle within, such a defeated lifestyle should not be the norm for the believer. Romans 7:7-25 is part of the experience, but not the whole. The warfare of chapter 7 is only a precursor to the concept of "more than conquerors" in 8:37. Human determination and self-reliance are shown as helpless in chapter 7 so that divine enablement and destiny can be realized in chapter 8. The only time Romans 7 becomes our experience is when we fail to assimilate to ourselves the work and provision of the Spirit so vividly and extensively expounded in the very next chapter.

What should we do, however, when we "slip back one chapter"? What do children do when they are learning to walk? They fall, and at times, scrape their knees rather severely. But we'd never encourage them to sit there and lick their wounds. We would make them get off their duffs and try again . . . and again . . . and again. We notice that as they gain confidence and a bit of experience, the time between falls become longer, until they are able to run around the house, even getting into things we wish they wouldn't.

When we stumble, the Holy Spirit comes along, pulls us up by His strong hands, dusts the dirt from our backsides and says, "Go again and grow up!" Remember, He's our coach, not our critic. He really wants us to make it.

A young man named Troyal, decided to accept a scholarship to Oklahoma State University for track and field—javelin throwing, to be exact. Since athletics did not seem to be his real calling, however, Troyal asked himself this question: "If God came to earth with a box containing the reason for my life inside, what words would I most like to find?"

It didn't take Troyal long to decide that the box would contain two words: "the music." He picked up a little guitar (his voice wasn't half bad), some great songs he'd written and set off for Nashville, Tennessee.

On his first venture in the music business, Troyal got nowhere. He returned to Oklahoma City. Two years later, he tried Nashville again. He worked at a boot shop, while his wife worked at a dry cleaner. One night he showed up at an audition evening at the Bluebird Café. A Columbia Records scout caught Troyal's act and signed him to a record contract. Troyal Garth Brooks, now the best-selling country and western artist of all time, found the race he wanted to run and didn't quit until he had won.

What is in your box? It may look like a lot of round pegs in square holes. God has something wonderful for each of us. Too often, however, we give up or, worse yet, see the challenge as too great and quit trying. We allow sin and doubt to sell us to failure as POWs.

When the psalmist David needed help, he penned Psalm 121: "I look to the mountains; does my strength come from mountains? No, my strength comes from God, who made heaven, and earth, and mountains. He won't let you stumble, your Guardian God won't fall asleep. Not on your life!" (vv. 1-3, *The Message*).

We may feel like we are losing the battle, but our Lord is not there just to begin the attack— He fights alongside us. He's here for the duration of the war (our destiny). He can make us into victorious witnesses of His life and grace.

Just keep reading!

LESSONS ANYONE?

1. In what ways did the "dos and don'ts" of the Law rouse the passion for sinning in our hearts? Why do you think this is so?
2. Do you believe Paul's experience, described in Romans 7, was preconversion or was it a present experience?
3. In your own life, what is the "don't" that gives you the greatest problem? What form and forum does that battle take? How are you making progress?
4. What should we do when we fall short of God's expectancy in our obedience? How do you normally deal with repentance and restoration?

Chapter 16

In All These Things: Part I

Romans 8:1-13

We have now come to the fourth major span in the bridge called "the Letter to the Romans." In Romans 1:17, Paul declares that the righteous shall live by faith; in 3:21-31, he explains that God is both just and the justifier of all who believe (apart from the Law); and in 5:1-8, he spells out the process that has begun in our lives through the love of God. Now, in chapter 8, we discover there is no condemnation, no defeat and no separation from that love. Through Jesus Christ we cease being the wretched and commence being the winners.

Whereas in chapter 7 the word *I* continually recurs, in this chapter the focus is not on self-help but the Spirit's help. There is the total absence of any imperative or command. It is all about divine provision, not about human persistence. There is a rest, not a restlessness; it is a "being carried along" rather than "carrying the load."

One of my favorite movies is *Driving Miss Daisy*. In the film, the chauffeur (Morgan Freeman) receives constant instructions from Miss Daisy (Jessica Tandy) on where to go and how to get there. Knowing better, the driver simply replies, "Yes, Miss Daisy," and with tender care and attention, takes the best roads. Upon arrival at their destination, Miss Daisy sometimes recognizes his wisdom.

What a picture of Romans 8. We sit in the backseat making demands on God, while He continues developing our Christian character through better roads (experiences), better care (lessons and teachings) and greater attention (provision and protection). Could it be that being led by the Holy Spirit is simply the choice to sit in the backseat and leave the driving to Him?

The development of our Christian character will be accomplished through specific things that the Holy Spirit is doing in our lives that "work together for good to those who love God, to those who are the called according to His purpose" (8:28).

He Frees Us to Live (vv. 1-4)

There are no greater words in Holy Scripture than these: "There is therefore now no condemnation to those who are in Christ Jesus" (v. 1). In this context, *katakrima* (condemnation) carries with it the idea of "penal servitude." It would be ludicrous if a man or woman who had been sentenced to death received a pardon and then chose to remain in prison. Likewise, since there is no condemnation now or in the future, why do we choose to remain locked up in the cell of the flesh rather than enjoy the pleasures of freedom provided by the Spirit of God?

We are "in Christ Jesus." We have been redeemed by His righteousness (Romans 3:21-31). We are linked relationally to Him as the branch is to the vine (John 15:1-7) and as the body receives life from the head (1 Corinthians 12:27; Ephesians 1:23). His Spirit dwells in us (1 Corinthians 6:15, 19; 12:13). His life is appropriated and experienced in reality by faith (Ephesians 3:17; Galatians 3:26, 27).

But like Miss Daisy's car, the rubber has to meet the road. Otherwise, these great principles turn into empty platitudes we neither understand nor experience. How can we even begin to see such a light at the end of the tunnel?

The answer is in the words "law of the Spirit of life in Christ" (v. 2). For years I carried the emphasis of being "in Christ" over to the next three verses, and missed the importance of the term *Spirit of life in Christ*. This is not some nice religious phraseology; it is a concrete reality.

By whose power did Jesus live His earthly life and perform His earthly ministry? According to Philippians 2:8, though He was God, "He humbled Himself." In other words, He emptied (*kenoo*) Himself, forgoing the privilege of acting as deity on His own. He did not empty Himself of His deity, for if that took place, He no longer could have fulfilled the demands of the Cross. He was not some sort of divine neurotic, who sometimes acted as God and at other times slipped into humanity. At all times, while being the God-man, our Lord would not allow Himself to act independently, though He had both the ability and authority to do so.

Instead, *Jesus Christ was begotten by the Holy Spirit* (see Matthew 1:20; Luke 1:35; John 1:14; Hebrews 7:26; 10:5). The human nature of the Christ child was through the work of the Spirit. It was not a new being who was called into life as in all other cases, but One who had existed from eternity and who now entered into vital relation with human nature. Remember the Christmas carol, "Silent Night," and the phrase, "Jesus, Lord, at Thy birth"?

Jesus Christ was energized by the Holy Spirit (see Isaiah 11:2; John 3:31-36). In Christ's birth, the Holy Spirit effected not just a separation from sin, but He endowed Jesus' human nature with glorious gifts, powers and faculties. The Holy Spirit also caused these gifts to be exercised, and gradually, to enter into full activity.

Jesus Christ was anointed by the Holy Spirit (Acts 10:38). We often see the water baptism of Jesus as being simply the right thing to do (Matthew 3:15). In another sense, the act of Jesus fulfilling righteousness was an initiation of our Lord into the priesthood as required in Leviticus 8:6, 10, 12. Since Christ was fully man, even in His office, He had to be installed according to human custom. The washing of the priest was symbolic of the Holy Spirit. It is of no small significance that God's voice from heaven stated Christ's messianic function as the Son of God. The dove from heaven anointed Him to serve.

Jesus Christ offered Himself through the Holy Spirit (Hebrews 9:14). Christ did not redeem us by His sufferings alone, but this passion was accomplished by His love and voluntary obedience. The Holy Spirit enabled Him to finish that eternal work whereby our souls are redeemed.

Jesus Christ was quickened by the Holy Spirit (Romans 1:4; 8:11; 1 Peter 3:18). The Holy Spirit performed a peculiar role in the Resurrection (see Ephesians 1). Though not directly referenced, the Spirit's work in Christ's exaltation is implied.

In each of the above, the Holy Spirit was either an agent or a perfecter of Christ's relation to us. What was the wisdom of God in doing this? While Christ was the Son of God by nature and divine assignment, we are sons of God by grace alone. For Christ to act according to His own prerogative as God and then to ask us to be like Him would have been unfair and impossible, because we do not possess His divine nature. But by living according to the law of the Spirit of life—the Holy Spirit—and then, following His ascension, sending that same Holy Spirit to dwell in us, Jesus made spiritual life attainable. Hear this! As believers, you and I have the same Holy Spirit dwelling in and upon us as did the Lord Jesus Christ!

That's why Romans 8:3, 4 reads: "For what the [Mosaic] law could not do in that it was weak through the flesh [impossible to keep], God did by sending His own Son in the likeness of sinful flesh . . . that the righteous requirement of the law [a perfect life] could be fulfilled in us who do not walk according to the flesh but according to the [Holy] Spirit." Christ's life by the Spirit makes our life by the Spirit possible!

We now can be Christians—Christlike in life and deed. Thus, we understand our Lord's excitement about getting back to heaven in order to send "another Comforter" (John 14:15, 16, KJV). It explains His words about "greater works" (v. 12).

It is the Holy Spirit's work to regenerate us (John 3:5; Romans 8:16; Galatians 4:6). We are inwardly energized by the Holy Spirit (1 John 2:27). We are outwardly anointed and empowered by the Holy Spirit (Acts 1:8; Luke 24:49). Our offering of service is by the work of the

Holy Spirit in us (Romans 12:1, 2; Titus 3:5, 6; 2 Corinthians 3:3-6). In the future, it will be the Holy Spirit who raises us up to heaven and presents us to God (Romans 5:5; 2 Corinthians 4:14).

That's why Paul can state in Romans 8:31: "If God is for us, who can be against us?" The reality is no condemnation, but accomplishment. His commands have now become our enablings.

To run and work the law commands,
Yet gives me neither feet nor hands;
But better news the gospel brings;
It bids me fly and gives me wings.

He Alerts our Minds (vv. 5-8)

When we walk according to the Spirit, He makes us aware of what He expects. He begins by capturing our attention, our desires and our pursuits.

According to the apostle, that's where the battle begins. Those who live according to their own way focus on the things of the flesh—their inabilities, their perceptions and prejudices. The word *carnal* has to do with the things of this world. It is centered on what we will eat, what we will drink, what we will put on, and who will notice us (Matthew 7). It discerns the weather but can never understand "the signs of the times" (16:3). It is having more friendship with the world than with God (lust, murder, covetousness, anger, arguing, greed—see James 4:1-4). It is the lust of the flesh, the lust of the eyes and the pride of life that cause us to be *foolish* (1 John 2:16). It is exactly what God warned Adam and Eve would happen if they ate of the Tree of Knowledge of

Good and Evil. Their new understanding became too heavy to bear and it crushed them.

But since we are "in the Spirit"—allowing Him to act as president as well as resident—we set our minds on the things that the Holy Spirit desires to reveal to us. We allow our understanding to be renewed (Romans 12:2). We think soberly and honestly about ourselves (v. 3). We pray in the Spirit with understanding (1 Corinthians 14:15). We will know the hope of His calling (Ephesians 1:18). We will have the same attitude as Christ (Philippians 2:5). Our mind will be set on things above (Colossians 3:2). We will think on what is true, noble, just, pure, lovely and of good reputation (Philippians 4:8). We will walk as children of light, redeeming the time and understanding the will of the Lord (Ephesians 5:17).

He Gives Life to Our Mortal Bodies (vv. 9-13)

The very fact that the Holy Spirit indwells you—for He has entered the life of every person who has accepted Jesus Christ—is the assurance of your salvation. Nothing more is needed.

Paul explained it this way to the Ephesians:

> He came and preached peace to you who were afar off and to those who were near. For through Him we both have access by one Spirit to the Father. Now, therefore, you are no longer strangers and foreigners, but fellow citizens with the saints and members of the household of God, having been built on the foundation of the apostles and prophets, Jesus Christ Himself being the chief cornerstone, in whom the whole building, being joined together, grows into a holy temple in the Lord, in whom

> you are also being built together for a dwelling place of God in the Spirit (2:17-22).

The apostle also wrote that our bodies are temples of the Holy Spirit (see 1 Corinthians 3:16; 6:19; 2 Corinthians 6:16; Galatians 4:6; and 2 Timothy 1:14). Jesus informed the disciples that the Spirit of truth would dwell in them (John 14:17).

Because the Holy Spirit dwells in us, and because we have become aware of His standard, He gives life to our humanity (mortal bodies) to bring forth life and freedom. We are totally in His debt (Romans 8:12). In other words, there is not an additional thing needed in order to live a holy life according to His will. Any words to the contrary are simply excuses.

We have the privilege of choice. But we do not have the prerogative of outcome. If we live according to the flesh, our experience will be frustration and death. If we live according to the Spirit, we will experience freshness of life until we make it (v. 13; see also 1:16).

I'm sure this was a conversation piece between Paul and his friend Peter as they were together in Rome. Listen to Peter's words:

> Grace and peace be multiplied to you in the knowledge of God and of Jesus our Lord, as His divine power has given to us all things that pertain to life and godliness, through the knowledge of Him who called us by glory and virtue, by which have been given to us exceedingly great and precious promises, that through these you may be partakers of the divine nature, having escaped the corruption that is in the world through lust. But also for this very reason, giving all diligence, add to your faith

> virtue, to virtue knowledge, to knowledge self-control, to self-control perseverance, to perseverance godliness, to godliness brotherly kindness, and to brotherly kindness love. For if these things are yours and abound, you will neither be barren nor unfruitful in the knowledge of our Lord Jesus Christ (2 Peter 1:2-8).

Several years ago I was invited to visit Edwards Air Force Base just outside Lancaster, California. This base is where many of our country's new experimental aircraft are tested and where many of the space shuttles landed upon their return from space. At the time, one of our Foursquare chaplains was stationed there and conducted what he called "The Ministry of God's Presence," right there on the flight line. Having been in the U.S. Air Force in my younger days, I found the personal tour exciting.

Because of the type of clearance I had during my time in the service, we were allowed to tour one experimental site that I later learned was the beginning of the "stealth" era. The guide told us that the aircraft could fly twice the speed of sound at an altitude of 500 feet, and the hundreds of thousands of sensors on the front edge of its horizontal stabilizers could measure the moisture in the air, even recording the density of a snowflake. The computers inside the craft could also rectify 270 simultaneous malfunctions within a microsecond.

If this was not enough to give my brain a power surge, my mind defaulted when I heard that the plane could turn straight upward and with the help of stealth power could reach an altitude of more than 20,000 feet in less than a minute. During that 60-second burn, the amount of power expended would have been able to light the entire city of Los Angeles for a 24-hour period.

Forty-five minutes later on my way home, as my 4-cylinder Buick Skyhawk was trying to gather sufficient horsepower to pass a slow truck coming over the 4,000-foot Escondido Summit, I remembered what I had just heard. Compared to what I was now experiencing, I could hardly fathom the magnitude of human genius and the convergence of forces to create such power. I finally gave up and exclaimed, "God, that's awesome!"

Inside, a small voice said, "Piece of cake." Then the Holy Spirit reminded me of the prayer He inspired the apostle Paul to pray for the church in Ephesus:

> That the God of our Lord Jesus Christ, the Father of glory, may give to you . . . that you may know . . . what is the exceeding greatness of His power toward us who believe, according to the working of His mighty power which He worked in Christ when He raised Him from the dead and seated Him at His right hand in the heavenly places, far above all principality and power and might and dominion, and every name that is named, not only in this age but also in that which is to come. And He put all things under His feet, and gave Him to be head over all things to the church, which is His body, the fullness of Him who fills all in all. And you He made alive (Ephesians 1:17—2:1).

Paul could also write: "He who did not spare His own Son, but delivered Him up for us all, how shall He not with Him also freely give us all things?" (Romans 8:32). And I add, "even our destiny."

LESSONS ANYONE?

1. From other New Testament letters, check out the phrase "in Christ" or "in Christ Jesus." What understanding do you gain from these passages about your position as an heir of God and joint heir with Christ?

2. Do most Christians fully realize and truly believe that the same Holy Spirit who energized Christ also lives to energize them?

3. How do we discover the mind of Christ? What hinders us from doing so?

4. Describe what it means to be led by the Holy Spirit. Is it the same as being "in the Spirit"? Explain.

Chapter 17

In All These Things: Part II

Romans 8:14-27

As the songwriter wrote, "Who could ask for anything more?" When it comes to the work of the Holy Spirit detailed in Romans 8:1-13, how could there be any more? There is!

He Assures Us That We Are His (vv. 14-17)

In the previous chapter I alluded to the movie *Driving Miss Daisy* as a great illustration of what it means to be led by the Holy Spirit. As Paul continues his description of the Holy Spirit's work in us, he begins with the word *led*, which literally means "driven." It is not the driving of a herd (compulsion), nor the irresistible influencing (manipulation) of a group, but it is guiding and suggesting, so that we might willfully respond and submit.

Nor can I go any further without calling your attention to the conjunction *for* throughout this chapter. It carries with it the collective concepts of "because" and "since." We might expand it to read, "The reason you will live and be happy is . . ."

"Is what? Is because you are the sons of God." This verse is not talking about making us sons, but the fact that we already are sons. Galatians 4:4-7 reads like this:

> But when the fullness of the time had come, God sent forth His Son, born of a woman, born under the law, to redeem those who were under the law, that we might receive the adoption as sons. And because you are sons, God has sent forth the Spirit of His Son into your hearts, crying out, "Abba, Father!" Therefore you are no longer a slave but a son, and if a son, then an heir of God through Christ.

When we look at the context in Galatians more closely, we find two words that are full of implications: *children* and *sons*. Whereas *children* denotes kinship, nature or origin, the word *sons* denotes a legal relationship, one of right and privilege. Rather than allowing His children to live in a slavish and anxious state of mind, God produces within us feelings of affection, reverence and confidence.

In a similar vein, Paul reminded Timothy: "For God has not given us a spirit of fear, but of power [confidence] and of love and of a sound mind" (2 Timothy 1:7). On that basis, Timothy could stir up those embers of God that had been given to him through the laying on of hands (v. 6). Because of that foundation, Timothy need not be ashamed of the testimony of the Lord, or of his spiritual father, Paul.

In Roman law, the rights of an adopted son were no different from those of a natural son. *Sonship* (adoption) is not based on our merit, but upon God the Father's declaration. We cry out with our hearts, "Abba, Father," and discover inheritance and intimacy.

Dunn makes this observation:

> It is generally accepted that 'Abba' was characteristic and distinctive of Jesus' own prayer life, as sense of intimate sonship on the part of Jesus, expressed as it was in the colloquial language of close family relationship.[1]

While the heavenly Father has declared us to be sons, the Holy Spirit bears witness—confirms and gives evidence of that declaration. And if we are heirs of God, then we are joint heirs with Christ. The word *heir* (*kleronomos*) implies the right of possession, the certainty of that possession, and the security of that possession. In 1 Peter 1:4, 5, Paul's friend Peter refers to our receiving an inheritance that is *incorruptible*, not exposed to destruction or defilement from the outside; *undefiled*, pure and genuine (a treasure purchased with integrity and expressed in integrity, not able to be polluted by man or broken by God); *unfading*, totally consistent, never wasting away; *reserved in heaven* for us while we are *kept on earth* for it. We have equal portions of everything Christ has inherited from the Father.

When talking about promises, some people say they must see to believe. When talking about our inheritance as believers, we reply, "You have got to believe it to enjoy it." However, before shouting too loud, we are made aware that being "joint heirs with Christ" includes His sufferings as well as His glory.

He Guarantees Glory Through Suffering (vv. 18-25)

As we read these words of great promise, we must keep in mind the future the Roman church was about to experience. Within seven years of the writing of this letter, both Peter and Paul were martyred, the city of Rome was burned to the ground, the Christians were blamed for the fire, and unprecedented persecution was unleashed.

Sufferings are not inconsistent with the promise of the gospel for two reasons: they will later be proven to be comparatively insignificant, and we will be sustained under them. To the church at Corinth, Paul writes:

> We do not lose heart. Even though our outward man is perishing, yet the inward man is being renewed day by day. For our light affliction, which is but for a moment, is working for us a far more exceeding and eternal weight of glory, while we do not look at the things which are seen, but at the things which are not seen. For the things which are seen are temporary, but the things which are not seen are eternal (2 Corinthians 4:16-18).

Earlier in this study, I alluded to the word *glory* as being God's divine intention for each of our lives. That intention will be realized through a process of revelation—a heavenly mystery or reality hitherto secret or unknown, but now seen in its full definition and destiny. According to Morris, *revelation* (*apokalupsis*) has the thought of a play in which the final curtain is drawn back to reveal the various actors transformed back into their real characters.

Now, throughout Romans 8:18-25, the apostle uses repeated phrases to produce a metaphor. He turns from the intensive care unit to the maternity ward. Listen to these phrases: "earnest expectation . . . eagerly waits" (v. 19); "will be delivered" (v. 21); "groans and labors with birth pangs" (v. 22); "groan . . . eagerly waiting" (v. 23); "eagerly wait for it with perseverance" (v. 25). The incubation period, as well as the anticipation of new birth, is the experience of both the creation (it groans in v. 22) and ourselves (we groan in v. 23).

Dunn talks about the frustration of creation:

> It is about an object which does not function as it was designed to do (like an expensive satellite which has malfunctioned and now spins uselessly in space), or, more precisely, which has been given a role for which it was not designed and which is unreal or illusory.[2]

The anticipation of the creation is the reversal of the curse. Fallen humanity had subjected it unwillingly (it had no choice in the matter). Creation now looks forward to the day it will be restored back to the rating "good," the evaluation of everything God had made before the Fall. Again, Dunn observes, "Creation is to be redeemed, not redeemed from. Because God made it, it has to fulfill the original purpose for which it was created."[3] Such will not be accomplished by a "green-earth" policy or by the Environmental Protection Agency. Humanity will have little to do with it; God will have everything to do with it.

For the believer in Jesus Christ, the anticipation is for the "redemption of our body" (v. 23). Once again, Christianity is truly a "body religion." When our minds became darkened, as in Romans 1, our bodies became sinful. When Christ died, it was truly a physical death (3:25). The promise to Abraham that he would be the "father of many nations" resulted in descendants (4:18). We are to present our bodies (physical members) as "instruments of righteousness" to God (6:13). Spiritual warfare takes place in the physical realm as well as the spiritual (ch. 7). Our bodies will be quickened (8:11), yet in a process toward the full realization of its "glorious liberty" (v. 21). And now that our minds are being renewed, we are to present our bodies as "a living sacrifice, holy, acceptable to God" (12:1, 2), which is both reasonable and acceptable—to God and to us.

According to Romans 8:24, successful canoeing through the rapids of this spiritual river is based on our perspective of what is taking place. Paul uses a complex sentence to deal with a complex truth: "For we were saved in this hope, but hope that is seen is not hope; for why does one still hope for what he sees? But if we hope for what we do not see, we eagerly wait for it with perseverance" (vv. 24, 25).

Without question, what takes place in the supernatural will always express itself in the natural. Equally true, that which is taking place in the natural will also have its source in the supernatural.

Having lived in Asia for many years, where animism is so prevalent, I've become acquainted with the "third world"—no, not developing countries, but a third dimension to reality. Allow me to explain.

Western philosophy and theology have traditionally divided reality into two realms—the natural and the supernatural. There are some things actual, and there are some things that are spiritual. These seem to be clearly defined and seldom intermingled. When events occur in our lives, we allot the cause or case to the appropriate category.

In many cultures, however, there is a "third realm," in which there is constant interaction and interrelationship between the natural and the supernatural. Many cultures have their shamans, good and bad; others have their council of the ancestors, and still others try to find the "third realm" through meditation and detaching themselves from the influences of the natural. To interact on all three levels is both the natural and supernatural thing to do! Thus, when such people become believers in Jesus Christ, they naturally anticipate, accept and appreciate the intervention of God in their lives through visions, miracles and other divine expressions.

Frankly, Western Christian church culture has not clearly acknowledged, defined or taught regarding the reality and relevancy of such experiences. Those who are seeking to identify and understand the "beyond and out there" turn to transcendental meditation, Eastern religion and even New Age. Moreover, when miracles do take place, they become the center of debate within the church, rather than the center of delight. We demand proof, and fail to see their purpose. When the church loses its supernatural touch, it also loses its natural touch.

When the believer understands the "what is," the "what will be," and the continuity of "what is happening in between," perspective, patience and perseverance—*hope*—results. Contrary to the view of many commentators, I firmly believe that verses 24 and 25 are not simply embracing promise of finally giving birth to new life, it is understanding what is taking place during the pregnancy. How those Roman believers would need that knowledge in a few years' time!

He Joins With Us in the Quest (vv. 26, 27)

The Holy Spirit has been given to us as a down payment ("firstfruits," v. 23), and as a "guarantee of our inheritance" (Ephesians 1:14). There's more to come, and there's more that He provides. He actually "makes intercession for us" with those same "groanings" (Romans 8:26)—the conception, the gestation and the birthing of all God has designed us to be.

There is a word that is often lost in the reading of verse 26. The word is *helps*. The Holy Spirit *helps* in our weaknesses. The Greek word, *sunantilambanetai*, was used in the Septuagint when God gave *support* to Moses by the appointment of 70 elders (Exodus 18:22; Numbers 11:17). The word's very construction contains the concept of partnership—assuming part of the responsibility, the transference of weight, bringing equilibrium, and the sharing of the load. You know, there is a difference between one man carrying a log by juggling it on his shoulder at the center and two men transporting that same log, carrying the weight at each end.

The reason He helps is because we "do not know what we should pray for as we ought" (v. 26). The road He takes to help us is by "making intercession . . . according to the will of God" (v. 27). He becomes the divine link between our lack of understanding and the fullness of God's intention. We are ignorant of what is really the best for us. We are unaware of what God is willing to grant to us. There is perplexity.

But the Holy Spirit fully comprehends God's destiny, His design and delight. He meets us at our point of need, approaching God at His point of omniscience and applies

His will to our woe with divine omnipotence. One such experience has become the Williams' life-sermon.

A Fresh Start for Carole

I couldn't believe my eyes! The letter read: "Ron, I'm sorry I cannot live with this burning pain in my body any longer. I love you so much: my sons, daughters (daughters-in-law) and grandchildren. I do not want to be a burden to anyone. Please forgive me! None of you are at fault, I'm to blame. The medication is too much for me. I wish there was another way out, but there is not. All my love, Carole."

At the bottom of the note were two postscripts: "This is the most selfish thing I have ever done—me a giving person" and the three words, "Echo Park Lake." We live across from Echo Park Lake, a beautiful yet dangerous tree-lined lake located in the heart of Los Angeles.

For several months prior to that morning of June 20, 1997, Carole had been suffering from what the doctors finally diagnosed as polymyalgia rheumatica, rheumatism of the muscles. Every muscle in her body became inflamed, causing great pain and discomfort. At times the pain became so acute that she had to be rushed to the emergency ward at a local hospital, only to hear the doctor on duty say they could find nothing wrong. Batteries of tests were taken, all with the same result.

Finally, the doctors (who were and are still outstanding doctors and our personal physicians) called us in. They asked if we would consider Carole taking a particular steroid-based medication that was not designed to cure the illness, but would relieve the pain and relax the muscles so that healing could occur. They also warned us that it was somewhat risky, that one out of every 250,000 women who took the drug would have severe reactions, in some cases, resulting in life-and-death situations. The plan was to give my wife the highest dosage possible, then to gradually lower the dosage to where she could withstand the pain.

Because of Carole's excellent health record, we agreed to the treatment. Unfortunately, Carole was the one in a quarter-of-a-million. Around 3:30 a.m. on that dreadful morning in June, while also experiencing an accompanying heart attack, which did not complete itself (according to enzymes later found in her lungs), the pain became unbearable. Carole dressed, walked across the street and literally jumped into the lake, trying to kill herself. I woke up three hours later, only to walk into our front room to discover the note.

Later I was to learn that before Carole could drown (she doesn't know how to swim), two men in a motorboat appeared. They were wearing hard hats, and they had a rope. They pulled my wife out of the water and called the police and ambulance, who took her to Queen of Angels Hospital in Hollywood, California. What is unexplainable is that, according to the Parks Department and the Echo Park management, there was no one on duty that morning. *Angels in hard hats?*

Having been notified by the police, I arrived at the hospital to find my wife in the Intensive Care Unit. She was fully alert and aware of what had occurred and why. The doctors confirmed her story and began to treat her, physically and emotionally. Miraculously, over the next five days, Carole was totally healed from both the rheumatism and the heart problem.

But her emotions were devastated. She was admitted to a mental health center in Glendale, California, and for the next three weeks, it was uncertain whether or not she would ever be released. While settling the suicide attempt with the Lord, she became convinced that all hope was gone. She distrusted all medicine. Her mind was convinced that she could no longer swallow food. It took the use of infrared video footage to prove to her that food was being digested. Finally, she became catatonic and for three days she sat in a chair simply responding with the words "It is too late."

Calling our three sons and their wives together on the second Thursday evening of July 1997, we discussed what would happen should Mom die. It was expected that she would lose the will to live, go into a coma and pass away. We also warned our second son, Mark, who then lived in San Mateo, California, and who had not yet seen his mother, that the scene the next morning would not be a pretty one.

At almost the same time we were meeting, an evangelist friend of ours, Barbara Yoder, was conducting services in South Africa. After receiving an email from one of my daughters-in-law, informing her of Carole's condition, she decided to ask the more than 1,000 people attending the service to pray. Listen to her email of July 12, 1997, which was received several days later:

> When I got up to preach, I asked to first pray for Carole. I did not tell them her name but a little bit about the situation . . . I asked the African pastor to lead us in prayer.
>
> What began to happen was awesome. The whole congregation stood to their feet and began interceding with

the pastor. I heard Pastor Jack Hayford teach a powerful lesson years ago on the power of clapping of hands. I explained to the people the power that there is in the clapping of hands Biblically. In unison, we began to clap and as they continued to clap, the power of God came even stronger. People began to shout. I have never seen anything quite like it. It was like the heavens were suddenly ripped open.

This praying and clapping went on for at least 30 minutes. As the power of God grew stronger, there was the presence of angelic hosts seen in the room. We released them even into Carole's room in the hospital to minister to her as an heir of salvation. People were so overcome by the presence and power of God they began to weep uncontrollably. God began loosing people from demonic powers. Demons began to cry out and as we took authority over them, I would point and the person would be released.

After 40-45 minutes, healing broke out. The Lord spoke to my heart that Jesus had come into our midst to "release" us. It is like you find a thread in the hem of a dress and when you pull it, the whole thing comes unraveled. God was saying that He would unravel the Enemy's works. We prayed for a little baby who was swollen with kidney disease and he was healed. Again, it was all as we prayed for Carole. I've never seen anything like it. I began to weep at the awesome manifestation of the power and presence of God. It had to be 45 minutes of focused prayer. All of this happening in the context of Carole.

The next morning, back in Glendale, California, Mark and his wife, Lynn, went into the ward, expecting to see

Carole still entrenched in that chair. Instead, they found her in bed resting. Mark said, "Mom." Carole recognized him, and said, "Hi, Son." She then began rubbing his forehead as she had done so often as she used to put him to bed as a child. Mark came back to the waiting room and simply remarked, "Pop, I think Mom's healed."

Five days later, my wife left the hospital totally healed by the power of God. Since that time, we have shared her story across the nation and even overseas, seeing hundreds of men and women set free from depression, disease and dysfunction. As He had promised in Romans 8:26, 27, the Holy Spirit had come alongside our groanings with His; He had identified with us and turned an extremely horrible experience into a glowing testimony of the faithfulness of God and His ability to bring His children through any circumstance.

There were also other gems of beauty that came out of that pile of ashes. Many lessons were learned by all of us. First of all, when the fury flies around you, it's OK to panic. Those who don't are either liars, angels or dead. It's OK to cry, even in public. You can be angry at what is taking place—just don't take it to bed with you. There will be a feeling of aloneness, and you must be given space to deal with that loneliness and to allow all those impacted by the event to have the same space.

Fix your mind on the things you know to be true, not on the things you don't know. Be honest. Sometimes Christians are the worst liars in the world. You do not have to fix blame on God, the devil, others or yourself. Do not superspiritualize every event. Sometimes the words "I don't understand" or "I don't know" will suffice.

You do not have to be in control. Recognize that not everything can be brought to an immediate conclusion. There are no quick fixes. When words don't come, hugs do. When decisions are having to be made, rely on your head, not on your emotions or ego.

Determine to be content. Your choice to be content rests inside, not with the circumstances. This does not mean you will no longer have unrest or doubt, but you can learn to keep yourself disciplined and determined to trust in the veracity of God.

Fill your mind with God's promises. Test all advice with God's promises; your destiny is based on God's thoughts about you rather than clever clichés. Here are some of the promises from the Bible, which God gave to sustain me over those three weeks:

> "When you pass through the waters, I will be with you; and through the rivers, they shall not overflow you. When you walk through the fire, you shall not be burned, nor shall the flame scorch you. . . . Since you were precious in My sight, you have been honored, and I have loved you; therefore I will give men for you, and people for your life" (Isaiah 43:2, 4).

> "Israel, I created you, and you are my servant. I won't forget you" (44:21, *CEV*).

> "Israel, I am your Lord, I am your source of life, and I have rescued you" (44:24, *CEV*).

> "But Israel, I, the Lord, will always keep you safe and free from shame" (45:17, *CEV*).

"I will soon come to save you. I am not far away and will waste no time" (46:17, *CEV*).

"Since the day you were born, I have carried you along. I will still be the same when you are old and gray, and I will take care of you. I created you. I will carry you and always keep you safe" (46:3, 4, *CEV*).

"People of Israel, I am the holy Lord God, the one who rescues you. For your own good, I teach you, and I lead you along the right path" (48:17, *CEV*).

The Lord said to me, "Israel, you are my servant; and because of you I will be highly honored." I said to myself, "I'm completely worn out; my time has been wasted. But I did it for the Lord God, and he will reward me" (Isaiah 49:3-5, *CEV*).

"The Lord God gives me the right words to encourage the weary. Each morning he awakens me eager to learn his teaching; he made me willing to listen and not rebel or run away. . . . But the Lord God keeps me from being disgraced. So I refuse to give up, because I know God will never let me down" (50:4, 5, 7, *CEV*).

"Everyone crying out in pain will be quickly set free; they will be rescued from the power of death and never go hungry. I will help them because I am your God, the Lord All-Powerful, who makes the ocean roar. I have told you what to say, and I will keep you safe in the palm of my hand" (51:14-16, *CEV*).

> "You won't need to run. No one is chasing you. The Lord God of Israel will lead and protect you from enemy attacks" (52:12, *CEV*).

One morning, there were two promises that stood out. First was the promise God gave me in Isaiah 55:3, that God will give me the same love and loyalty He gave to David in His mercies. Second was a promise to Carole, that according to His Word, in Isaiah 55:11, His Word will accomplish all that He sent it to do.

> Our holy God lives forever in the highest heavens, and this is what he says: Though I live high above in the holy place, I am here to help those who are humble and depend only on me (57:15, *CEV*).

> Your honesty will protect you as you advance, and the glory of the Lord will defend you from behind. When you beg the Lord for help, he will answer, "Here I am!" (58:8, 9, *CEV*).

> The Lord says: "My people, I promise to give you my Spirit and my message. These will be my gifts to you and your families forever. I, the Lord, have spoken" (59:21, *CEV*).

And on the morning she was to be released by the psychiatrist, without previous notification, I read these words:

> "Victory" will be the name you give to your walls; "Praise" will be the name you give to your gates (60:18, *CEV*).

One day, in my journal during this experience, I wrote the following:

"There is spiritual warfare being waged. Our role is to allow the Cross to cover us and then allow the Cross to deal with the Enemy of our souls. While we take our authority, we are fully aware that our only authority is the blood of the Cross, our love of the Savior and the declaration of our testimony. Hallelujah, though I feel so tired, exasperated and extinguished, I'm still more than a conqueror.

Part of spiritual warfare is that of suffering. Look at Peter and Paul. This is a thought I want to probe further—the fact that our suffering in Christ actually becomes a weapon against Satan. For every trial, there will be a reciprocal triumph. Thus, there is going to be a great deliverance.

Oh, my soul, rest in God. Turn from your carnal ways and lusts and allow a freshness of His person, power and restoration to be your portion. Recognize the promise He has given you, even before the year began and take heart. You will find Him; and He will hear you.

Do not try to interpret prophetic promises. You can't force them to take place, they must occur in the manner in which God designs. Simply deal with the spiritual forces with prayer and patience. Desperation can often lead to deception.

Watch for the little miracles, not the big ones. I've come to call them the "Miracles of the Moment." The very first day, there were 10, ranging from God waking up two of our sons at the time Mom needed them the most, to my meeting a coworker at the very moment I needed someone to help me, to friends and stories of God's sovereign moving of people to pray for us. The San Mateo (California) Foursquare Church began praying around the clock for our family, beginning at the very time Carole became catatonic.

During a Communion service at the Florence Avenue

Foursquare Church in Santa Fe Springs, California, I saw a vision of the blood of Jesus streaming from the table of the Lord out of the building and into my wife's room, bringing healing. Then there was the junior high student who, without any knowledge of what was going on in our family, came to Mark, our second son, at camp and stated, "I need to pray for your mother."

Learn to lean on others for help. It is not wrong or unspiritual to seek counseling. Learn to listen, yet without superimposing your trauma on those about you . . . or taking it out on them. Learn to trust God . . . and those who know. By learning to lean, you learn the lessons of how to identify with and minister to others in the days ahead.

When answers don't come, release God to do what He knows best. During the time of Carole's hospitalization, I came across a poem written by a 6-year-old lad named Matthew Stepanek, "Mattie," who was suffering with a rare form of muscular dystrophy:

Dear God,
I was going to thank You tonight for a beautiful sunrise,
That was pink behind the fog down the hill,
And for a wonderful rainbow,
That I ran under pointing to all my favorite colors,
And for such a great sun, dear God,
That sprinkled orange across the water.

I was going to thank You tonight for all those special gifts,
Except that none of them happened.
But do You know what?
I still love You, God.

And I have lots of other things
That I can thank You for tonight,
Even if You didn't give those very special gifts to me
today.
It's OK, God,
Because I'll look for them all again,
When my tomorrow comes. Amen.

From *Heartsongs* by Mattie J.T. Stepanek. Copyright © 2001 Mattie J.T. Stepanek. Reprinted with permission from VSP Books/Hyperion.

What a "To Do" list the Holy Spirit works in our daily lives!

- He alerts our minds (vv. 5-8).
- He gives life to our mortal bodies (vv. 9-13).
- He assures us that we are His (vv. 14-17).
- He guarantees glory through suffering (vv. 18-25).
- He joins with us in the quest (vv. 26, 27).

All these "things" are working together "for good to those who love God, to those who are the called according to His purpose" (v. 28). It sure turns us "mighty worriers" into His "mighty warriors!"

LESSONS ANYONE?

1. What are the benefits of being a child of God? Are there any responsibilities in His family?

2. How do you define the word *suffering* in this passage? How do problems in the Christian's life correspond with faith?

3. From your own experience, what is the difference in looking at suffering from a "maternity ward" perception rather than the "morgue"?

4. List three major lessons that were reinforced in your life from Carole Williams' testimony. Why were they significant?

Chapter 18

In All These Things: Part III

Romans 8:28-39

Take a look at the use of the word *things* throughout the remainder of Romans 8. In verse 28, "all things" work toward the accomplishment of God's purpose in us. In verse 31, conclusions are drawn regarding "these things," and in verse 32, God freely gives us "all things." Even in those negative experiences—"all these things"—we can be more than conquerors (v. 37) and no "created thing" will be able to separate us from the love of God (v. 39). There must be something God is trying to say to the Roman believers . . . and to us!

Again, Paul and Peter sound so much alike. Peter writes that God's "divine power has given to us *all things* that pertain to life and godliness" (2 Peter 1:3). There is absolutely nothing more needed; nor will anything more be added! Other than heaven, God has given the believer everything needed (see Romans 1:17: "The just shall live by faith").

Therefore, we know (vv. 28-30), we declare (vv. 31-37), and we act (vv. 38, 39). In the same way as in Romans 6, we know, reckon, present, and then we apply the provisions the Holy Spirit has so abundantly made possible.

We Know (vv. 28-30)

What we know is crucial. There seems to be much discussion as to how the words should be interpreted. Some manuscripts indicate that "in all things God works for the good"; others read, "God works all things." Still others translate it: "He makes intercession for the saints according to the will of God and he makes all things work together . . ." Leon Morris quotes Luther as commenting, "The Spirit makes all things, even though they are evil, work together for good."[1]

It is also key to note the use of "He" in the passage. In verse 27, the "He" refers to God the Father, "who searches the hearts," and the pronoun in verse 28 implies it is "His purpose." In verses 29 and 30, there can be no other subject than God the Father. It is safe, then, to conclude that Paul has made a sudden shift from the person of the Holy Spirit to the purpose of "Father God," whom we call "Abba!" (v. 15).

Whichever view or translation you wish to accept, it is evident that Paul is not talking about some sort of "Christian fatalism." It is never to be understood that "all things are good," or that "God causes all things to take place." I would never want to blame everything I experience on God, for most of my difficulties have to do with my own stubbornness, inadequacy and simply being alive in a yet unredeemed world.

However, three conclusions can be reached:

1. Though we may not have caused a particular event to happen, there is nothing that is going to confront us today that God cannot use for His glory.

2. Though we may not have caused a particular event to happen, there is nothing that is going to confront us today that God cannot take and extend His kingdom through it.

3. Though we may not have caused a particular event to happen, there is nothing that is going to confront us today that God cannot take and make it work for our growth as His children. Whether "all things" refer to the sufferings which we experience or the work of the Holy Spirit in us, we know that "the Christian is not dependent on the Micawberish hope that something will 'turn up'; his confidence rests rather on the outworking of God's purpose through all the contradiction and frustration of the present to its intended end."[2]

Why can we conclude this? Because we are those "who love God" and who are "the called" to complete His divine destiny and purpose in our lives. Note the divine dualism between God's sovereignty and man's free will. As the sinner approaches the door of salvation, he responds to the sign on the doorpost that reads "Whosoever will, may come." Having entered the door to the kingdom of God, he looks back and notices a new sign, "Chosen before the foundation of the world." Though it is impossible to explain, it should never be a matter of debate but of delight. God did not choose us to the exclusion of others. But He did include us! And He has designed a destiny uniquely shaped to each one of us.

Five verbs make up the beauty of verses 29 and 30. First, He *foreknew* who and what we were going to be. God's foreknowledge is never casual. In other words, nothing is ever going to happen simply because God knows it will. He knows it beforehand, because it is going to happen. Because He knows certain things are going to occur, He prepares a response beforehand. That response has a goal that is included in the very next verb.

"For whom He foreknew, He also predestined . . ." Predestined to what? "To be conformed to the image of His Son, that He might be the firstborn among many brethren" (v. 29). In spite of the numerous theological debates regarding predestination (over which discussions are endless), the term *predestined* is used only three times in the New Testament:

1. To be conformed to Christ's image (8:29)
2. To experience the adoption of children (Ephesians 1:5; see also ch. 3)
3. To obtain an inheritance (Ephesians 1:11).

There is never an indication that someone is predestined to salvation, but all believers are predestined to become an expressed image (Greek, *eikon*, icon) of Jesus Christ. Rather than destroying the sovereignty of the Almighty, *God's Highest Delight* (read my other book) is revealed.

With this aim, God begins to put process to His purpose. He *called* us to Himself. He issued the invitation. Then He *justified* us and *glorified* us. God has placed us into a process whose end is guaranteed. His destiny in us is absolutely certain.

I can never read these verses without remembering a trip in 1985 to the city of Suzhou, China. Established several millennia ago, the city is often referred to as the "Venice of the Orient," because it is built on a series of canals. I was filled with awe as I stood on a bridge built by those who accompanied Marco Polo and tried to identify with men and women who for centuries walked the same path. It was in this city that the vast majority of Chinese artisans and philosophers worked or learned their art.

A friend and I were invited to the studio of one of the most famous sculptors in China. There we saw a huge piece of jade that stood about 6 feet tall, 4 to 5 feet wide, and of equal depth, worth hundreds of thousands of dollars. The veins of grey and white color running throughout the green surface were exquisite. Yet, the sculptor had carved chunks, large and small, out of the jade. He seemed to be totally without a plan.

I asked him what he was making. "A man," he replied. "In a few months, it will be placed in the national museum in Beijing." When asked about his plans, he pointed to his head and reminded me that he was a master craftsman. (By the way, from reports, he did meet his deadline.)

With my reasonably fluent Cantonese and horrible Mandarin, I expressed shock: "I don't understand why you seem to be so unorganized. If it were me, I'd start in one section, finish it completely, and then proceed to the next after the first part was perfect."

With a gleam in his eye, he smiled and responded, "I recognize two things: your Mandarin needs a lot of work, and you have no idea how to work with precious stones. If I followed your suggestion—perfecting one section before proceeding to the next—I'd ruin my work. You see, this stone is precious because it is still one piece. The stone could not withstand too much carving on the same part. It would break, rendering the entire stone worthless. Thus, I work a bit here, take a lot out over there, and keep the angles balanced. The work proceeds according to the texture of the jade. Remember, I'm a master craftsman. When I'm finished, it will be more valuable than it was in its original form. And, it will be a man, just like I've envisioned."

Returning to my hotel, I felt embarrassed by my rudeness and obvious stupidity. Then, I received another of those life lessons from the Lord.

"Ron, isn't that the way I work with your life? I never perfect one aspect of your life before going to another. If I did, you couldn't stand the pressure. You'd break! That is not My plan or purpose.

"You see, you are even more valuable than any piece of jade. Therefore, this week I work on your worry, anger and self-esteem. Next week, I deal with stewardship, pride and love. The third week, I might return to some of those things already mentioned, or I might strengthen your faith. There are times I simply shave away small pieces of the old life. Other times, I dig deep at the expense of causing you pain, and remove large chunks.

"But Ron, when I'm through with you and you enter the gates of My city, you'll look like a man. Remember, I'm the ultimate Master Craftsman. As a matter of fact, My son, you'll look just like Jesus!"

Our only response is, "Yes, God, complete it *according to Your purpose.*"

We Declare (vv. 31-37)

I like the words used in the *New English Bible*: "With all this in mind, what are we to say?" (v. 31). While our response encompasses the teaching of the entire letter, I also believe there are some conclusions that seem to rise out of the immediate context.

"If God is for us, who can be against us?" (v. 31). If God has freed us to live by the Holy Spirit (vv. 1-4), and if His purpose is to make us like Jesus, then we must never doubt His feelings and His faithfulness to see that purpose realized. There will be those who oppose us; but in spite of their efforts and affects upon our feelings, we return to the fact that "He who has begun a good work in you will complete it until the day of Jesus Christ" (Philippians 1:6). When knocked down, we get back up and continue the journey. We can know God's attitude toward us.

"How shall He not with Him also freely give us all things?" (v. 32). As illustrated in His request of Abraham to sacrifice Isaac, God provided a perfect Substitute to be sacrificed on the altar of the Cross. He gave His ultimate and the price was not cheap. When Jesus died on Calvary, God placed on Him the sins of every man, woman or child, of all time. According to Isaiah 53, our Lord was "smitten"—beaten—by His just Father. All the punishment every person would experience in hell converged on the shoulders of our Lord. It was so terrible, the mercy of God caused the darkness to fall over the site, so that humanity would never have to see or experience it.

If this is the case, then why do we wonder if God is capable or willing to quicken our minds and our bodies to make us capable of fulfilling His standard and expectations? We can expect God's ability to be present and plentiful. If you don't believe it, then reread Romans 1:5; 3:24; 4:4, 16; 5:2, 15, 17, 20, 21; 6:1, 14, 15. It is free and graciously given.

"Who shall bring a charge against God's elect?" (v. 33). If the heavenly Father has adopted us, if we are joint heirs with Jesus, if the Holy Spirit continues to bear witness to these truths, then who cares what the devil or anyone else accuses or lays charge against us? We can expect God's acceptance to secure our future.

While the application of this verse is regarding the response of the believer to the sufferings and challenges that are part of the Christian process, I will always remember my third week in the ministry. I received a telephone call from one of the precious elderly people who were assisting us in planting a church in Delta, British Columbia, just outside the beautiful city of Vancouver.

The lady was upset at something I had done that was in contrast to the way she would have desired. In exasperation, she finally forsook all decency and declared, "You are nothing but a green student!" On the other end of the phone was this three-week-old pastor, with tears in his eyes, who could only answer, "There's no one who knows that any more than I do, but I've been called!"

Today, nearly four decades later, I'm still a green student. But I've been called, and that is the only foundation I have to stand on.

How many times have we heard the devil whisper in our ears, "You are only a weak, green Christian." To our accuser we can respond, "But we've been called! Not only that, we've been justified and on our way to becoming everything you aren't!"

"Who is he who condemns?" (v. 34). If the Holy Spirit identifies with us on earth, and if Christ identifies with us in heaven, at God's right hand, and if both know the

Father's will, then there's no question regarding God's awareness of our situation. Christ, who died, rose from the dead, ascended and now intercedes, is our adequacy.

"Who shall separate us from the love of Christ?" (v. 35). No matter what comes our way, there's always God's access that receives us, and reminds us that we are only pilgrims in this world. He then assures us that the worst thing that could ever happen today is that we would die and go to heaven! What a hope! What a destiny!

In verse 35, Paul also begins a prophetic description of what the future holds for the Roman congregation:

- *Tribulation* has to deal with pressure, like grapes having all the juice squeezed out of them.
- *Distress* carries the concept of being chased into a corner, with no room for maneuvering.
- *Persecution* is just that—beatings and physical opposition.
- *Famine* is their being placed in precarious situations, as believers some seven years later were exposed and driven out of their homes, outcasts of society.
- *Nakedness* would be experienced as believers in their nakedness were made into human lamp posts to light the streets of Rome at night.
- *Peril* has the idea of danger of any kind.
- *Sword* has the reality of death itself.

"Yet in all these things, we are more than conquerors . . ." (v. 37). When hell has unleashed its fury and the devil has spent all his demons, when the world has taken its

highest toll and death has completed its ultimate role, the believer in Jesus has only begun to fight. The *New English Bible* declares: "Overwhelming victory is ours." Instead of causing harm, God turns these things into our health, our banner of victory and the rejoicing of our souls.

We Act (vv. 38, 39)

It is with such strong and unwavering confidence that we act with boldness. Our existence (life or death) is based on God's loving purpose for us. He takes the fear of death, pain and trials and makes them gateways to eternity so that we might declare (actually ridicule death itself), "Death is swallowed up in victory. O Death, where is your sting?" (1 Corinthians 15:54, 55).

It is with such strong and unwavering confidence that we wage spiritual war against the rulers and authorities, who try to usurp dominion over the world in which we live and for which Jesus died. It is a fight. We do so with the "whole armor of God, that [we] may be able to stand against the wiles of the devil. For we do not wrestle against flesh and blood, but against . . . the rulers of the darkness of this age, against spiritual hosts of wickedness in the heavenly places" (Ephesians 6:11, 12).

It is with such strong and unwavering confidence that we proceed without concern about the *present* problems and *future* uncertainties *(things to come).* We redeem time, making it our friend rather than our foe. We perceive what is taking place in our world, knowing the signs of the times and making full use of them. We are not dependent on the futurists, but on the One who holds the future in the palm of His hands.

It is with such strong and unwavering confidence that we take heart, whether we be honored with wealth or splendor *(height)*, or should we find ourselves in the lowest circumstances of depression, poverty, contempt or lack *(depth)*. The accolades of this life are of little importance. It's hearing the divine pleasure: "Well done, good and faithful servant."

A missionary doctor had spent 40 years of his life ministering in the primitive villages of Africa. Finally, he decided to retire. He wired ahead that he would be returning by ship and gave the date and time of his arrival.

As he was crossing the Atlantic, he thought back over all the years he had spent helping to heal the people of Africa, both physically and spiritually. Then his thoughts raced ahead to the grand homecoming he knew awaited him in America, because he had not been home in 40 years.

As the ship pulled into port, the old man's heart swelled with pride when he saw the homecoming that had been prepared. A great crowd of people had gathered, and there was a huge banner saying, "Welcome Home." As the man stepped off the ship onto the dock and awaited a great ovation, his heart sank. Suddenly he realized the people had not gathered to pay tribute to him, but to the U.S. president who had been aboard the same ship, returning from a safari.

He waited in anguish with his heart breaking. No one had come to welcome him home. As the crowd disbursed, the old man was left waiting alone. Tilting his face heavenward, he spoke these words: "O God, after giving all those years of my life to my fellowmen, was it too much to ask that one person—just one person—be here to welcome me home?"

In the quietness of his heart, he heard the voice of God whisper, "You're not home yet!"

In Matthew 19:29, our Lord made this promise: "And everyone who has left houses or brothers or sisters or father or mother or wife or children or lands, for My name's sake, shall receive a hundredfold, and inherit eternal life."

Many times people serve the Lord, day in and day out, and never receive the honor they deserve. Recently, a friend of mine was discouraged and expressed disappointment in not being recognized for the work that had been accomplished. After hearing the hurt, I simply replied, "Aren't you glad that God keeps 'good books'?" Yes, He does and will reward each of us for our faithfulness.

LESSONS ANYONE?

1. Does God bring suffering on His people? Does Romans 8:28 mean we are to be Christian fatalists?
2. What "chunks" of jade has God, the Master Craftsman, been carving out of your life lately, to make you into His image? How are you responding?
3. List the questions in Romans 8:31-35. Underneath each question, briefly write how each question relates to those "things" mentioned earlier in the chapter that the Holy Spirit does in your life. Why are these significant at this point in your life?
4. Should Christians be discouraged? How do you deal with your "down" experiences or moments?

Chapter 19

But What About the Jews?

Romans 9:1-29

Following such a mountaintop experience as recorded in Romans 8, we would almost be tempted to say, like Peter, "Lord, it is good for us to be here. Let's make three tabernacles and pitch our tents here for the rest of our lives" (see Matthew 17:4). But remember the response of our Lord after the Transfiguration when He immediately took the disciples to a valley where they were confronted by a demon-possessed lad and the tax collector. The ecstasy of seeing God's glory carries with it His expectancy that we deal with the hard realities of human need.

That's exactly what takes place in the abrupt transition from Romans 8 to 9. "[Nothing can] separate us from the love of God" (8:39) is immediately followed by "I have great sorrow and continual grief" (9:2). The magnificence of Romans 1—8 does not seem to be the experience of the

Israelites. Dare we ask the questions: "Did God fail? Did His Word have absolutely no effect?" Paul did.

An Overview (chs. 9-11)

While Paul's purpose of the letter to the Romans is to meld the hearts and minds of the Jewish and Gentile believers into one mutual bond, the fact of the matter is, Israel was the nation God had chosen as His people. In light of the gospel, should that relationship be written off as a thing of the past or as a good intention gone bad?

Paul has shown great grace toward the Gentiles in this letter, including them in his definition of the "Israel of faith." On the other hand, he has come down hard on the Jews regarding their self-righteousness and apostasy. Wasn't he one of them?

In explaining chapters 9-11, many have superimposed their own presuppositions and come up with an answer that God is God; He has made a choice to include whom He wants in His redemption (and whom He doesn't want). Humanity becomes pawns in a divine chess game God plays against Himself. Such conclusions make God unfair, unrighteous and unmerciful.

Yet, God's dealings with Israel in the past *had been* fair, righteous and full of mercy (ch. 9). His acts toward Israel *are still* fair, righteous and full of mercy (ch. 10). The fulfillment of His redemptive promises regarding Israel in the future *will be* fair, righteous and full of mercy (ch. 11). Paul is talking about the veracity of God's character, not about a vicarious moving of certain individuals toward a predetermined, fateful end.

It is on the veracity of God's mercy that all of us can now "present [our] bodies as a living sacrifice" (12:1).

There are four underlying questions being asked:

1. Paul, don't you care about your countrymen anymore?
2. How is it that the people of God missed the gospel, yet those who weren't even interested in God found it?
3. Is Israel not responding because the people haven't heard? Or is it because they don't understand?
4. What will happen to the Jews? Has God given up on them forever?[1]

God's Mercy Was Seen Through His Promise (9:1-8)

Paul begins with his heart: "I tell the truth . . ." (v. 1), and there are three witnesses to that fact. This shows his intimate relationship with Christ, his conscience agreeing to the genuineness of his feelings and the Holy Spirit, who is giving the inspiration.

The *truth* brings "great sorrow and continual grief" (v. 2). Sorrow carries the connotation of emotional distress; grief is the mental anguish that causes such distress. For Paul, it was *continual*; actually, according to the Greek, it was *adialeiptos*—"unceasingly increasing in intensity." It was so intense that inside the apostle was a "seriously meant but unrealizable wish"[2] that he could take their punishment upon himself.

Paul uses the word *accursed* (v. 3; Greek, *anathema*). To the Gentiles of that day, *anathema* was anything set apart or consecrated to the gods in the temples as spoils of war, images or statues. To the Hebrews, it was what was set apart to God for destruction with no possibility of reclamation.

Paul says that he would be willing to be devoted to death, willing to suffer the bitterest evils, forgo all pleasure, and endure any privation or toil, if it would bring his countrymen to the knowledge of Jesus. There is no doubt as to his commitment to the Jews.

It is the same commitment Moses expressed to Jehovah in Exodus 32:32, regarding God having mercy on Israel. The deliverer from Egypt was now delivering the divine Law to God's people, written by the finger of Jehovah himself. He had just come from the mountaintop, negotiating and pleading with God not to destroy Israel, who were back in the valley substituting a golden calf for the glorious Creator. Moses saw their sin for himself and his "anger became hot, and he cast the tablets out of his hands and broke them at the foot of the mountain" (Exodus 32:19). He destroyed the idol, rebuked Aaron and administered judgment. It was not a good day for the people—or for Moses!

White-hot with anger, Moses was also hot with compassion. He goes to God and offers this prayer: "Oh, these people have committed a great sin, and have made for themselves a god of gold! Yet now, if You will forgive their sin—but if not, I pray, blot me out of Your book which You have written" (Exodus 32:31, 32).

Paul is saying, "Do I love my beloved Israel? You bet your bottom shekel!"

In one of our churches in Hong Kong, there is a wonderful family named Leung. The dad, Michael, and the mother, Barbara, are psychiatric nurses. They have two grown children, Joyce and Ronald.

When Joyce was very young, the doctors informed the parents that the girl needed an operation. Blood needed to be donated. Ronald, who was 7 or 8 years of age, offered to give blood. He went into the hospital room, got up on the bed, and allowed the nurses to attach all the tubes. The process of transfusion began.

Suddenly, Ronald seemed puzzled. He looked up at the nurse and asked, "Just when is it that I'm going to die?" To his relief, the reply was, "You won't, at least not yet!" When questioned later, it was discovered that Ronald's original expectation was that by giving his blood, he was going to die for his little sister.

"Hot with sorrow and grief" over his kinsmen according to the flesh, Paul was also "hot with compassion." An example for all of us!

There is a sudden change in Paul's terminology. In the early part of the letter, Paul used the term *Jews* to emphasize their distinctiveness over against everyone else. Now, he uses *Israelites*, the covenant name given to those descendants of Jacob whose name was changed to *Israel*, "prince with God."

Along with that name came privileges. First, there was adoption—they had been selected, chosen from other nations. They had experienced the "glory"—the divine presence of God that led them out of Egypt and finally came to rest on the ark of the covenant in the first Temple. There had been the *covenants* made and reaffirmed to Abraham, Isaac and Jacob. There was the day when, from Mount Sinai, God gave them the Law (Exodus 20). In great detail, they had been given instructions regarding the Tabernacle, offerings and how to serve Jehovah. And how about the promises concerning the Messiah? It was a magnificent privilege to be the people through whom the Anointed One would come. Paul's "kinsmen according to the flesh" (v. 3, KJV) were also Christ's kinsmen "according to the flesh" (v. 5).

Israel's rejection in no way implies that God had gone back on His original design or desire. The people of the covenant were not based on physical relationship, but on the covenant relationship God made with Abraham regarding Isaac, the child of promise (see Romans 4:16). It would be a matter of faith, not nationality. There was a difference between comprehensive Israel and those who are of the promise. Now, even Gentiles have a place within that covenant relationship.

In the end, God did bless Ishmael (Genesis 21:18) and promised to make a great nation out of his loins. The Palestinians are the result.

God's Mercy Was Seen Through God's Purpose (vv. 9-13)

In Genesis 15, Abraham complained to God about the Creator's seeming delay in giving him an offspring. God promised that the heir would come "from [Abraham's] own body" (v. 4). He then reaffirmed to Abraham the covenant He had made (see ch. 12).

Knowing his wife, Sarah, was barren, a plan was carried out to have a son through Sarah's maid, Hagar. At age 86, Abraham became the father of Ishmael. It would be 14 years more before God would open Sarah's womb and Isaac would be born. It would not be through human endeavor that redemption would come, but through divine enablement. What man could not do, God did! That's called "mercy."

Every reader of the Book of Genesis is moved by the great love story between Isaac and Rebekah, though we'd never want to obtain a wife that way. Abraham's servant chose a young lady and brought her home. Isaac saw her beauty. Rebekah dismounted her camel and ran to her Prince Charming, and they lived happily ever after. Right? Wrong!

Rebekah was also barren. Isaac pleaded with God and the Lord opened Rebekah's womb (25:21). Unlike her mother-in-law, however, Rebekah conceived twins. Esau was the oldest by a heel, and Jacob came about a foot short.

During the pregnancy, God told Rebekah that there would be two nations conceived and that "the older shall serve the younger" (Genesis 25:23; Romans 9:12).

Picking up this history, Paul reminds us that both had been conceived not only by the same man, but at the same time. Neither had done anything wrong. If God's favor was based on physical lineage, then both sons would inherit the covenant relationship. If privilege was given on the basis of who came first, Esau would have been the chosen one. But God's mercy to Israel would come through His sovereign choice. It was a decision man could neither earn nor in any way control.

Did God's statement to Rebekah cause Esau to sell his birthright? My suggestion is that it did not. Again, the foreknowledge of God is never causal, only informative. The events surrounding the selling of Esau's birthright in Genesis 25:27-31 support this. It was Esau's desire for Jacob's stew that began the transfer. Through the conniving of Rebekah, Isaac passed his blessing to Jacob (27:1-41). Each decision was the choice of individuals. Esau did receive a blessing from his father that included wealth, but it also resulted in violence and the serving of his younger brother. Today, the conflicts between the Arab world and Israel remain. Who can match the wealth of either of these two nations?

In the previous portion of Romans 9, it was Isaac; in verses 10-13, it is Jacob. Both had no natural claims on divine favor, still God's merciful purpose came to them.

To rightfully understand verse 13, we must look at the context in which the original statement was made. The apostle is recalling the prophet Malachi, who wrote this statement nearly 1,600 years after Jacob and Esau lived (1:2, 3). He wasn't talking about individuals, he was talking about the nations of Israel and Edom, which came forth from them. Paul is using this verse to prove that the prophetic statement in Romans 9:12 had actually come to pass, just as God said it would. Today, we would write, "And it was so."

We must also come to grips with the word *hated.* The word literally means "to regard and treat with less favor." It is not a feeling—it is a choice. A better word might be "selected or chosen." It has the same connotation Jesus used in Luke 14:26, when He demanded those who follow Him to "hate his father and mother, wife and children, brothers and sisters, yes, and his own life." Matthew 10:37-39 gives a clearer definition: "He who loves father or mother more than Me is not worthy of Me. And he who loves son or daughter more than Me is not worthy of Me. And he who does not take his cross and follow after Me is not worthy of Me. He who finds his life will lose it, and he who loses his life for My sake will find it." We would never attribute to our Lord the encouragement to hate as we understand the word *hate*.

Since 1988, in the denomination I serve, there have been the selection of two different presidents to lead the Foursquare family. The first selection saw three pastors—all equally loved and equally qualified to lead our denomination—as potential presidents. The second saw only two possible choices. Through a deliberate process, the leadership and ministers of our church sought God's will as to the person who would lead us in the capacity of president during the ensuing years. A choice was made, but not to the rejection of the other men who allowed their names to be considered. Actually, their participation in the process moved them to a higher level of dignity and respect from their peers. When all was said and done, everyone agreed that "it seemed good to us . . . to send chosen men to you . . ." (Acts 15:25).

The choice was not the *rejection* of others (as today's term is understood), but the *selection* of specific individuals for a peculiar purpose.

If mercy came to Jacob, who had no original rights, then God's mercy can reach to everyone, both Jews and Gentiles who have entered into faith in Jesus.

God's Mercy Was Seen Through His Preservation (vv. 14-18)

There is a great caution. We must never dilute the fact that God has elected us; there are predetermined aspects of our lives, and there are times God treats people differently. Yet, such choices are not based on favoritism (unrighteousness). They are based on a divine design that reaches beyond human comprehension.

One of those choices was regarding the person Moses. Remember our earlier discussion regarding this prince of

Egypt, who was standing in the gap for Israel? Because of Moses' intercession, God delayed the original judgment and instructed the children of Israel to prepare to leave Mount Sinai. Before leaving, however, Moses presented God with a condition: "If Your Presence does not go with us, do not bring us up from here" (Exodus 33:15). This impertinent young leader dared to ask the Lord to show him His glory (v. 18).

God responded in graciousness: "I will make all My goodness pass before you, and I will proclaim the name of the Lord before you. I will be gracious to whom I will be gracious, and I will have compassion on whom I will have compassion" (v. 19). God would protect Moses by only showing him the hind parts of His glory. This exceptional unveiling of God, even though it was His back, would suffice Moses' needs.

Using this illustration, Paul accomplishes two goals. He is first reemphasizing the character of the God of Israel. Dunn suggests this:

> The God of Israel is first and foremost a God of mercy and compassion. The covenant name (Yahweh) signifies that His choice of Israel was motivated solely by pity and compassion. The central motivation in election is God's compassion; His purpose has the primary object of showing mercy.[3]

God has the right to do whatever He wishes, and His wishes are full of mercy.

Second, there are some who serve God's purpose consciously and voluntarily; others do it unconsciously and involuntarily. Such is the case with Pharaoh, as recorded in Exodus 9.

Exodus 7:1-5 records that Moses and Aaron would speak to Pharaoh. God would harden Pharaoh's heart and multiply the signs and wonders in the land of Egypt (v. 3). Moses obeyed, and in their first meeting, Pharaoh asked for a miracle. Both Moses and the magicians of Egypt caused their rods to be turned into serpents. But Pharaoh's heart grew hard (v. 13).

In that same chapter, we read about the fish dying in the river, followed by another statement in verse 22 that Pharaoh's heart grew hard. In chapter 8, there were the plagues of frogs, lice and flies. In chapter 9, we read where the livestock was struck and finally, there was hail. Note the responses of Pharaoh: "he hardened his heart" (8:15); "Pharaoh's heart grew hard" (v. 19); "Pharaoh hardened his heart" (v. 32); and "the heart of Pharaoh was hard" (9:35).

Now the tables are turned—in 9:12; 10:1, 20, 27; 11:10; and 14:8, we read that the Lord hardened Pharaoh's heart.

It appears that there are two causes for the hardening of Pharaoh's heart—the king himself by his own rebellion and reluctance, and the Lord in response. Certain facts remain:

1. God was going to accomplish a great purpose by Pharaoh's existence and conduct.

2. God did not prevent Pharaoh from repenting or doing evil.

3. The monarch acted on his own free will.

Both Moses and Pharaoh were used by God to preserve the nation of Israel—all because of God's mercy. In addition, through both of these men, the truth of God's existence was spread even further among the surrounding nations. It is not by chance that later (Romans 11:25), it will be observed that through the "hardening" (*NIV*) of Israel, the gospel spread to every corner of the Gentile world.

God's Mercy Was Seen Through God's Patience (vv. 19-24)

Immediately, we hear the complaint: "Why does He still find fault? For who has resisted His will?" (v. 19).

What the plaintiff fails to remember is that "it is the God-defying rebel and not the bewildered seeker after God whose mouth He so peremptorily shuts."[4] Haldane adds, "That God does all things right there is no question, but the grounds of His conduct He does not explain to His people. Much less is it to be supposed that He would justify His conduct by explaining the grounds of it to His enemies. No man has a right to bring God to that."[5]

The apostle Paul quotes from Isaiah 29:16. The prophet had just chastised Israel for spiritual blindness and obedience, thinking God would excuse them. Isaiah declares, "Surely you have things turned around! Shall the potter be esteemed as the clay; for shall the thing made say of him who made it, 'He did not make me'? Or shall the thing formed say of him who formed it, 'He has no understanding'?"

Paul uses a popular illustration in Jewish thought: that of the potter with his clay (see also Psalm 2:9; Isaiah 41:25; 45:9; Jeremiah 18:1-6). In Romans 9:21, he refers to "vessel[s] for honor," those fitted for a more noble, ornamental and refined purpose; and "vessel[s] . . . for dishonor," those designed for common use. Paul does not speak of vessels being destroyed, only being put to different uses. The function of the vessel differs, not the material.

It is with great patience and long-suffering that God endures those who are worthy of His wrath (1:18) in order to make known His abundant glory upon those who have received His mercy. It is those whom He has prepared beforehand, through history and through life, who will be conformed to His image and comforted with His hope—not only the Jews, but we who are Gentiles.

Three Comments Regarding God's Mercy (vv. 25-29)

Hosea 1:10; 2:23. In Hosea 1, the prophet was instructed to marry a harlot, Gomer, the daughter of Diblaim. In time, she gave birth to a son, and Hosea acknowledged the child as his and named him Jezreel. But Hosea was convinced that the second and third children were not his own. The names he gave them expressed his disillusionment: the daughter he called *Lo-Ruhamah* ("not the object of my affection or mercy") and the son, *Lo-Ammi* ("no kin of mine"). This was a life-parable of the broken relationship between God and His people, Israel.

Because of the mercy of God, those who had not been His people (*Lo-Ammi*) and those who had not been the objects of His affection (*Lo-Ruhamah*) have now become His sons (*ammi*) and the center of His love (*ruhamah*). In relation to the Jews, God looks forward to the day when the restoration is complete, and they once again become the focus of His mercy. For the Gentiles, we rejoice because we have been included. As John 1:11-13 so aptly puts it:

> He came to His own, and His own did not receive Him. But as many as received Him, to them He gave the right to become children of God, to those who believe in His name: who were born, not of blood, nor of the will of the flesh, nor of the will of man, but of God.

Isaiah 10:22, 23. Though at the time Israel had been taken into exile to Assyria, Isaiah foresaw a day when there would be a remnant—a small minority—who would survive God's judgment. They would constitute the hope of Israel's restoration. This theme had already been a living sign to the people of that day when Isaiah named his son Shear-Jashub, which means "a remnant shall return." They are not an accidental leftover, but an integral part of God's mercy.

The time of that restoration was not a delay and it would be carried out in a righteous manner.

Isaiah 1:9. If God had not been merciful and planted some seeds of the remnant, there would be no future hope. Israel would have ceased to experience the presence of God. But there is a future, as seen by the Jewish believers in Rome.

A Part of Today's Remnant Finds God's Mercy

Max Federmann says that one of the first words he learned in his Jewish home was *shalom*, meaning "peace." Growing up as a Jew in Germany as Adolph Hitler came to power, Max remembers the horror of November 1938, when Nazi storm troopers marched through his village, destroying the property of every Jewish family.

He experienced intense hatred when he saw his father and older brother carried away to a concentration camp, where they were starved and tortured. His brother finally escaped to China, and his father was later able to get to London. But the rest of the family were not able to escape and when Germany invaded Poland, they lost all hope.

At age 16, Max escaped to Yugoslavia and then to Italy. When the war was over in 1945, Max and his wife returned to Frankfurt in search of his family. He was joyfully reunited with his younger brother. His mother and younger sister had been killed at Auschwitz. The pain became so great that living in Germany became impossible. He and his own family migrated to the United States. However, not long after that, his older son was killed in a car accident. In anger, Max denounced God, "How can You be a good God and bring such pain to me? I will have nothing more to do with You!"

When Max's wife and 14-year-old son received Jesus Christ as their Savior, Max felt rejected and refused all invitations to attend church. As the mom and son read their Bibles, Max turned to his Hebrew Bible. One day, he read Isaiah 35:5: "Then the eyes of the blind shall be opened," and he knew God was talking about him. When he reached Jeremiah 31:31, that God promised to make a "new covenant with the house of Israel and with the house of Judah," he had to look at the New Testament. It was not long before Max recognized the *shalom* of God in sending Jesus, the Messiah, to forgive his sins. This Jew found the completion of his faith.

Max continued to grow in Jesus Christ and became a leader in His church in Burbank, California. His heart was flooded with love, and his life story led many people to find the same hope. Today, Max's son pastors a Foursquare church in Lompoc, California.

All because God had not given up on His people!

LESSONS ANYONE?

1. Why do you think the Jewish believers might question Paul's love for his kinsmen? How is his compassion an example for today's believers?
2. In light of Paul's accounts of Isaac and Ishmael, Jacob and Esau, what does this tell us about today's struggle between the nation of Israel and its Palestinian and Arab neighbors? Do you believe any peace process will settle the situation?
3. How does knowing God is ever present with us impact our daily living, our speech and choices?
4. Read afresh the history of Hosea and God's request. How should this impact the attitude of Gentile believers toward God's inclusion of them in His plan?

Chapter 20

Then, What's the Problem?

Romans 9:30—10:21

Don't forget the four basic underlying questions Paul is trying to address in Romans 9—11 (see previous chapter).

The first one was asked, in essence, by the Jews: "Paul, don't you care about your countrymen anymore?" Paul's answer in Romans 9 was that he would be willing to be sacrificed if it resulted in the Jews recognizing their Savior. God's mercy had been shown throughout Israel's history, in spite of their unbelief.

Now, he seems to answer the next two questions: How is it that the "people of God" missed the gospel, yet those who weren't even interested in God "found it"? Is Israel not responding because they haven't heard? Or is it that they don't understand?

Using a chain of illustrations from the Old Testament, Paul certifies that Israel did have sufficient understanding

(9:30—10:5); that the gospel was plainly accessible to God's chosen people (10:6-13); that there was ample opportunity for Israel to respond (vv. 14-18); and that God's arms of mercy are still outstretched to this beloved nation (vv. 19-21).

Sufficient Understanding (9:30—10:5)

Here is one of those "What shall we say then?" moments! The first "What then?" nailed down the fact that both Jews and Greeks—all—are under sin (3:9). Verse 27 concluded that a man is justified by faith apart from the deeds of the Law. In 4:1, "What then shall we say . . . ?" was the lead-in question. The answer is that Abraham himself was justified by faith, and so are we because we are his children by the promise.

The question was repeated when Paul told us we should no longer continue in sin (6:1), that we have a better master (v. 15), and that we are in a spiritual battle with the old nature (7:7). In 8:39, Paul nailed down the fact that nothing shall separate us from the love of God.

Here, the next nail is driven in the coffin of excuses. The reason for Israel's failure to obtain the righteousness God had designed for them was because "they did not seek it by faith, but as it were, by the works of the law" (9:32). In other words, that which was to be a *plumb line* to show them their sinfulness actually became the *bottom line* of their self-righteousness. They literally stumbled over what was meant to be a blessing to them. What was to be stepping-stones to God's people in their quest for righteousness became their stumbling stone.

The apostle links two familiar scriptures from the prophecy of Isaiah to illustrate his point. While warning them about the impending deluge from Assyria that would sweep away Israel's excuses and false security, God speaks through the prophet about the source of true safety: "Behold, I lay in Zion a stone for a foundation, a tried stone, a precious cornerstone, a sure foundation; whoever believes will not act hastily [panic]" (Isaiah 28:16).

Paul connects this promise to Isaiah 8:14, 15 to show what really took place: "He will be as a sanctuary, but a stone of stumbling and rock of offense to both the houses of Israel, as a trap and a snare to the inhabitants of Jerusalem. And many among them shall stumble; they shall fall and be broken, be snared and taken." Psalm 118:22 had foreseen this: "The stone which the builders rejected has become the chief cornerstone."

Writing to the church at Corinth, Paul wrote: "For Jews request a sign, and Greeks seek after wisdom; but we preach Christ crucified, to the Jews a stumbling block [scandal] and to the Greeks foolishness" (1 Corinthians 1:22, 23).

We dare not miss, however, the fact that Paul places Isaiah 28:16 at the end of this statement. There is the hint of a righteous remnant about whom he had talked in Romans 9:27: the hope of the future embodied personally in the promised Messiah, the prince of the house of David.

Paul never condemned the Israelites without soothing the gaping wound with the salve of the mercy of God still available for them. It was Paul's desire and prayer that Israel be saved (10:1).

If anyone could understand firsthand how someone could have a zealous enthusiasm for God but not understand why, Paul could. Listen to his own testimony:

> My manner of life from my youth, which was spent from the beginning among my own nation at Jerusalem, all the

> Jews know. They knew me from the first, if they were willing to testify, that according to the strictest sect of our religion, I lived a Pharisee. . . . Indeed I myself thought I must do many things contrary to the name of Jesus of Nazareth. This I did in Jerusalem, and many of the saints I shut up in prison, having received authority from the chief priests; and when they were put to death, I cast my vote against them. And I punished them often in every synagogue and compelled them to blaspheme; and being exceedingly enraged against them, I persecuted them even to foreign cities (Acts 26:4, 5, 9, 11).

There was a sincere passion that was not enlightened, wise or correct in its essence. It was also a voluntary ignorance (see Romans 1:20, 22; 2:17-24). The Israelites persisted in confiding in their own merits and advantages as a Jew as grounds for acceptance with God.

Paul refers back to the conclusion of Romans 3:20, 28, 31, that Christ was the fulfillment of the Law. If anyone chooses to find justification by works, that person has the responsibility to keep all of the Law's requirements. Any error is "one too many." "In other words," says Paul, "to base your future on your perfection is both impractical and impossible."

I like the comment attributed to John Calvin: "It is better as Augustine says to limp in the right way than to run with all your might out of the way."

"To whom much is given, from him much will be required" (Luke 12:48) was spoken by our Lord when He came to the end of a discourse regarding faithful and evil servants. Peter had asked the Lord if His parable was to the people of Israel or only to the disciples. Jesus didn't give a specific answer, but He left the principle open for all to interpret. The disciples were responsible because they had been taught directly by Jesus. The Jews to whom Jesus had been talking were also responsible because of the mercy, types and shadows, and promises that had been given to the world through them.

Paul's words should sober us Gentiles regarding our responsibility to God. Think about it! If the Jews were responsible because of their unique relationship with God, then doesn't it stand to reason that we who came in the door by the long-suffering of God because of the Jews' disbelief are even more responsible? Or will we remain willfully ignorant?

Plainly Accessible (10:6-13)

A second excuse raised by those who had willfully stumbled over the cornerstone was that the gospel was too remote and too difficult. In rebuttal, Paul draws from the life of Moses and Deuteronomy 30:12, 13. But to understand the apostle's rationale, we go back even further in the Hebrew writings.

The earliest writing in Scripture is probably the Book of Job. Though Job's comforters were lousy counselors, their words reflect the mind-set of the earliest times. One of the counselors, Zophar the Naamathite, was certain that if Job would simply repent, God would show him the error of his ways. In doing so, he stated: "Can you search out the deep things of God? Can you find out the limits of the Almighty? They are higher than heaven—what can you do? Deeper than Sheol—what can you know? Their measure is longer than the earth and broader than the sea" (Job 11:7-9). God was too high to be available and too deep to be understood.

Over the passage of time, the phrase "higher than heaven and deeper than Sheol" became a popular way of saying something was too remote to be relevant and too mysterious to be comprehended.

When Moses gave his "last will and testament" to the people of Israel as they were about to enter the Promised Land, he made this declaration:

> The Lord your God will make you abound in all the work of your hand, in the fruit of your body, in the increase of your livestock, and in the produce of your land for good. For the Lord will again rejoice over you for good as He rejoiced over your fathers, if you obey the voice of the Lord your God, to keep His commandments and His statutes which are written in this Book of the Law, and if you turn to the Lord your God with all your heart and with all your soul. For this commandment which I command you today *is not too mysterious for you, nor is it far off. It is not in heaven, that you should say, 'Who will ascend into heaven for us and bring it to us, that we may hear it and do it?' Nor is it beyond the sea, that you should say, 'Who will go over the sea for us and bring it to us, that we may hear it and do it?'* But the word is very near you, in your mouth and in your heart, that you may do it (Deuteronomy 30:9-14, italics mine).

Paul now turns the idiom into the incarnation. Note Romans 10:6, 7, where Paul adds the words "that is, to bring Christ down from above" and "that is, to bring Christ up from the dead." The gospel is not too remote or too difficult to understand; as a matter of fact, it is near and clear! The incarnation of Jesus "put a face on God"—"He who has seen Me has seen the Father" (John 14:9); and Jesus was "declared to be the Son of God . . . by the resurrection from the dead" (Romans 1:4). Nothing more was needed.

The Jews need not find lofty heavens; God's righteousness is just as near as their mouth and can be clearly embraced by their hearts. There was absolutely no grounds to their "buts."

The message is clear, but what about the application? It is just as plain and simple. It is by the confession of faith in Christ's sufficiency (not His slavish responding to our hedonistic wants and lusts, as some preach). Read the repetitive words in 10:6-12: *speaks* (v. 6), *mouth* (v. 8), *confess* (v. 9), *confession* (v. 10), *call/calls* (vv. 12, 13). The doorway to our salvation is in the heart that expresses itself in public speech or forum.

In Matthew 10:32, 33, our Lord clarified the word *confession*: "Therefore whoever confesses Me before men, him I will also confess before My Father who is in heaven. But whoever denies Me before men, him I will also deny before My Father who is in heaven." Revelation 3:5 foresaw this: "He who overcomes shall be clothed in white garments, and I will not blot his name from the Book of Life; but I will confess his name before My Father and before His angels." It is also not coincidence that Luke 12:8 remembered the same quote from Matthew 10, but included the angels.

Paul once again marvels: "Whoever believes on Him will not be put to shame [embarrassed or panicked]" (Romans 10:11). Whether we are Jew or Greek, the same Lord who has descended from heaven and ascended again, and who has descended into the grave and ascended again, continues to pour out His rich (*generous*, remember

Romans 6:23, "the donation/gift") mercy upon all who call upon him. We call it "salvation." Hallelujah, the message is just as simple as that!

Ample Opportunity (vv. 14-18)

There are some who believe the next two verses have a strong missiological tone to them. In principle, there's absolutely nothing wrong in using verses 14 and 15 to that end. Still, we must remember the context in which Paul is writing: it is to answer the excuses of the Israelites while laying down principles for the entire church in Rome.

Paul is also responding to further possible arguments: "Maybe they didn't have ample opportunity to hear? Remember, before they can call upon the Lord, they must believe. They can't believe unless they've heard, and there can't be a preacher unless one is sent."

Again, like the scholar he is, this former Pharisee immediately launches into Old Testament scriptures for his answer.

The gospel was heralded. He quotes Isaiah 52:7 and Nahum 1:15. "How beautiful upon the mountains are the feet of him who brings good news, who proclaims peace, who brings glad tidings of good things, who proclaims salvation, who says to Zion, 'Your God reigns!' Your watchmen shall lift up their voices, with their voices they shall sing together; for they shall see eye to eye when the Lord brings back Zion" (Isaiah 52:7, 8).

Here is a description of watchmen on the walls of the city of Zion during times of war and exile. They daily awaited the appearance of runners who brought news from the battlefield or land of captivity back to loved ones at home. Suddenly a runner appeared, but he was not running. He was bent over with a depressed demeanor. His feet carried bad news, messages of despair and death.

On the other hand, should the runner be waving his arms and running with all his might, good news was at hand; no matter how dirty and bruised his feet were, they were absolutely beautiful. The day will come when One whose feet were nailed to a cross will come proclaiming "Our God reigns!" and we will consider them the most beautiful feet that ever walked on God's creation. Yes, the message has been preached!

But it was not heeded. Paul refers to Isaiah 53:1: "Who has believed our report? And to whom has the arm of the Lord been revealed?" As the messenger arrived in the city and reported the victories at the front, there were always skeptics. These persons can always refuse the report simply because they don't like it. You see, saving faith comes by truly hearing the report of the gospel, and that comes only through the Word (report) of God.

The gospel had been amply available. It had been heard clearly. In Romans 10:18 the apostle quoted Psalm 19:4 as a grand finale. "Their sound has gone out to all the earth." The emphasis is on the word *sound*, for it is the tone of a symphonic instrument. There is nothing confusing or complicated—it is clear.

The last part of the verse states: "And their words to the ends of the world." The focus here is that the gospel had been spread to every part of the civilized world. There's nothing remote; the gospel is as near as one's heart and mouth. It has come to all the same way, both Jew and Gentile, even to Rome.

Still Outstretched (vv. 19-21)

Throughout this chapter, the apostle used the lives and words of Moses and Isaiah to answer the challenges of unbelieving Jews. He relates how Moses recounted the disobedience and rebellion of the people who had been delivered out of Egypt.

> And when the Lord saw it, He spurned them, because of the provocation of His sons and His daughters. And He said: "I will hide My face from them, I will see what their end will be, for they are a perverse generation, children in whom is no faith. They have provoked Me to jealousy by what is not God; they have moved Me to anger by their foolish idols [vanities]. But I will provoke them to jealousy by those who are not a nation [Lo-Ammi]; I will move them to anger by a foolish nation" (Deuteronomy 32:19-21).

In other words, God is giving the children of Israel a taste of their own medicine. He literally makes them jealous through His mercy to the Gentiles.

God made Israel an offer. While the gospel was so clear that it could be understood by the Gentiles, and so near that those who didn't even seek still found Him, God's mercy is still outstretched to His beloved Israel. Paul quotes Isaiah 65:1-3:

> I was sought by those who did not ask for Me; I was found by those who did not seek Me. I said, "Here I am, here I am," to a nation that was not called by My name. I have stretched out My hands all day long to a rebellious people, who walk in a way that is not good, according to their own thoughts; a people who provoke Me to anger continually to My face.

The Pharisees and the scribes came to Jesus complaining that He was associating, even eating with the tax collectors and the sinners. (I'm sure there's not a connection between sin and the IRS!) In response, Jesus told the parable of the shepherd leaving his flock in order to save one lost sheep. He talked about the rejoicing of a woman who found a lost coin that had been so valuable to her. He concluded with the parable of the prodigal son, a perfect illustration of the nation of Israel.

While not relating the entire story found in Luke 15:11-32, I call your attention to the location of the father when the son returned home. The Scripture says, "But when he was still a great way off, his father saw him and had compassion, and ran and fell on his neck and kissed him" (v. 20). The father was not standing at the gate with arms folded in judgment and condemnation, but he was running to greet the son with open arms, ever yearning to embrace him.

All of us who have found Jesus understand the outstretched hands of God's mercy. They have embraced us. He has kissed us with His welcome. And we are "home."

LESSONS ANYONE?

1. In your opinion, why was the gospel so hard for the Jews to comprehend and receive? Are there any lessons from their past for the church today?

2. From the personal testimony of Paul, the letter writer, does sincerity of heart and zeal have any merit in one's pursuit of God? What does this speak to us about the "revelation" of the gospel in one's heart?

3. Relate the belief in one's heart with the confession of their mouth. What did Jesus say about the mouth and the heart connection?

4. When Jesus told the parable of the prodigal son (Luke 15), was He making reference to the nation of Israel or each of us individually? Briefly review the parable and draw at least three principles for application in our lives today.

Chapter 21

Israel—Y2K Compatible

Romans 11:1-36

There are moments of history that leave an indelible imprint on our memories. I remember as a young lad sitting in front of my father's Zenith console radio listening to the funeral of Franklin D. Roosevelt. I will never forget the days of drama as the assassination of John F. Kennedy unfolded. Nor the "out-of-this-world" pictures of Neil Armstrong taking that "small step" that became a "giant leap" on the moon. Should the Lord tarry and we live long enough, those in the next generation will ask, "Where were you when the millennium turned?" One thing I will remember is that as the world entered the 21st century, I was at this point in my writing regarding Israel.

What a difference 100 years make! In 1900, the population of the United States stood at 76,306,387; the projected population by midnight, December 31, 1999, was 274,634,000. In 1900, worldwide population stood at

1.6 billion; projected world population as we entered the year 2000 was 6.03 billion. In 1900, the average income of American workers was $438 per year; today, that average annual income is nearing $18,800. Average hourly wage for Americans working in the manufacturing industries at the beginning of the 20th century stood at 21.6 cents; today it stands at $13.84.

At the beginning of the century, the speed limit on New York City streets was 8 miles per hour, and 4 million pounds of horse manure covered those same streets every day. At the close of the century, the speed limit is 30 miles per hour with 1,086,180 cars making their way into New York City each morning. In 1900, the average life expectancy for Americans was 47.3 years. In 1997, the last year for which information is available, the average life expectancy was 76.5 years.

In 1900, the population of Los Angeles was 102,479; today, in the city of Los Angeles, there are 3,485,000 people. At the beginning of the 20th century, there were 377 stock issues listed on the New York Stock Exchange; there are now 3,336 stock issues listed on that same exchange. In 1900, the public debt in the U.S. reached $2.1 billion; as we entered 2000, our public debt reached $5.7 trillion. In 1900, the average American owed $27.52; today, the projected per capita debt is nearly $21,000. For you who are driving the freeways every morning, you'd be interested to know that over the past 100 years, the number of cars in the United States has risen from 8,000 to more than 200 million.

The months that have led up to this moment have been filled with doomsday prophecies regarding the "Y2K Bug," which, in fact, never materialized. People stockpiled cash and cases of food just in case the world's computer systems reverted back to the year 1900, and their future was filled with chaos and catastrophe at the strike of midnight. The question was, "Are you Y2K compatible?" Thanks to the spending of over $510 billion in adjusting old and implementing new computer data, we were.

What does all this have to do with Israel? They do not even follow the calendar of the Western world. The Hebrews date their calendar back to their idea of Creation: 3761 B.C. (If we figure the year 2000 has significance, then what about their 5761?) Doesn't sound too apocalyptic, does it?

But while the world has changed over the centuries, even millennia, and we are still quibbling about where we stand on the calendar, there are two certainties: We are definitely living in the end times, and God's love and plan for Israel have not changed one iota.

Paul now answers the fourth question (see chapter 19 of this study): "What will happen to the Jews? Has God given up on them forever?" Again we hear Paul's response, "Certainly not!" He employs three arguments:

- God has not rejected His people—there are still some who believe, including Paul himself (vv. 1-10).
- Israel's present rejection of the gospel has enabled salvation to come to the Gentiles (vv. 11-24).
- The nation of Israel will fully experience God's original, gracious intention (vv. 25-32).

With such a magnificent future, the apostle breaks forth in glorious praise to a wise and magnanimous God (vv. 33-36).

God Has Not Given Up on His People (vv. 1-10)

The first proof of this fact is Paul himself. He was an Israelite—a member of the very race God had chosen as His covenant people. He was of the natural seed of Abraham, the fountain of that race. And if that wasn't enough, he was born into the tribe of Benjamin, the only son of Jacob who was born in the land of Israel, where the holy city Jerusalem is located. Benjamin was the one tribe that remained faithful to Judah. As was the custom of the time, Paul was probably named in honor of Saul, the first king of Israel who had come from this tribe. A more true-blue Israelite you couldn't find.

Moreover, seeing all that Saul did prior to his conversion, if God was going to reject anyone, it would have been him. Yet, look who is writing the letter—what a proof that God has not "cast away His people whom He foreknew." Israel had not been repelled, pushed away or spurned. Paul was living proof of the indestructible existence of a believing remnant in all periods of Israel's history.

Let us look at Elijah's time. In 1 Kings 18, the prophet, who had previously predicted the drought, went before King Ahab and declared that it would once again rain in the land of Israel. He was immediately summoned to a "Challenge of the Gods" on Mount Carmel. What a mismatch! After the priests of Baal pleaded before their gods all day, Elijah approached the altar and offered a prayer of 64 words. The fire of the Lord fell and consumed not only the sacrifice, but also the wood, stones, dust and water that had been poured around the base of those stones. Talk about a mountaintop experience!

But in chapter 19, Queen Jezebel's words dampened Elijah's elation. She declared that within 24 hours, she would have the prophet's head. Elijah fled to the desert. Feeling lonely and forlorn, this man of God sat under a juniper tree and prayed to die (sound like anyone you and I know?). An angel from the Lord allowed this weary prophet to get some sleep, then provided food and water for him. The meal was sufficient to carry Elijah along for 40 days and nights, as he found refuge in Mount Horeb—the mountain of God.

There the Lord asked, "What are you doing here?" This mighty man of God's response was, "I have been very zealous for the Lord God of hosts; for the children of Israel have forsaken Your covenant, torn down Your altars, and killed Your prophets with the sword. I alone am left; and they seek to take my life" (1 Kings 19:10). His complaint was repeated again in verse 14.

God's answer was simple: "Yet I have reserved seven thousand in Israel, all whose knees have not bowed to Baal, and every mouth that has not kissed him" (v. 18). Elijah was not the only one; there were many others who had remained just as faithful. Likewise, in Paul's time, there were those Jews who had remained faithful and had responded to God's grace by faith (Romans 11:5).

This reminds me of a bumper sticker I saw on the car of a Jewish person here in Los Angeles. For months, a para-church organization had very successfully used an evangelistic outreach titled, "I Found It," referring to the answer that is found in our Savior, Jesus Christ. In response to the slogan's implication, a Jewish person had placed a decal on his bumper along with a Star of David that declared, "I Never Lost It!"

Whether or not they were believing Jews, this fact remains: there are still members of the nation of Israel who have "never lost it." But it was not earned, it was completely given by grace. In verse 6, Paul references previous statements he had made in Romans 3:21-31 and 4:4. The majority of the Jews had tried to "earn" God's favor by their own merits. Yet "the elect," those who placed their trust in Christ (see 11:5), had been given such grace based solely on the merit of Christ's righteousness, His completed work on the cross and resurrection.

Because of their unbelief, the Jews "were hardened" (v. 7, *NIV*). Paul uses the word *poroo*, a kind of marble. It also means "to petrify," or in medical terms, "to cause a callus to form in order to bring healing." It should be recognized, however, that God's hardening in verse 7 is in direct response to Israel's stumbling and rebellion in 9:32.

In 11:8-10, Paul stated that this had been foreseen in the Old Testament. He combined the event of Deuteronomy 29:1-4 and the declaration of the prophet Isaiah (v. 10). Because Israel had refused to walk with Him into the Promised Land as Joshua and Caleb had encouraged, the Lord did not give them a heart to perceive and eyes to see and ears to hear. For 40 years they wandered in the wilderness. Years later, because of Israel's refusal to obey God, Isaiah observed, "For the Lord has poured out on you the spirit of deep sleep, and has closed your eyes, namely, the prophets; and He has covered your heads, namely, the seers. The whole vision has become to you like the words of a book that is sealed" (vv. 10, 11). What a contrast to the gospel being a blessing, near and clear!

King David described the result in Psalm 69:22, 23, as quoted by Paul in Romans 11:9, 10: "Let their table become a snare and a trap, a stumbling block and a recompense to them. Let their eyes be darkened, so that they do not see, and bow down their back always."

First of all, what was meant to be a blessing became chaos and destruction. David was a shepherd who lived outdoors most of his life. When it came time to eat, he would loosen his tunic and spread his garment out before him as the "tablecloth" on which to place his food. It was to be a time of rest and refreshment from the day's toil. However, being suddenly ambushed by animals or human predators, he tried to rise and defend himself only to see his tablecloth become a tunic of death. It became a snare and a trap that hindered his maneuverability.

Second, what was meant to be the fulfillment of their anticipation of their redemption became the stick ("stumbling block"; Greek, *scandalon*) that set off the trap and captured them like animals. It was God's "recompense," or repayment, for their willful ignorance. To this day, being blind to the gospel has become their heavy burden.

Israel's Rejection: the Gentiles' Redemption (vv. 11-24)

Is Israel's "stumbling" final and fatal? Is Israel like a runner who sprawls on his face, putting him out of the race? Are the Jews beyond recovery?

Paul's response is, "Certainly not!" Actually, their fall will come full circle: salvation has come to the Gentiles and the salvation of the Gentiles will make Israel jealous, resulting in the Jews' redemption. By the way, Gentiles, you ought to be grateful to the Jews. It is a classic illustration of how "all things work together" (8:28) for both the Jew and the Gentile.

Because of Israel's rejection, the possession and blessing (riches) God had given to Israel had been passed to the world, in particular, the Gentiles. This cannot be seen negatively, but positively. God's desire and Paul's delight would be that there be full inclusion, in quantity and in quality.

For centuries, rather than placing Israel as a source of blessing, even we in the Christian church have hated, criticized and even demeaned the Jews. That's why Paul turned to the Gentile believers in Rome to initiate a fresh perspective.

In 11:13, Paul became the apostle to the Gentiles—the "ethnics." As a matter of fact, he accepted this divine assignment with great esteem. But his ultimate hope was that by whatever means (this is actually a Greek idiom that could be translated "in the hope that"), the Jews would be provoked to jealousy.

In Acts 22:21, Paul related God's call upon his life: "Then [the Lord] said to me, 'Depart, for I will send you far from here to the Gentiles.' " He later wrote to the church in Galatia: "It pleased God, who separated me from my mother's womb and called me through His grace, to reveal His Son in me, that I might preach Him among the Gentiles" (Galatians 1:15, 16). There was no question in Paul's mind about the focus of his ministry. Still, he boldly proclaimed the gospel so that at least some of the Jews would be saved.

The word *jealousy* is used in Romans 11:11 and again in verse 14. In his notes on Romans 11:10-12, Steve Schell, Foursquare pastor and theologian, gives great clarity: "To provoke to jealousy, to stimulate to follow, to excite to emulation is to be taken not in a negative but in a positive sense of seeking after what was lost and has now been given to the Gentiles."

The restoration of Israel to favor with God will be glorious. Lenski writes: "Great is the marvel that the casting away is reconciliation of the world; certainly equally great and like life from the dead is the fact that many are still received."[1]

In verse 16, Paul begins to illustrate the principle just stated. He uses two very understandable metaphors: the dough that made up the cakes to be offered as the firstfruit of the heave offering (Numbers 15:17-21); and that of the olive branch, which was the imagery of Israel (see *branches/root*: Job 18:16; Jeremiah 17:8; Ezekiel 31:7; Hosea 9:16; *a spreading vine*: Psalm 80:8-18; Jeremiah 2:21; Ezekiel 17; *the messianic hope*: Isaiah 1, 10, 11; Jeremiah 23:5; 33:15; Zechariah 3:8; 6:12). The firstfruits and the root refer to the patriarchs to whom the covenant of the Lord and the divine blessings of Jehovah had been given and passed on to the nation.

In the illustration of the vine and branches, some of the branches were broken off as had been prophesied by Jeremiah: "The Lord called your name, Green Olive Tree, Lovely and of Good Fruit. With the noise of great tumult He has kindled fire on it, and its branches are broken" (11:16). In their place, the Gentiles had been grafted in among those who remained faithful. They became sharing partners of the blessings of God's people and the richness of His mercy. Therefore, rather than considering themselves superior to their Jewish brothers and sisters, the Gentile believers in Rome must remember that it is because of the Jews that they even have access to the Vine—Jesus Christ.

We should never think of the rejection of the Jews without being struck with the awe of our being included and blessed among them. As Charles Wesley so eloquently penned: "And can it be that I should gain an interest in the Savior's blood?" We are left absolutely speechless, but eternally thankful to God and to the Jews.

There is a warning. The Gentiles dare not become proud and belittle the Jews. If God didn't spare the original branch, then He can break off the wild branch! Barrett explains it this way: "The moment the Gentile begins to grow boastful, he ceases to have faith and therefore becomes a candidate for 'cutting off.'"[2]

There is a balance between the goodness and kindness of God and His severity and justice. Paul warns that there is the possibility for one who has experienced the grace of God, should they fail to continue in that grace, to be cut off, like the chopping down of an entire tree (see Matthew 3:10; 7:19; Luke 13:7, 9). Hodge writes:

> Our security does not depend upon our now enjoying the blessings of the church of God, but is dependent on our continuing in divine goodness or favor; doing nothing to forfeit its favor; its continuance being suspended on the condition of our faith alone.[3]

At the same time, those Jews who do not continue in unbelief will again be grafted in. As a matter of fact, God is extremely willing to do just that.

Throughout the theological world, there has been much debate regarding the matter of unconditional eternal security (i.e., that after accepting Jesus Christ, no matter what these persons do, their salvation is secured). On the other side of the coin are those who daily walk in fear that they will suddenly commit a sin that will cause God to cast them away. It is important to recognize from these verses that it is not God who causes the separation; it is the unwillingness of the person to accept the goodness of God. If belief in Christ is the doorway into the glorious redemption provided for us, then only unbelief—a willful rejection—can be the exit from that grace. We should believe in that "eternal security" of God's love that our Lord wants us to daily experience; at the same time, we should never become presumptuous of this relationship.

Paul's warning sobers those Gentile believers in Rome who considered the Jews as those "ignorant, legalistic adherers of the law." It was those legalistic adherers who were the "natural branches" and partakers of the tree where the Gentiles received the good news of the gospel.

Israel Will Experience God's Original Intention (vv. 25-32)

The apostle let his readers in on a mystery, not an undisclosed secret, but what is now revealed by divine agency. A good example of such a mystery is found in Daniel 2:18, 19, 27-30, where Daniel informed King Nebuchadnezzar that "there is a God in heaven who reveals secrets, and He has made known to [you] what will be in the latter days. Your dream, and the visions of your head upon your bed, were these" (v. 28).

Many believe Paul was not predicting any unique future conversion of the Jewish nation, but he was emphasizing their blindness until the Gentiles all come in. This view was championed by authors about the time of the Reformation.

The second view, one which has been embraced throughout every age of the church, is that Paul is predicting a great and general conversion of the Jewish nation, which would take place at the end of the age. Only then will these prophecies be fulfilled.

As we look at the flow of the letter, we see that Paul has hinted that some of the natural branches would be once again "grafted into their own olive tree" (Romans 11:24). There is also a comparison between the "blindness in part" (v. 25) and "all Israel will be saved" (v. 26). The *all* must be understood as Israel as a whole, but not necessarily every individual member. It is what is known today as the collective *we*. Other scriptures use the same terminology (1 Samuel 7:5; 25:1; 1 Kings 12:1; 2 Chronicles 12:1; Daniel 9:11).

James D.G. Dunn concurs: "The salvation of Israel in the sense of the restoration of those scattered throughout the Diaspora was a common enough theme of Jewish expectation (Deuteronomy 30:1-5; Nehemiah 1:9; Jeremiah 23:3; 29:14; Ezekiel 11:17; 36:24; Micah 2:12; 4:6-7; Zephaniah 3:19-20; and Zechariah 10:8-10)."[4]

The prophet Isaiah (59:20, 21) had prophesied this: "The Redeemer will come to Zion, and to those who turn from the transgression in Jacob." The apostle turns the words to forecast the future, when Jesus Christ returns and touches down on the Mount of Olives and will once again remove the blindness and unbelief of the people of Jacob (Israel). Israel will come to the same encounter with the reigning Lord as Paul did with the resurrected Lord. Moreover, what the Jews (even the disciples) had considered to be a national or political covenant will in fact be a spiritual restoration (see Isaiah 27:9).

As far as the gospel is concerned, the Jews were regarded and treated as enemies so that the Gentiles could be included. But in reference to God's plan for them (the election), they are still to be regarded as His "peculiar people" because of their relationship to the patriarchs. The gifts (see

Romans 9:4, 5) and the calling (unique position) of being God's special people will be fully completed, based on His faithfulness, steadfastness and reliability.

> Remember Gentile believers, when you were disobedient, you obtained mercy through the disobedience of the Jews. Now they are disobedient and through the mercy you have found, they too will be restored. Somehow in God's wisdom, all of us have been confined in the prison called "disobedience" The only exit door from this prison has the inscription, 'Mercy!' Yes, you are profitable for each other (see 11:30-32).

To God Be the Glory! (vv. 33-36)

The realization of God's mercy catapults Paul into an orbit of praise. The combination of the two words *depth* and *riches* creates the picture of a treasury that has no bottom. Wisdom and knowledge show how God aptly turns His understanding into the fulfillment of His will. His decisions (judgments) and His works (ways) are beyond comprehension, yet they are very real.

Verse 34 is a quote from Isaiah 40:13, 14: "Who has directed the Spirit of the Lord, or as His counselor has taught Him? With whom did He take counsel, and who instructed Him, and taught Him in the path of justice? Who taught Him knowledge, and showed Him the way of understanding?" God's ways are far beyond ours.

There is no way anyone can put God in his debt or repay Him for what He has accomplished. First Chronicles 29 records the moment King David gave God praise for the privilege of providing for the building of the temple in

Jerusalem. Having recognized God's sovereign authority and strength, the king humbly confessed, "But who am I, and who are my people, that we should be able to offer so willingly as this? For all things come from You, and of Your own we have given You" (v. 14). Here (v. 36) in the first doxology of the letter to the Romans, Paul adapts this concept and makes this conclusion:

All things are OF HIM: they come from Him;
All things are THROUGH HIM: they live by Him; and
All things are TO HIM: they end in Him;
TO HIM be glory forever!

LESSONS ANYONE?

1. How does unbelief in a Christian's experience normally manifest itself ? How does unbelief cause one to stumble?

2. What attitude should today's believer hold toward the people of Israel? Does this imply that we must accept all actions that national Israel takes? What will be Israel's destiny in the end times?

3. Explain a proper view of eternal security in light of the warning that Paul makes to the Gentile believers in chapter 11.

4. What should it mean to the believer to live in light of Jesus Christ's soon return?

Chapter 22

Therefore, by the Mercies of God

Romans 12:1-8

"I beseech you therefore, brethren, by the mercies of God . . ." (v. 1). These are some of the most quoted words in the Bible. Many feel they should be the climax of Paul's discussion regarding the mercy of God in Romans 11. Others make these words a gateway into the practical conclusions of the apostle's letter to the Roman believers. Most likely, Paul's intention was to accomplish both purposes. Without mercy, there is no redemption; without practical living, there is no relevance.

"I beseech you therefore, brethren, by the mercies of God . . ." is like a pebble thrown into a pool of water that sends forth concentric ripples to the ends of the lake. For the purpose of our study, I would like to suggest those concentric ripples as being the following:

- Our body (12:1)

- Our mind (v. 2)
- Our view of ourselves (vv. 3-5)
- Our gifting (vv. 6-8)
- Our attitudes toward fellow believers (vv. 9-13)
- Our relationship to the world (vv. 14-21)
- Our relationship with civic authorities (13:1-7).

Present Your Bodies (v. 1)

Paul reaches back to Romans 6 and, like the copy icon on your computer, carries forward the verb *present.* It has to do with the making of an offering. In this case, it is our "bodies" that are to be offered. Again I suggest that while the word *body* includes our whole life, it is our bodies that become the expression of the vitality (or lack of) that is resident in our hearts.

Of course, each of us is fully aware that the problem with "living sacrifices" is that they keep climbing off the altar! Therein lies the difference! Whereas the Old Testament lamb had no choice in the matter, we who know Jesus become both the offerer and the offering. The "after altar" result will be the ever renewing of life, not death. As one has suggested: "To be a Christian means to give as much of myself as I can to as much of Jesus Christ as I know."[1]

Continuing with the motif of the altar, verse 1 says such a sacrifice will be *holy*, given over totally to God to be consumed by Him; *acceptable to God*, clothed in Christ's righteousness, a sacrifice in which God delights; and it is *reasonable service*, the logical act of worship expected from such a sacrifice. *Service* has often been translated as "worship." Rather than narrowing the concept of worship down to a weekly 60-minute session of spiritual aerobics in which we release our faith and frustrations, worship in Paul's day had to do with a wholistic lifestyle and perspective. One writer put it this way: "If I were a nightingale, I should be singing as a nightingale; if a swan, as a swan. But as it is, I am a rational being, therefore I must be singing hymns of praise to God."[2] And I add, "living in praise and service."

Be Transformed in Your Mind (v. 2)

The actions of the body will always be shaped by the attitude of the mind. In Romans 1, when humanity became pointless in thought and willfully ignorant in heart, the body became exceedingly sinful, going man's ways. But Jesus came to *totally change* the process and to *change totally* the perspective. When the mind is once again renewed or enlightened, the body becomes exceedingly submitted, going God's ways.

Such a perspective does not come from conformity. The Christian's principles are never established by consensus. It is not a posture or attitude that can be adapted to whatever is convenient. It does not begin with outward conformity to a particular custom. It begins with the inward condition of the heart that changes the lifestyle to match the character of Jesus Christ.

All of us understand the word *metamorphosis*. To be *transformed* is to continually yield to every word of God's Holy Scriptures and every work of God's Holy Spirit. The direction we are heading is more clearly defined in Philippians 3:20, 21: "For our citizenship is in heaven, from which we also eagerly wait for the Savior, the Lord Jesus Christ, who will transform our lowly body that it may be conformed to His glorious body, according to the working by which He is able even to subdue all things to Himself."

The result of such a metamorphosis of our thinking is that we will learn to *prove* God's will. Actually, the better translation is "approve by testing." The tendency of the believer will be more than WWJD (What Would Jesus Do?). It would ask, WWJE (What Would Jesus Expect?). We will allow the Holy Spirit to work in us and then respond to His work. We will "work out [our] own salvation with fear [respect] and trembling [care]; for it is God who works in [us] to will and to do for His good pleasure" (Philippians 2:12, 13).

Such a transformation of the mind will result in our doing God's will. It will be good for us, acceptable to God, and completely consistent with what God has designed for our destiny.

The process of approving God's will is not always easy, but it is best. Some time ago, a friend of mine who is battling cancer, shared the following with me:

> A man found a cocoon of an emperor moth. He took it home so that he could watch the moth come out of the cocoon. On the day a small opening appeared, he sat and watched the moth for several hours as it struggled to force its body through that little hole. Then the moth seemed to stop making any progress. It appeared as if it had gotten as far as it could and it could go no farther. It just seemed to be stuck.

The man, in his kindness, decided to help the moth, so he took a pair of scissors and snipped off the remaining bit of the cocoon. The moth easily emerged. But it had a swollen body and small, shriveled wings. The man continued to watch the moth because he expected that, at any moment, the wings would enlarge and expand to be able to support the body, which would contract in time.

Neither happened! In fact, the little moth spent the rest of its life crawling around with a swollen body and shriveled wings. It was never able to fly.

What the man in his kindness and haste did not understand was that the restricting cocoon and the struggle required for the moth to get through the tiny opening forced the fluid from the body of the moth into its wings. It prepared the moth to be ready and capable to fly once it had achieved its freedom from the cocoon. Freedom and flight would only come after the struggle. By depriving the moth of a struggle, the man had deprived the moth of health.

My friend then concluded: "Sometimes struggles are exactly what we need in life. We would not be as strong as we could have been otherwise."

For nearly four decades, I have counseled young men and women regarding the will of God for their lives. Now, much older and somewhat wiser, I have concluded we will never know the will of God before we take that leap of faith. Only after the step of faith is taken can we look back and confirm (approve) that it truly was the right way to go. You see, if God was going to show us everything *up front*, He would have never asked us to live *by faith*. That's part of being a living sacrifice.

Think Soberly (vv. 3-5)

In Romans 2, Paul condemned the judging of others; in chapter 7, during the spiritual wrestling between the flesh and the spirit, there was no sober thinking. In Romans 12:3, Paul implies that through the divine wisdom and dealings of God, each one of us has received a *measure* (the Greek meaning is "measuring rod") by which we can recognize and realize our place in the body of Christ.

In thinking soberly, it is not possible for the believer to live in isolation. When individuals place their trust in Jesus Christ, the Lord of the church places them in a larger dimension of experience as part of His body—the church. The Christian individual in community with other believers has always been in God's thinking and part of His pattern.

Look at 1 Corinthians 12:12-30; Ephesians 1:23; 4:4-16; 5:23-30; Colossians 1:18, 24; 2:19; and 3:15. I especially like the phrase *being many,* found in Romans 12:5. It should be read: "belonging to one another." You and I never had a choice in the matter. Unity in Christ is not a future aim, it is an already accomplished fact.

When writing to a congregation that had been torn apart by the words of two women, Paul concludes: "*Since* there is encouragement in Christ, *since* there is enablement by love, *since* there is fellowship of the Spirit, *since* there should be affection and mercy, fulfill my joy by having the same attitude, same love, same togetherness and same understanding" (Philippians 2:1, 2, paraphrased).

Thinking soberly (v. 3), therefore, is my understanding of the unique grace God has given me as His child, and how I must work together with other believers as members of His body.

Let Us Use Our Gifts (vv. 6-8)

There have been many ways of interpreting and illustrating what Paul is saying in verses 6-8. We recognize that the Holy Spirit placed the potential of natural giftedness into the creation of the world. He then gave natural talents to each individual in the formation of their personality, adaptivity, abilities and interests. As a matter of fact, in their unsaved state, many people today use that creativity for selfish and sinful reasons. Even Jesus once admitted that the children of darkness are often wiser than the children of light.

When men, women and children find Jesus as their Savior, their abilities are not suddenly altered. Actually, those natural tendencies are intensified by the Holy Spirit extensively for the development and fulfillment of Christ's body. In addition, special and specific endowments are given by the Holy Spirit to new believers that allow them to fulfill responsibility and practice in the church. The apostle Paul alludes to these in Romans 12:6-8.

Finally, there are those particular times and instances when the Holy Spirit would make His presence known in the church through very special manners in order to supply a particular need at that given time. We would call those, "the gifts of the Holy Spirit," and they are listed in 1 Corinthians 12.

I adapted the following section from the lecture notes by Reverend Don Pickerill.

> Motivations are the real factors behind our decisions and actions. They explain why we do the things the way we do. When people know what moves them, they discover a clue of understanding in themselves, their feelings and actions.

As we look at the gifts (I like to call them "gracelets" or portions of grace) listed in verses 6-8, there is a command to use any or all of the grace God has bestowed upon us. However, there will usually be a group of gifts in this list we find most comfortable. We feel the most fulfilled and fruitful when we know our strengths and focus on them. According to the Scripture, the important thing is that we "use them."

There are some people who are gifted with prophecy. They have the ability to declare truth with great insight. Like John the Baptist, their whole motivation is to make sure the spiritual tone of the church is right. It takes faith to "step out on a limb," and often, these people are misunderstood as being too "black and white" about matters.

There are those in the church who are servers. You've seen them; they are full of practical assistance and, without prompting, demonstrate love by doing those things that need to be done. They can, however, be like Martha, Mary's sister, and become so busy that they fail to enjoy the service of the Lord.

Others are teachers. Their greatest joy is clarifying truth and imparting knowledge. Facts and validated truth are their bailiwick, so they are students. Like Apollos in Scripture, they meet the mental needs of the congregation.

Exhorters are like teachers in that they impart truth. But they are unlike teachers in that their joy comes from the personal progress of the student. They have the ability of encouraging people to grow. They are the Barnabases of the congregation, stimulating faith and maturity in the personal lives of believers.

When we study the life of Abraham, we find the patriarch always giving something away. And there are those in today's church who do the same thing. They have the ability of gaining and giving away material assets. They supply the financial and material needs of the congregation.

Then there are the facilitators. I like to think of them as the "traffic controllers." Instead of doing the work themselves, these people are most effective in organizing and leading. They have the ability to see long-range goals and to place others into the right functions. They are the Nehemiahs of the congregation and continually help the church become effective.

Finally, the most special people of all are those who meet the emotional needs of the congregation. They have the unique ability to feel the hurts of others and identify with their need. They offer personal support and sympathy. Who could be a better example of the merciful person than the Good Samaritan?

How do these giftings work together? Suppose a young lad came into the church sanctuary, carrying a cone with a double scoop of Hagen Daas ice cream. Suddenly, something startles him and he drops the ice cream all over the floor.

Now imagine the response each would make. The prophet would inform the child that it was not right to eat ice cream in the house of God. The server would immediately get a mop and a bucket of water. The teacher would explain

> what started the problem and what caused the cone to fall. The exhorter would comfort the kid, telling him to hold it tighter next time. The giver would hand him a few bucks and tell him to go buy another ice cream cone after church. The facilitator would have teams organized to clean the rug, clean the boy and take care of whatever else needed to be done. Finally, there would be the merciful brother or sister who would put his or her arm around the lad and say, "I know just how you feel. I've dropped ice cream in church before!"

Each one of these gracelets are vital to the body of Christ. They make the church complete and the individual believer fulfilled. That's the way God designed us . . . and His church.

Behind the Scenes

It is intriguing how Paul is setting "line upon line, precept upon precept" before both factions in the church at Rome. Having laid the theology in chapters 1-11, he now builds upon that foundation to bring the congregation back together in heart and mind. They will give up their own stubbornness as a living sacrifice. They will allow the Holy Spirit to transform their thinking about their place in God's economy—the church. They will recognize that the essence of Christianity is that of giving away what God has given, and that sacrifice is to be in relation with the entire body of Christ.

Paul is not finished. There are still stones to be inserted into the altar of sacrifice, especially the way Roman believers are to treat each other and those outside the church. To be a living sacrifice is going to take the mercy of God!

LESSONS ANYONE?

1. How does the Bible define worship? In what way does finding the will of God, which is holy, acceptable and mature, relate to one's worship?

2. What is the difference between having your thinking conformed and being transformed? How does this fit the motif of God's mercy as presented in Paul's letter to the Romans?

3. In your daily living, what have you found that helped you find God's will for your life and for your decisions? Do you believe we will always have to know God's will before we proceed? What role does "sober thinking" play in finding God's will?

4. Every believer expresses a little bit of all the motivational gifts found in Romans 12. Prayerfully consider which three gift types you most closely resemble. Out of the three, which gift seems to be most dominant at the present? How are you presently using it to serve the Lord and His church?

Chapter 23

The Beatitudes of a Living Sacrifice

Romans 12:9-21

The year was 1981 and I had traveled to Japan from Hong Kong to attend the 30th anniversary of the Foursquare Gospel Church in that nation. It was a special treat for me to travel to the northernmost island of Hokkaido, to the city of Hakodate. Twenty years earlier I had been stationed in Japan as a linguist with the U.S. Air Force. In fact, a few hundred kilometers south, on the tip of the island of Honshu, I had assisted a Baptist chaplain in establishing a Baptist church in the town of Omisawa.

As we drove across the countryside, many memories returned. The houses, rice paddies and customs of the people brought to mind many personal experiences. To top it off, during a special prayer conference at the anniversary celebration, I happened to be seated next to a lady who had just come from the town of Omisawa and had spoken in the Baptist church just three days earlier.

Jerry and Barbara Cook, close friends who at that time pastored a large congregation in Gresham, Oregon, joined me. As happens when preachers get together, we began sharing our hearts about denominational matters and for some reason, I began to complain about some of the decisions our leadership had made. As I was busy pontificating my views, Jerry graciously took hold of my hand and remarked, "You know, Ron, God never blesses us for being right in our opinions. He blesses us for being right in our attitudes." It was a lesson I have never forgotten.

Having beseeched the Roman believers—both Jews and Gentiles—to present their bodies, be transformed in their thinking and ready to use the gifts God had bestowed upon them, Paul gives practical instruction regarding attitudes toward fellow believers (vv. 9-13) and toward the unbelievers yet outside the church (vv. 14-21).

To Live With Saints Here Below (vv. 9-13)

"To live with the saints in heaven, oh, that will be glory. To live with the saints on earth, now that's another story." The reason? Our brothers and sisters in the church are not perfect yet . . . and neither are we!

Note the strong emotional elements in these four verses:

- Love genuinely (v. 9)
- Abhor evil—be horrified (v. 9)
- Cling to good—glue yourself (v. 9)
- Brotherly love with kindness (v. 10)
- Family affection, giving respect and preference to others (v. 10)

- Eagerness to be diligent (v. 11)
- Aglow with enthusiasm (v. 11)
- Rejoicing with hope (v. 12)
- Patient when afflicted (v. 12)
- Faithful in prayer (v. 12)
- Unselfishly meeting others' needs (v. 13)
- Commitment to embracing others—hospitality (v. 13).

Each of these words implies relationship. When relationships are established, the emotional element of our Christianity makes its presence known. Emotions control much of the Christian experience. Those emotions can either be beneficial or a blight. It depends on who controls them.

If we are honest with ourselves, it is this emotive aspect of our belief system that usually gets us in trouble. Very few church problems can be traced to error in doctrine or lack of pastoral skills. Most of the difficulties in the body of Christ are due to our unwillingness to get along with others. Believers choose their home church because of taste, not truth. People commute to a church 50 miles away, simply to be with friends, and with very little thought on how to win their neighbors for Christ. And woe to the pastor who breaks into their private world with a new slant on traditional truth. In America, at least, members have learned to vote with their feet, by uprooting their pet doctrine and finding another congregation that agrees with them. Rather than becoming "fishers of men," they have become "changers of aquariums."

If we look closely at verses 9-13, we discover what Galatians 5:22, 23 lists as the fruit (harvest) of the Holy Spirit. That which gives credibility to our giftedness (Romans 12:6-8) is our character (vv. 9-13).

In advising his spiritual sons, Timothy and Titus, Paul lists 20 different qualifications that should factor into the choosing of church leadership, whether it be the office of pastor or deacon. Of the list, there is only one qualification that has to do with ability, that of being able to teach. The other 19 qualifications have to do with the character and reputation of the person. If today's church followed this pattern, not only for church leadership, but in church life, there would be a lot less problems and, by the way, a lot more converts.

To Live With Unbelievers Here Below (vv. 14-21)

Paul reminds the church at Rome that the world is watching. Too often, it is not the message that is being rejected, but the way believers live or express their faith. It all boils down to believers' character, not their charisma.

The church must sincerely and truthfully pray God's blessing over those who seek to do harm to the cause of the gospel (v. 14). In Matthew 5:43, 44, Jesus raised the standard of the Old Testament law: "You have heard that it was said, 'You shall love your neighbor and hate your enemy.' But I say to you, love your enemies, bless those who curse you, do good to those who hate you, and pray for those who spitefully use you and persecute you." In Galatians 6:10, Paul himself suggested, "As we have opportunity, let us do good to all."

The way the church changes the world is by winning one convert at a time. If we want to change the vote, we must first change the voter. Rather than demanding that the world and those who oppose us give us our rights, we need to lift them up before the Lord. We will make more headway by praying than by parading.

The church must sincerely care for the unbeliever (Romans 12:15). Someone has said, "The Christian is the only fisherman who fishes without hooks; they simply give the bait away." Emerton says it this way:

> The Christian is to take his stand beside his fellowman, to have time and room for him in those experiences in which he is most truly himself, in his real human joy and his real human sorrow, and to strive to be both with him and for him, altogether and without reserve, yet without compromising with his evil or sharing, or even pretending to share, the presuppositions of this age which is passing away.[1]

Whatever service is rendered must be done in a spirit of humility, no matter the recipient. I like Paul's choice of words, "Do not set your mind on high things, but associate with the humble" (v. 16). It is not our opinion of ourselves that matters, but what the world thinks of us. Leon Morris quotes Bishop Haldane as saying, "Self-conceit is an evidence of weakness of mind and of ignorance."[2]

Retribution or evil have no place in the Christian's thinking or doing (v. 17). Think beforehand what will bring good in the sight of all men. Provide a good example.

There are times when two events take place simultaneously that are in direct contrast to each other. During the second week of January 2000, the U.S. national headlines were filled with the foul words of Atlanta Braves pitcher, John Rocker. The public outcry against his racist remarks and obnoxious opinions was immense.

At the same time, an article was published in the *LA Times* on January 9, 2000, that carried the story of another ballplayer, Randy Flores. Randy was a star pitcher who helped the University of Southern California Trojans reach the finals of the 1995 College Baseball World Series. He was a ninth-round pick of the New York Yankees, and during the '99 season he pitched in the AA League on the East Coast. His father, Ron, is the pastor of the Foursquare Church in Pico Rivera, California.

Each January, the church conducts a baseball clinic. This past year 200 kids, ranging from 6 to 15 years of age, gathered at the El Rancho High School to be instructed in the fundamentals of baseball.

An amazing fact was that the *Los Angeles Times* ran the half-page news story about Randy on the front page of their sports section. The point that *Times* writer Diane Ducin made was that in a day when there is questionable influence on today's youth by even the most well-known athletes, it was refreshing to see a humble young man, who has not rejected his Christian principles, help the neighborhood kids who lived near his father's church. Yes, the world is watching and recognizing the difference between good and evil.

"As much as depends on you, live peaceably with all men" (v. 18). Leon Morris quotes Colin Brown: "To 'live peaceably' is descriptive of that state in which a man does not disturb others, and is not disturbed by them. The first is always in our own power, the second is not."[3]

Believers must leave judgment and punishment to God (v. 19). The apostle refers to two Old Testament passages. In the first giving of the Law, the prohibition of revenge was emphasized. Moses wrote: "You shall not take vengeance, nor bear any grudge against the children of your people, but you shall love your neighbor as yourself: I am the Lord" (Leviticus 19:18). When it was given the second time, the source and surety of retribution were introduced: "Vengeance is Mine, and recompense; their foot shall slip in due time; for the day of their calamity is at hand, and the things to come hasten upon them" (Deuteronomy 32:35).

Solomon, the wisest man to grace the face of the earth, wrote these words: "If your enemy is hungry, give him bread to eat; and if he is thirsty, give him water to drink; for so you will heap coals of fire on his head, and the Lord will reward you" (Proverbs 25:21, 22).

It is interesting that in quoting the Proverbs passage, in Romans 12:20, Paul does not include "and the Lord will reward you." Whether the omission was intentional or not, those who read this letter would have been well acquainted with the words. Within eight years following their reception of this letter, the statement just written by the apostle would become one of the most important pieces of divine admonition and advice the believers in Rome would ever remember.

As they were set afire as lamp posts, they could comfort one another—"And the Lord will reward you." As they were clothed in animal skins and shoved into the coliseum to be eaten alive by wild beasts or killed by gladiators, they could find hope—"And the Lord will reward you." As they wept over their loved ones as they buried them in the catacombs, they could rest assured—"And the Lord will reward you."

Oh yes, both Peter and the writer of this letter would repeat "And the Lord will reward you" as they were martyred in the city of Rome. Today, the Roman Empire is only a memory, but the kingdom of God has spread to every corner of the earth. "Do not be overcome by evil, but overcome evil with good" (Romans 12:21).

You and I are the only gospel the world reads. The question is, "How are they understanding what they read?" Paul's friend, Peter, said it this way: "Honor Christ and let him be the Lord of your life. Always be ready to give an answer when someone asks you about your hope. Give a kind and respectful answer and keep your conscience clear" (1 Peter 3:15, 16, *CEV*).

LESSONS ANYONE?

1. Briefly study other passages in the New Testament that talk about the fruit of the Spirit, such as Galatians 5 and 1 Corinthians 13, as well as other letters of Paul. List them and consider how such qualities should be lived out in the church, in the workplace and, above all, in the home.

2. How important is character and integrity as compared with someone's abilities and charismatic personality? What relationship does character have to someone's service or ministry?

3. In what ways are you being a witness and light in your immediate neighborhood? Why has God placed you where you are presently living?

4. How should the church express the fruit of the Spirit in a society that views it as part of today's social problem rather than a part of its solution?

Chapter 24

What About Nero?

Romans 13:1-14

In the last few verses of Romans 12, Paul contrasted between good and evil. He concluded by admonishing the believers in Rome to "not be overcome by evil, but overcome evil with good" (v. 21). One of the biggest "evils" they were facing was the Roman emperor, Nero himself.

From the events that had happened eight years before, in particular the expulsion of the Jews by Claudius, Paul was concerned that the church might become entangled in the extensive political maneuvering prevalent at that time in the empire's capital.

Moreover, Paul was no stranger to injustice administered by the state. It had taken place in Jerusalem with the Lord Jesus; it had happened to Paul as recorded in 2 Corinthians 11:23; and there seems to be an intuition in Paul's writing that it would soon happen to the believers in Rome.

With a sense of urgency, the writer addressed three duties the church must maintain in a hostile society:

- Respect for authority (vv. 1-7)
- Love for one's neighbor (vv. 8-10)
- Walk as children of light (vv. 11-14)

Respect for Authority (vv. 1-7)

Paul was aware of the words of Jesus: "Render to Caesar the things that are Caesar's, and to God the things that are God's" (Mark 12:17). He remembered the Hebrew scriptures and writings: "By me kings reign, and rulers decree justice. By me princes rule, and nobles, all the judges of the earth" (Proverbs 8:15-16); "Your dominion was given you from the Lord, and your sovereignty from the Most High" (Apocryphal book, Wisdom of Solomon 6:3, *RSV*).

Paul was convinced that all authority, direct or delegated, comes from God. God is firmly in control of history, and there is no position of rulership unless God permits it. The Almighty also sets the boundaries of that authority and makes recompense accordingly.

Most likely, the apostle recalled Daniel's words to Nebuchadnezzar: "The Most High rules in the kingdom of men, gives it to whomever He will, and sets over it the lowest [humblest] of men. . . . until you know that the Most High rules in the kingdom of men, and gives it to whomever He chooses" (Daniel 4:17, 25, 32). Immediately thereafter, God took the kingdom from the wicked king and gave the authority to Belshazzar, who was equally as bad. Remember the handwriting on the wall?

The actions of every believer in Rome were to be "subject" to the authorities. There was no question about the implications. In 1 Corinthians 16:16, Paul used the same Greek term to tell the believers in Corinth that they were to come under the authority of the household of Stephanas and Paul's coworkers, who had been sent to assist them. In Ephesians 5:21, 22, that same submission was to be worked out between the husband and wife, giving due recognition and respect to each other.

But Nero!? Look at 1 Timothy 2:1-4:

> Therefore I exhort first of all that supplications, prayers, intercessions, and giving of thanks be made for all men, for kings and all who are in authority, that we may lead a quiet and peaceable life in all godliness and reverence. For this is good and acceptable in the sight of God our Savior, who desires all men to be saved and to come to the knowledge of the truth.

Sounds like Romans 13:1, doesn't it? Though we don't understand how it works, there's something about praying for those in authority, even tyrants, that brings a quiet and peaceable life to the believer. It also provides a strong witness in their understanding of the truth to those without Christ.

But Nero!? Titus 3:1, 2 states, "Remind [the believers] to be subject to rulers and authorities, to obey, to be ready for every good work, to speak evil of no one, to be peaceable, gentle, showing all humility to all men." In verses 8 and 9, Paul reminded Titus, "This is a faithful saying, and these things I want you to affirm constantly, that those who have believed in God should be careful to maintain good works. These things are good and profitable to men.

But avoid foolish disputes, genealogies, contentions, and strivings about the law; for they are unprofitable and useless." Giving respect to authority keeps the church focused on that which is good and profitable, rather than vain and useless activity.

But Nero!? Peter also lived in Rome. His conclusion?

> Therefore submit yourselves to every ordinance of man for the Lord's sake, whether to the king as supreme, or to governors, as to those who are sent by him for the punishment of evildoers and for the praise of those who do good. For this is the will of God, that by doing good you may put to silence the ignorance of foolish men—as free, yet not using liberty as a cloak for vice, but as bondservants of God. Honor all people. Love the brotherhood. Fear God. Honor the king (1 Peter 2:13-17).

The church's humble response and submission to authority silences the excuses of the unsaved.

Nineteen hundred years later, some may have questioned, "But Mao!?" It was in 1949 that Chairman Mao Tse-tung assumed dictatorship over the People's Republic of China. For the next 27 years, he isolated the country, both nationally and philosophically, from the rest of the world. His rule was filled with murder, political intrigue and every type of atrocity imaginable. If we studied Mao's leadership, we will find that he was always just one step ahead of his adversaries.

At the time of the liberation in 1949, the number of believers in China was less than 2 million. In the years that followed, great persecution ensued. Many believers lost their lives for the cause of the gospel, and hundreds of pastors were imprisoned. For many years, the outside world watched and wondered if the church in China was still in existence.

Following the death of Mao and his comrades, the world was provided a peek into the People's Republic. They discovered that the number of believers in China had increased from less than 2 million in 1949 to an estimated 70 million believers by January 1, 1979. Though deprived of its buildings and finances, the body of Christ had grown by 35 times! If such a rate of revival had taken place in the Western Hemisphere, every person living in the United States, Canada and Mexico would have been saved, along with one-half the population of Central and South America. Moreover, for the first time in the 5,000-year history of China, there was a common language, a common transportation system and common technology that made it more convenient to publish Bibles and preach the gospel.

As mentioned earlier, during a visit to northern China in 1998, a government official admitted to me that in China, there are now twice as many believers in Jesus Christ as there are Communist Party members. That nation is asking for teachers who have a Christian standard of living to move to their country to teach English and supply professional expertise to the economy. The history of the church in China over these past 60 years is absolutely phenomenal, but that must be left for another book and another time.

Did God make a mistake in 1949? I think not! Across the world, the atheistic socialism of communism is crumbling, while the church of Jesus Christ is growing at an unprecedented rate. The price has been severe, but the result is worth it!

According to Paul, rulers are placed in authority

because of humanity's sinfulness. But to good people, because God is over those rulers, and because "all things work together for good" (Romans 8:28) for the believer, even the most horrible tyrant in Rome later marveled at the commitment of those who gave their lives for Christ and to one another.

Such a reaction, according to 13:5, is not only politically wise, but brings inner hope and satisfaction. Dunn explains:

> The morally responsible person and good citizen will recognize the need for government in society as a divine ordinance: resistance to this divinely ordered authority will provoke in such a person such a pang of conscience; and prospect of such moral discomfort should dissuade them from civil disobedience.[1]

For Paul, one practical expression of respect and honor was found in paying taxes. While Paul seems to make a distinction between direct and indirect taxation, the bottom line is that by paying what is owed to any person, the believer exhibits an attitude of respect that is pleasing to God and good for all.

Love Your Neighbor (vv. 8-10)

I like the explanation Leon Morris provides regarding verse 8:

> We may pay our taxes and be quiet. We may give respect and honor where they are due and have no further obligation. But we can never say, "I have done all the loving I need to do." Love is a permanent obligation, a debt impossible to discharge.[2]

The word *owe* must be understood as both an indebtedness and an obligation. In Luke 7:47, Jesus said: "Therefore I say to you, her sins, which were many, are forgiven, for she loved much. But to whom little is forgiven, the same loves little." To both the Jews and Gentiles in the Roman church, there had been much mercy and forgiveness. Therefore, like Paul (Romans 1:14), they were indebted to the world and to God.

Paul cites five of the Ten Commandments that have to do with our relation to our neighbor. He concluded by quoting Leviticus 19:18: "You shall love your neighbor as yourself." There were three times when Jesus referred in some form to this verse. The first was in answer to the rich young ruler who came seeking eternal life. Jesus answered, "You shall love your neighbor as yourself" (Matthew 19:19), and then ordered the man to sell his possessions and give to the poor.

The second occasion was in answer to the question of what was the greatest commandment in the Law (Matthew 22:34-39). Jesus quoted Leviticus 19:18, and then stated that everything the Law and the Prophets taught surrounded our love for God or for our neighbor.

There is a third passage we often overlook. In His Sermon on the Mount, Jesus made this statement: "You have heard that it was said, 'You shall love your neighbor and hate your enemy.' But I say to you, love your enemies, bless those who curse you, do good to those who hate you, and pray for those who spitefully use you and persecute you" (Matthew 5:43, 44).

As Paul asked the Romans to love their neighbor, he also confronted them with the reality that even those who took an adversarial posture toward them—their enemies—were in reality their neighbors.

I have often heard Corrie ten Boom share the story about being sent to a Nazi concentration camp during World War II for hiding Jews in her home in Holland. Corrie found, as Isaiah promised, "a hiding place from the wind and . . . tempest" (Isaiah 32:2). After the war, Corrie was used of God in a mighty way.

On one occasion, she was asked to come to Munich, Germany, to minister to a group of believers. As she entered the room, her eyes immediately focused on a gentleman, a former Secret Service man who had stood guard at the shower room door in the processing center at Ravensbruck. Suddenly, all the pain and humiliation came flooding back—the roomful of leering, mocking men, the heaps of clothing and the pain-wracked face of her sister who had died under the atrocities. Throughout the service, Corrie's mind was divided between the truth of God she was proclaiming and the awful memories of her past.

Following the service, the man came to thank Corrie for her gospel message. He put out his hand to shake hers, and the angry, revengeful thoughts boiled inside her.

Suddenly, Corrie recognized the sinfulness of her thoughts. Jesus had come to earth to die, even to redeem this wretched man. She then thought, *Am I going to ask for more?* She prayed, "Lord Jesus, forgive me and help me forgive him." She tried to smile, but couldn't bring herself to raise her hand to shake his.

She prayed again: "Jesus, I cannot forgive him. Give me Your forgiveness." As she took the hand of the former Secret Service officer, a most incredible thing took place. From her shoulder, down along her arm and through her hand, a current seemed to pass to the man. There sprang in her heart an overwhelming love for this man who was once her enemy.

Corrie commented, "When God tells us to *love* our enemies, He gives, along with the command itself, the *love* itself."

Walk as Children of Light (vv. 11-14)

While Paul remembers where we came from, he continues to remind us where we are going. Such is the basis for our attitudes toward those in authority over us. In loving our neighbors, even our enemies, we now walk as children of light. In 1 Thessalonians 5:1-8, this same apostle writes the following:

> But concerning the times and the seasons, brethren, you have no need that I should write to you. For you yourselves know perfectly that the day of the Lord so comes as a thief in the night. For when they say, "Peace and safety!" then sudden destruction comes upon them, as labor pains upon a pregnant woman. And they shall not escape. But you, brethren, are not in darkness, so that this Day should overtake you as a thief. You are all sons of light and sons of the day. We are not of the night nor of darkness. Therefore let us not sleep, as others do, but let us watch and be sober. For those who sleep, sleep at night, and those who get drunk are drunk at night. But let us who are of the day be sober, putting on the breastplate of faith and love, and as a helmet the hope of salvation.

In a footnote, Morris quotes Chrysostom as suggesting this:

> As soon as it [night] is actually departing, we hasten to one another, and say, 'It is day now!' And we all set about the works of the day, dressing, and leaving our dreams, and shaking our sleep thoroughly off, that the day may find us ready . . .[3]

Both of the above statements vividly illustrate the words of Paul in Romans 13:11-14. We are to put off those things associated with the night, such as *revelry*—actually a festive procession in honor of Dionysius that always resulted in drunkenness and orgies; *licentiousness and lewdness*— the lack of chastity and unbridled intercourse which accompanied the activities at the temples; and even *strife and envy*—dissension, contention and rivalry.

As the end of time drew near, they were to put on Christ and His righteousness, not only in standing but also in practical living.

By including strife and envy in the list above, the apostle elevated the core problem in the Roman church to equal status with the extreme sinfulness in the heathen temples. He most definitely was setting up the Roman believers to later hear the conclusion of the matter (14:1—15:6).

I remember one of my instructors in college illustrating verses 11-14. He was driving through a farming area in Ohio, when he came upon an old barn. Looking like it had come right out of a Norman Rockwell painting, on the sides of the barn were painted the words: "The end is near! Jesus is coming! Hallelujah!"

But what impressed him was that the barn had just been newly painted!

As believers, we are to live our lives in a hostile society with enthusiastic expectancy of His coming, yet with exemplary example until Christ appears. As another person has observed, "It is just like a gentleman with nothing to be ashamed of."

LESSONS ANYONE?

1. Compare Paul's view of church and state (as stated in Romans 13) with the disciples' response to authorities in the Book of Acts (5:29) that the believer ought to obey God rather than man. Does this give license for civil disobedience?

2. What is the responsibility of the church and the individual believer toward those who serve as civil and national authority?

3. How are the Ten Commandments to be lived out in a life of faith and grace?

4. From the testimony of Corrie ten Boom, review her struggle with forgiveness, and draw three principles to live by in relation to others. How strong is your forgiveness factor?

Chapter 25

Since You Are Strong . . .

Romans 14:1—15:7

By trade, Paul was a tentmaker. He had also been a lawyer and was well acquainted with rational debate. In the Book of Romans, he melds the art of argument with the touch of divine inspiration and brings the believers in Rome to the core of their problem.

Again, let's remember the Golden Gate Bridge motif Dr. Richard Mouw has suggested for the letter to the Romans. On either end are the words, "obedience to the faith" (Romans 1:5; 16:26), and there are the supporting spans at 1:16, 17; 3:21-26; 5:1-5; 8; 12:1, 2; and 14:1. In Romans 1:16, 17, whether one be Jew or Gentile, the gospel of Christ is "the power of God to salvation for everyone who believes. . . . " The apostle explicitly proves that the heathen Gentile and the self-righteous Jew are equally guilty before God. He concludes that "every mouth be stopped, and all the world may become guilty before God" (3:19).

To those who think they are more spiritual than others, they had better remember where they have come from. It's because of God's mercy that they haven't received what they truly deserve.

The second supporting span gives us the good news that God is both "just and the justifier of the one who has faith in Jesus" (3:26). The purpose of the Law was to point out our sinfulness; placing our faith in Jesus Christ brought the removal of God's wrath, the entering into a new relationship with Him, and the completion by God's mercies of everything God had been promising all along, even in the Law and the Prophets. Whether Jew or Gentile, what we could never have done on *our* own, God did through *His* own—the Lord Jesus Christ.

"Having been justified by faith" (5:1), we stand before God on the foundation of His grace and boast (rejoice) in the hope of fulfilling His unique destiny for us. We begin the process that brings in actuality what we anticipate in faith, through the "love of God [which] has been poured out in our hearts by the Holy Spirit who was given to us" (v. 5). Becoming in practice what we already are in position begins with the love of God in Romans 5 and concludes in chapter 8, for nothing "shall be able to separate us from the love of God which is in Christ Jesus our Lord" (8:39).

Romans 9—11 reminds the Jews that throughout their history, God's mercy protected and preserved them, in spite of their unwillingness to accept it. Actually, His mercy is available to them in their present disobedient and contrary state. And God still has a glorious destiny for Israel in the future. By the way, Gentiles, you'd better be thankful for those Jews, because it is through them that God's grace has come to you. What a span on which to hang our hope!

True faith will always be expressed in right thinking (our minds, Romans 12:2), right living (v. 1), and right relationships (12:3—13:14). We will see ourselves as God sees us (12:3-5); we will use the graces and giftings He has given us for the benefit of others (vv. 6-8). The character of the Holy Spirit will govern our actions toward fellow believers (vv. 9-13) and in our witness to the world (vv. 14-21), even toward those in governmental authority over us (13:1-7). Whatever is accomplished will be in responsible living, with an eye toward the soon coming of the Lord (vv. 8- 14).

Finally, Paul reminded the Roman believers that strife and envy in the church is just as serious as the extreme sinfulness that is being practiced in the heathen temples. Pride and disputing are tearing away the fabric of the body of Christ at a time when it faces its greatest challenge.

Who Are the Strong?

There is much debate about who are the weak and who are strong in this passage. From the Gentile perspective, the weak were believers who were not walking in liberty, but were still using religious crutches (such as the Law, rituals or religious calendars—namely, the Jewish observances) to sustain their walk with Christ. The Jewish perspective identified the weak as being those unspiritual, disrespectful and unappreciative Gentiles who had discarded all the traditions the original church members had held dear.

May I suggest that Paul's definition of the strong extended to those who felt they were mature believers. It was to their standard of freedom or responsibility that every other believer was expected to conform. The strong believed it was the obligation of the weaker brother and sister to comply and achieve the expectations of the more mature in the church—sort of a "catch-up-with-the-others" style of Christianity.

The apostle totally disagrees with this line of reasoning. Rather than adherence being the responsibility of the weak, acceptance is the responsibility of the strong. Those who think they are strong must embrace the burdens of the weak and ensure that nothing causes them to stumble.

My, how today's church needs to hear this message! And my, how today's world needs to see this message! The sectarianism, competition and denominationalism that have reared their ugly face in today's Christianity do not help believers grow in the grace of the Lord. Nor do they present an accurate picture of the compassion and grace Jesus Christ came to bestow to those who are lost.

Since You Are the Strong, Receive the Weak (14:1-13)

In his book, *St. Paul's Epistle to the Romans*, Griffith Thomas wrote the following:

> Fellowship must not be broken for trifles, since we have no right to insist on such slight conditions of communion; indeed, the feat of breaking the bonds of fellowship between those who are under the lordship of Christ ought to act as one of the strongest deterrents.[1]

Paul sides with neither the Jews nor the Gentiles; he is concerned with unity. His focus is not on the person's weakness in knowing the basic Christian faith, but on the person's present faith that prohibits trusting God without reliance on the observance of certain practices. It is the church's responsibility to accept the latter into fellowship, recognizing unreservedly (without qualifiers, see v. 1) that they are brothers and sisters in Christ.

The issues discussed in this passage concern peripheral matters—not issues of moral conscience, but religious habits. First, he deals with the dietary laws, which for Jews was not simply a matter of clean and unclean food. The Jews' loyalty to God was most vividly expressed in their refusal to eat the food of the Gentiles, especially food that had been dedicated to or tainted by idolatry.

Paul says that while there is nothing intrinsically wrong with eating such food, we are not to look down or hold with contempt someone who does not eat it. On the other hand, he who refuses to eat such food should not judge someone who does. If God has received that brother or sister, why can't we?

Then there was the matter of days. Dunn states the principle well in this statement:

> This references a concern on the part of some Jewish Christians and others who had been proselytes or God-worshippers lest they abandon a practice of feast days and sabbath commanded by Scripture and sanctified by tradition, a central concern lest they lose something of the fundamental importance within their Jewish heritage, something close to the heart of the distinctiveness of the whole Jewish and now Jewish-Christian tradition and identity.[2]

Note the number of times the phrase "to the Lord" is used in verses 6-9. No one should be forced to live according to another person's conscience, nor should they pattern their own conduct by their own will or for their own purposes. It is the Lord's will and glory that should set the standard for believers' conduct. Being free in Christ never means freedom from His lordship. It is not spiritual autonomy.

Griffith Thomas states a good rule of thumb to live by: "*Yes*, if I can enjoy it to the Lord and while giving Him thanks for it; *No*, if I cannot receive it as a gift from His hand and bless Him for it."[3] All the while, we accept our brothers or sisters for the way they choose to serve the Lord.

There is a sobering fact: the one who chooses to act in a certain manner, and those who would dare to pass judgment on that individual, will all stand before the judgment seat of Christ. The *bema* in Gentile government was a raised, open place in each city, reserved for delivering speeches in public assembly or passing judgment among disputing parties or felons. It was at the *bema* in Tyre and Sidon that King Herod usurped the worship of the people away from God and was eaten by worms (Acts 12:20-23).

In 2 Corinthians 5:10, Paul wrote these words: "For we must all appear before the judgment seat of Christ, that each one may receive the things done in the body, according to what he has done, whether good or bad." It is not simply a judgment of our failures, but also an open place of recognition and reward for one "doing the will of God from the heart, with goodwill doing service, as to the Lord, and not to men, knowing that whatever good anyone does, he will receive the same from the Lord, whether he is a slave or free" (Ephesians 6:6-8).

God keeps good records. He is the supreme authority. We can depend on two things about His omniscience: He knows truly, and He truly knows.

These instructions were as pertinent to the Jews and the Gentiles of the first century as they are appropriate for Christians in the 21st century. We must do nothing that would cause our brothers or sisters to trip or stumble in their walk with Christ. Rather, we should be in front of them, clearing the path, to make their journey as easy as possible.

"It's not sin, it's just different!" This statement ascribed to Dr. Bob Pierce, the late founder of World Vision, continues to cross my mind as I think of the many occasions when the conflict between my cultural definition ran a collision course with that of my Chinese brethren, whom Carole and I served in Hong Kong. Sometimes, my concepts gave way to avoid confrontation; other times, my brethren swerved their views just in time; and on a few occasions, the collision was almost fatal.

One thing that came in conflict with my own personal conscience was that the Chinese believers seemed ambivalent toward drinking alcoholic beverages at certain occasions, such as beer with barbecue at picnics, and especially, offering brandy at wedding feasts. Though in principle the church never approved of such, nor did it allow alcohol to be consumed at its functions, the practice was reasonably common in individual family situations, especially in ceremonials such as births and wedding feasts. Because of peer criticism or judgment from some of my missionary colleagues serving in other parts of Asia, I constantly prayed that no member who got married would invite those missionaries as guests to a wedding feast during their frequent visits to Hong Kong. At times, I suffered from social paranoia.

Inquiring into both practices, I learned that in the society, beer was considered a soft drink rather than a means toward revelry. It cut the aftertaste of barbecue left in your mouth. Moreover, the brandy had a twofold significance: life and joy. Normally, there was no excessive drinking. If so, it was disciplined.

I refrained from outwardly expressing my personal conviction or trying to impose my standard upon the Chinese; however, it was interesting that in my family's personal contacts with those who did indulge in such practices, we were never once offered an alcoholic beverage. Over the long period of time, even at wedding feasts, those who were from our churches soon became identified by the absence of brandy at their table. Whether it was the Holy Spirit's work in their lives, or simply the fact that they respected my cultural (and in my case, spiritual) conviction, I could not discern.

Looking back on the situation, I ask which was the greater sin: the small bit of alcohol that passed through their lips and, incidentally, assisted their digestion of a huge, starch-filled meal, or the judgmental attitude of my peers and me when there was no specific Biblical prohibition of the action? Could it be that in the latter years, their abstinence in my presence was a greater act of love in not causing their brother to fall than my feelings of anger and personal embarrassment?

Since You Are the Strong, Respect the Weak (14:14-23)

William Barclay has written: "Unless a church is a body of people who, in love, consider one another, it is not a church at all."[4] Another person said, "Love is a self-sacrificial action." Love continues to act in spite of feelings or misunderstandings. In this passage, such insight becomes a challenge. The one who is strong is to love the weaker brother no matter how the weaker brother is walking out his life with the Lord. The weaker brother is to feel the same toward his stronger brother.

Two main issues arise:

1. Do not grieve the weaker brother.

2. Do not destroy God's work in him.

The position that needs to be maintained in a community of believers is that of servanthood. It has often been recognized that a Christian is a most dutiful servant of all, subject to all.

F.F. Bruce added:

> It is good to be strong in faith and emancipated in conscience, but Christians are not isolated individuals, but members of a fellowship; it is therefore the responsibility of all, and especially of those who are stronger and more mature, to care for the well-being of the fellowship.[5]

Paul states that we are not to *grieve* our brother by our conduct. The word picture here was often used of cavalry or light troops harassing an army. Paul is not talking about a minor irritation or disagreement, he is referring to wounding a person's conscience and potentially destroying the equilibrium of his or her faith. An individual's freedom to eat food or act in a certain manner never carries with it the license to do it at the expense of a brother's spiritual welfare.

Again, Dunn's explanation carries the day: "The conduct of the more liberal toward 'the weak' is not to be determined by the 'superior' insight of the 'strong,' or by what they think is best for the 'weak,' but by the actual effect of their conduct on the 'weak.'"[6]

The attitude of believers (or lack of it) toward each other in the church will either attract or repel those outside the church. This includes our freedom to do what we want and dare to call it God's will. Our reputation should attract the lost and our goodness should edify them. While we are careful not to cause our brother to stumble, we must be careful not to cause our unbelieving neighbor to stumble as well.

The kingdom of God is the righteousness of life that springs from faith in the finished work of Christ (chs. 1-4). Peace is both peace with God and experiencing the peace of God that rises from a sense of God's mercy ruling the heart (chs. 5-8). Joy in the Holy Spirit is more than a delightful feeling. It is a confidence in God sustained even in persecution (chs. 8-12). It is not by chance that in Romans 14:18, the apostle uses the words *acceptable* to God and *approved* by men. Sounds like a *living sacrifice* to me (see 12:1, 2)!

Strengthening others should be the standard in determining our relationships and mutual interdependence. In 14:13, we are cautioned "not to put a stumbling block . . . in our brother's way." In verse 15, we must be careful not to destroy with our food our brother's faith in Christ's sufficiency. Verse 16 tells us that we are not to let our actions, though good, be misunderstood and misstated as evil. And in verse 20, we are not to destroy what God has already accomplished in another's life by demanding our own way.

It seems that while there are a lot of "can-do's" permitted for the stronger and more mature believers, there is an equal amount of "but-don'ts" to which we must adhere.

The reciprocal principle in respecting others is the respect we have for ourselves. We should never act in such a way that causes us to feel guilty, to waiver between opinions or be condemned by our own standards (conscience). Christian liberty emanates from faith. Faith brings the freedom for us to discern God's will for ourselves. And if they know to do good and fail to do it, for them it is sinful.

Throughout my ministry, I have been approached with the question, "Is it all right to . . .?" or, "Is such-and-such a sin?" My initial response is to ask this question: "Why are you asking the question in the first place?" My advice usually has been, "If you have any doubts, DON'T!"

The following Scriptural principles need to be included in our "choice making." I call them the "all things, but" rules.

1. *The Principle of Expediency.* First Corinthians 6:12 says, "All things are lawful unto me, but all things are not expedient [helpful]" (KJV). Is the ethical decision you are about to make the fastest way to the highest standard of life? Or will it deter you from God's best?

2. *The Principle of Control.* The second part of verse 12 tells us this: "All things are lawful for me, but I will not be brought under the power of any." Will your action become habitual? Will you control it, or will the day come when it will control you? It is easier not to start than to have to dig your way out of addiction of any kind.

3. *The Principle of Contribution.* In 1 Corinthians 10:23 we again read these words: "All things are lawful for me, but not all things are helpful." Does your decision or action contribute to your well-being, or is it feeding upon your basic lusts and desires? What will it add to your life?

4. *The Principle of Edification.* The latter part of verse 23 cautions us, "All things are lawful for me, but not all things edify." The word *edify* means "to build upon a foundation."

On what foundation is your decision or action built? Will it strengthen or weaken your faith?

5. *The Principle of Worship.* In verse 31 Paul continues with these words: "Therefore, whether you eat or drink, or whatever you do, do all to the glory of God." Will your decision or action bring honor to Christ's name? Would you do it if He was here beside you? Remember, He is!

6. *The Principle of Evangelism.* Verses 32 and 33 give further admonishment: "Give no offense, either to the Jews or to the Greeks or to the church of God, just as I also please all men in all things, not seeking my own profit, but the profit of many, that they may be saved." Through these acts, will people come to know Jesus? Are you thinking of them, or only of yourself?

7. *The Principle of Love.* In 1 Corinthians 16:14, we read these powerful words: "Let all that you do be done with love." This includes love to God, to yourself and to others.

8. *The Principle of Conscience.* Romans 14:22 says, "Happy is he who does not condemn himself in what he approves." Can you do it without feeling guilty afterward? Do your inner feelings agree with what the Holy Spirit and your personal standards are suggesting?

By the time you have processed your moral and ethical decisions and actions through this grid of principles, you'll have no question as to what is right or wrong. You will actually be making judgments between what is simply good and what is the very best!

Since You Are the Strong, Remember Christ's Example (15:1-7)

What Paul is suggesting is utterly opposed to our human tendencies, even though we are redeemed. Note the word *please* in the first three verses. In verse 1, we are not to please ourselves, but carry the burdens of the weak. In verse 2, we are instructed to please our neighbors, looking out for their own good.

True Christianity focuses on others. Verse 3 says: "For even Christ did not please Himself."

William Barclay makes this comment: "When the Lord of Glory chose to serve others instead of to please Himself, He set the pattern which every one who seeks to be His follower must accept."[7]

Paul asks the Roman believers to get beyond their petty differences and be like Christ. As our example, Christ bore the weaknesses of others as He walked in freedom. F.F. Bruce writes the following:

> It is so easy for those who are quite clear in conscience about a course of action to snap their fingers at critics and say, "I'll please myself." Their right to do so is unquestioned, but that is not the way of Christ. His way is to consider others first, to consult their interests and help them in every way possible.[8]

The apostle quotes from Psalm 69:9, which calls attention to the willingness of the Messiah to be the representative of God in His incarnation, death and resurrection. The reproaches leveled against God fell upon the righteous Sufferer. Likewise, Paul admonishes the Romans to serve their brothers by bearing them up, despite the difficulty involved.

Two disciplines are required to follow in Christ's steps: patience and comfort. According to verse 4, the Old Testament was written with patient endurance and encouraging comfort in order to give us hope. God, who is full of patience and encouragement, desires to make us like-minded—full of forbearance of one another and ready to comfort each other at all times. Then when difficult times arrive, we will be of one mind, presenting a consistent witness to the glory of our Lord Jesus Christ.

"Learning the lesson of the sampans" is the way I describe this portion of Paul's teaching. During the years our family lived in Asia, we experienced an average of two major typhoons per year. I will always remember Typhoon Rose, which had gusts of winds approaching 200 miles per hour. I literally saw glass bend and a strand of straw pierce through wooden telephone poles. Thank God for Hong Kong's weather-warning system, which almost eliminated the casualty rate during such horrendous storms.

We lived about 15 miles from Aberdeen Harbor, which is located on the seaward side of Hong Kong Island. When we first arrived in what was then the British Crown Colony, as many as 15,000 sampans (small motorized boats about 12' x 16' in length) and junks (larger fishing vessels about 25' x 40' and being driven by 400 hp engines) would be docked in the harbor shelter at any given time. With the approach of a typhoon, the number of vessels would swell to as many as 30,000, with families of four to five persons living on the sampans. It was their home, with nowhere else to find shelter.

Yet, with all the typhoons, only twice did people living on those sampans lose their lives because of the storm. Moreover, I do not recall a single sampan being sunk, once it had successfully made its way back to the typhoon shelter.

One day, while taking some visitors on a tour of Aberdeen via a sampan, I asked my driver-friend why there were so few casualties. He replied, "We support one another. For example, take sampan A, sampan B and sampan C. We pass strong ropes through steel rings mounted on the front of the boats, tying the three sampans together. The same is done on the stern of the boats. Then we add sampan D and do the same. The process continues until all the sampans are intricately linked to each other, with no less than four ropes connecting the huge number of vessels together. Should a sampan or a junk spring a leak or begin to capsize, the support of the others take up the slack."

A couple of weeks later, while using Romans 15:4-7 to deal with a problem in one of our churches, the lesson of the sampans hit home. If the believers in Jesus Christ could learn to be patient with one another and become encouragers rather than accusers, there would be fewer spiritual casualties within the church. A safety net would protect our brothers and sisters from the attacks of the Enemy of our souls and uphold them when leaks in their faith threatened to submerge them.

God supplies the grace needed to live with our brethren. He provides the strength needed for all that He calls His people to do, including living in unity. When God is placed first, above agendas and prejudices, He can move. The result is oneness in praise, purpose and proclamation of the gospel. He desired it for the Jewish and Gentile believers in Rome and He desires it for the church in the 21st century. As Psalm 133:1-3 states: "How good and how pleasant it is for brothers to dwell together in unity! . . . For there the Lord commanded the blessing—life forevermore." "Therefore receive one another, just as Christ also received us, to the glory of God" (Romans 15:7).

James 3:13-18 reads like this:

> Who is wise and understanding among you? Let him show

> by good conduct that his works are done in the meekness of wisdom. But if you have bitter envy and self-seeking in your hearts, do not boast and lie against the truth. This wisdom does not descend from above, but is earthly, sensual, demonic. For where envy and self-seeking exist, confusion and every evil thing are there. But the wisdom that is from above is first pure, then peaceable, gentle, willing to yield, full of mercy and good fruits, without partiality and without hypocrisy. Now the fruit of righteousness is sown in peace by those who make peace.

This is Bruce's assessment:

> If their community life was harmonious, God would be glorified by their united worship and united witness. Such a united witness at the heart of the Roman Empire would be an incomparable factor in the furtherance of the gospel.[9]

If the Jew and the Gentile believers in the Roman church were seen as a body of people joined in love, despite their differences, the onlookers of that day would have seen the miracle and confessed that God was real . . . that their destiny was real. It is no different today!

LESSONS ANYONE?

1. Would you consider yourself someone who is strong in the faith or weak? Why would you identify yourself as such?

2. Has there ever been a time when you made a deliberate choice not to have your own freedom because of the impact it might have on a weaker brother or sister? What was the result and benefit?

3. What "all things, but" rules have you found to be most effective in supporting your life choices and determining ethical principles?

4. What benefit do the principles of patience and encouragement bring to interpersonal relationships? How were they found in Christ? What do they say to today's security?

Chapter 26

The Matter of Hope

Romans 15:8-14

Just as in the lesson from the sampans (see chapter 25 of this book), there is some overlapping of the use of the word *now* (Romans 15:5, 8, 13, 14). Having concluded that Christ did not please Himself so that we, through patience and comfort, might have hope, the apostle inserts the connective *now* to draw a distinction or a resulting change of conduct. It's just like you and me when we exert our parental or relational authority: "Now, here's the bottom line . . . listen up!"

Paul points us to the matter of hope. He does this by means of a chain of praise (vv. 8-12) and a brief prayer (vv. 13, 14). Hope will be created by a change of attitude (vv. 4-7, mutual acceptance), and hope will be exchanged by deliberate action (vv. 8-14, mutual admonishment). There is the look to the past, (God's provision in Christ), as well as a view to the future (God's provision of the Holy Spirit).

Paul's Chain of Praise (vv. 8-12)

It is vital to see all problems in light of the bigger picture. Paul gives perspective to the local problem by drawing the Romans' attention to the overall purpose of Christ's servanthood (attitude) and God's mercy (action). From the tense of the verb *has become* (v. 8), we understand that Christ didn't just try to please Himself, He continued in His capacity as a servant of circumcision. He came as a servant—one of lowly service—in order to serve the Jews (see Matthew 15:24). The word *servant* in this verse does not mean slave. It denotes a minister, priest and provider. His goal was to confirm (make firm, prove reliability, bring fulfillment, prove the promises) what God had promised through the patriarchs. It actually confirmed God to be honest.

Moreover, Christ came as a servant so that the Gentiles might enjoy God's mercy and break forth in praise. What God had promised the patriarchs and the mercy shown to the Gentiles are not two different things, but one—*hope*.

That hope is expressed in a song of praise, which has the Jews singing to the Gentiles (v. 9), the Gentiles singing with the Jews (v. 10), the Gentiles singing to themselves (v. 11), and then both the Jews and the Gentiles singing together (v. 12). Morris makes a fine point: "[Paul] quotes from the Law, the Prophets, and twice from the Psalms, so that he calls all the recognized divisions of Scripture to witness to the point he is making."[1]

Paul first quotes Psalm 18:49, which was written by David on the day the Lord delivered him from all his enemies, in particular, the hand of Saul. He begins with expressing love to Jehovah, who is his Rock, his Fortress and his Deliverer. The songwriter shares his experiences of despair into which God intervened and gave light to his darkness. He declares, "The Lord lives! Blessed be my Rock! Let the God of my salvation be exalted. . . . Therefore I will give thanks to You, O Lord, among the Gentiles, and sing praises to Your name!" (vv. 46, 49).

When Paul quotes the Septuagint verbatim, he gives fresh meaning to the word *confess,* referring to praise, especially in the worship of the Temple, as well as to the word *Gentiles* as referring to *ethnos*—all nations. Think of it, King David is singing prophetically to all of us.

The second quote comes from Deuteronomy 32:43. Moses has just written his last message and is singing his last song. At the end of it, he issues the invitation, "Rejoice, O Gentiles, with His people!" Since God is bringing the blessings of salvation to both the Jews and the Gentiles, the marvel of God's mercy is that they can sing redemption's song together! By the way, Moses' next admonition to the Jews was to remember these words as they entered the Promised Land to possess it.

Third, we find Paul quoting from Psalm 117:1, 2. There is no reference to the Jews, only the Gentiles: "Praise the Lord, all you Gentiles! Laud Him, all you peoples! For His merciful kindness is great toward us, and the truth of the Lord endures forever. Praise the Lord!" The Gentiles have now become the choir!

I cannot help but think of these words: "for the Jew first and also for the Greek" (Romans 1:16); "of the Jew first and also of the Greek" (2:9, 10); "both Jew and Greeks" (3:9); "Yes, of the Gentiles also" (v. 29); "Not only to those who are of the law, but also to those who are of the faith of Abraham" (4:16); "I will call them My people, who were not My people" (9:25); "He might have mercy on all" (11:32).

Finally, Paul quotes from the prophet Isaiah (11:1, 10): "There shall come forth a Rod from the stem of Jesse, and a Branch shall grow out of his roots. The Spirit of the Lord shall rest upon Him, the Spirit of wisdom and understanding, the Spirit of counsel and might, the Spirit of knowledge and of the fear of the Lord" (11:1, 2; see also v. 10). Remember Jesse's household? It was a humble family of shepherds born of lowly estate. Yet from that family would come not only the king of Israel but the Messiah—the King of kings—who would reign over the world. The Jews could fix their hope on Him, and the Gentiles would find their redemption!

Three lessons rise from this song. First of all, we can lift our sights above the difficulties we discover in our local congregations or personal families to see that we are part of a larger plan of God. Our problems are not unique to us, but are common everywhere. Yet in it all, we can experience a foretaste of what will be the final unity of all creation at the end of time.

Second, we recognize that God's nature is inclusive, not exclusive. There is no place or any person who is separated from God's mercy. Believers are to be representatives of God's plan, especially when it comes to acting as salt and light in the community (at church, at home and at work) wherever God places them.

Third, to come into unity of the faith, yet with respect for variety in expression, is not a choice—it is a duty. How can God have a universal purpose contrary to the believer's individual preference? And we will find out in the next chapter how that universal purpose drove Paul's life . . . and should drive ours also.

Paul's Prayer and Confidence (vv. 13, 14)

As Paul begins to pray, we are immediately brought to his focus on God. Earlier in the chapter (v. 5), Paul addressed the "God of patience and comfort." Here, in verse 13, he calls our attention to the "God of hope." In 16:20, it will be the "God of peace." The way Paul addresses God is determinate. It is theology at its finest, applying the eternal nature of God to our temporal immediate need—making His reality relevant to ours.

The same is true with the other prayers recorded in the Epistles. In Ephesians 1:17, we see a church being bombarded by existential philosophy, yet trying to live in the real world. Paul prays to the "Father of glory"; and again in 3:14, "the Father of our Lord Jesus Christ." In Philippians, where the church is endangered by division and possible failure, Paul focuses on the God who completes all that He has started. In Colossians 1, Paul petitions a God of wisdom and strength to give the believers discernment in overcoming doctrinal heresy. In 1 Thessalonians, it is the election of God, and in 2 Thessalonians, it is God, the Righteous Judge, who restores hope to a church who had been misinformed about the second coming of our Lord. Paul's prayer in 1 Timothy 2 is founded on "God our Savior, who desires all men to be saved" (vv. 3, 4); and in his second letter, Paul prays for Timothy, to be confident that God has saved us with a holy calling. There could be no finer encouragement to a young preacher.

All that we are, think or will become in attitude and action is founded on God's design that we become . . .

> Partakers of the divine nature, having escaped the corruption that is in the world through lust. But also for this very reason, giving all diligence, add to your faith virtue, to virtue knowledge, to knowledge self-control, to self-control perseverance, to perseverance godliness, to godliness brotherly kindness, and to brotherly kindness love. For if these things are yours and abound, you will neither be barren nor unfruitful in the knowledge of our Lord Jesus Christ (2 Peter 1:4-8).

According to Gordon Fee, in his excellent book, *God's Empowering Presence,* this prayer in Romans 15:13, 14 focuses on four realities: (1) the God of hope will fill them with the Spirit's joy and peace as they (2) continue to put their trust in Christ, making it possible for the God of hope to cause them to (3) overflow with hope and as they (4) are empowered by the Holy Spirit.[2] Paul is resignaling joy and peace as the result of the Spirit's work (see Romans 14:17; Galatians 5:22).

I again quote from Fee:

> Paul returns, by way of prayer, to the basic eschatological framework of his theology. By their trust in Christ, God's people "already" know joy and peace and thus, live in hope, absolute certainty regarding the "not yet." The key to all of this, of course, is the Holy Spirit, who empowers life in the present and guarantees its future consummation—so much so that Paul prays for them to "overflow with hope" by the power of the Spirit.[3]

While writing this book, I had my 60th birthday. My wife surprised me with a party attended by more than 100 of my family, friends and fellow ministers. From my oldest sister (on whose 19th birthday I was born) to mentors whom God had placed in my life and protégés into whose lives God had placed Carole and me, those gathered, as well as the dozens of cards from others sending greetings, represented every season of my life until the present. One of my sons even authored a short volume titled "Sixty Things My Dad Taught Me," whether it was through word, act or error.

I was one of those babies born late in my mother's childbearing years. It was at a time when the world was just emerging from the Great Depression and entering into the great conflict of World War II. The world was also on the verge of some of the most unprecedented changes and challenges history would ever record.

Consider the changes those born before 1945 witnessed: television, penicillin, polio shots, frozen foods, Xerox, plastic, contact lenses, Nintendo and Sega, and the birth control pill. We were born before the invention of radar, credit cards, split atoms, laser beams and ballpoint pens—not to mention pantyhose, dishwashers, clothes dryers, electric blankets, air conditioners, drip-dry or permanent-press clothes . . . and before man walked on the moon.

My generation got married first and *then* lived together. In our time, closets were for clothes, not for "coming out of." Designer jeans were scheming girls named Jean, and having a meaningful relationship meant getting along with our cousins. Alternative lifestyles meant that you were planning to go somewhere new and enjoy a different kind of day!

We were born before these terms: gay rights, computer dating, cable psychics, career moms and commuter marriages. We were also before day care centers, group therapy and nursing homes. We never heard of FM radio, tape decks, electronic typewriters, Apple computers, email, Palm Pilots, electronic conferencing, yogurt or guys wearing earrings. A *chip* meant a piece of wood. *Hardware* meant hardware, and *software* wasn't even a word.

Back then, *tests* were for school, not AIDS. Pizzas, McDonald's and instant coffees were unheard-of. We hit the scene where there were "5 and 10 cent" stores, where you bought things for five and 10 cents. For one nickel you could ride a streetcar (without fear of getting mugged), make a phone call, buy a Pepsi or an ice cream cone, or enough stamps to mail one letter and two postcards. You could buy a new Chevy coupe for $600 . . . but who could afford one? A pity too, because gas was only 11 cents a gallon!

In our day, *grass* was mowed, *Coke* was a cold drink, and *pot* was something you cooked in. *Rock* music was Grandma's lullaby.

No wonder we are so confused! But we've made it!

Earlier, I used the phrase "season of my life." When you enter the "metallic age" (silver hair, gold teeth and lead bottom), you begin to recall your life by seasons. This was an accumulation of events, feelings and persons over a particular period of time that added a fresh dynamic in your growth as an individual, a believer or a minister, rather than by single, unrelated occurrences. Many of those seasons began with God making a "mistake" (or at least I felt so at the time); however, as the results of His mistake became clearer, I came to recognize that He was producing something in my life that was moving me toward a much higher destiny than I could have ever reached for myself. God's mistakes are still much better than all of my acumen! In reality, they are not mistakes at all, but proof of His protection and better way.

The problem that we as sons and daughters of God have in experiencing peace, joy and hope in our daily life is due to the tension caused by living in the immediate (the "now") and at the same time being moved into the "not yet" that God has designed. Change occurs around us and we panic. Because it is focused on immediate response, our faith seems shaken. Yet, when all is said and done, we still make it through and are stronger and better for it. Could this be how hope is produced?

A suggestion from an "old salt": God still "changes the times and the seasons . . . [and] gives wisdom to the wise and knowledge to those who have understanding" (Daniel 2:21). He is also the Lord of your "now."

LESSONS ANYONE?

1. What does the word *servanthood* mean to you as a believer? Also, discuss the priestly and provider aspects of being a servant in ministry.

2. "Defeated Christians are those who have lost their hope." Do you agree with this statement? What are the reasons people lose hope?

3. In going through the daily confrontations of life, how important is seeing the "big picture" before responding or reacting? Share a recent experience where you made a decision without seeing the larger perspective. What was the result?

4. Take a few moments and consider the impact your theology (understanding of God) has upon your prayer life, both in vision and in vocabulary. Does your view of the person of God have any relevance?

Chapter 27

As I Was Saying

Romans 15:15-33

Have you ever begun writing a letter and then, because of a "just-can't-let-it-go-by" thought, started down another line of thought? Finally, as you finish your "detour," you get back to what you meant to say earlier. To some expositors, that is exactly what happened between Romans 1:16 and 15:15. If so, it would read something like this:

> For I long to see you, that I may impart to you some spiritual gift . . . that I may be encouraged together with you by the mutual faith both of you and me. . . . I often planned to come to you (but was hindered until now). . . . I am a debtor. . . . I am ready to preach. . . . I am not ashamed of the gospel of Christ. . . . Nevertheless, brethren, I have written more boldly to you on some points, as reminding you, because of the grace given to me by God, that I might

> be a minister of Jesus Christ to the Gentiles, ministering the gospel of God, that the offering of the Gentiles might be acceptable, sanctified by the Holy Spirit. . . . But now no longer having a place in these parts . . . whenever I journey to Spain, I shall come to you . . . (Romans 1:11-16; 15:15, 16, 23, 24).

The divine parenthesis between 1:16 and 15:15 is more than "beside the point"; it is "right to the point." Paul has suggested to their memory with a delicate courtesy (v. 15, *reminding*) that since God's grace has covered all their sins and given them a destiny, they should express that grace to one another, giving great delight to all parties. Paul does not end on correction; he completes the thought with commendation. He recognizes they are "full of goodness, filled with all knowledge, able also to admonish one another" (15:14). In spite of their relational difficulties, the Roman church overall is in good shape.

"That I Might Be a Minister" (vv. 16-21)

The apostle also asserts his right to write as he has: "because of the grace given to me by God" (v. 15). There is always with the impartation of God's grace a divine assignment. For Paul it was that he might be a "minister of Jesus Christ to the Gentiles" (v. 16). In describing the call, he chooses a word he used in Romans 13:6 in talking about a civil magistrate. In the Septuagint (Deuteronomy 10:8) and in Hebrews 10:11, the same term is used for those who exercised the office of a priest. In other words, Paul considered himself to be a sacred officer of Jesus Christ. There is both the authoritative and the priestly aspects of his calling.

Every priest presents an offering. In Paul's calling, the offering was the Gentiles who had become obedient "in word and deed" (Romans 15:18) through Paul's words and deeds as he proclaimed the gospel. In other words, those for whom he had sacrificed his life as an offering had now given themselves as "living sacrifices" (12:1), set apart by the Holy Spirit. The Gentiles had become Paul's personal offering to God; they had become their own offering to God, acceptable and received (or sanctified, set apart).

I appreciate Fee's observation:

> Here, probably, is a final word to the Jewish contingent to "welcome the Gentiles" (15:7); those who were formerly unclean have now been sanctified by the Holy Spirit. This is Paul's version of "do not call unclean what God has cleansed" (Acts 10:15).[1]

Whether we are a member, minister or missionary, our assignment is clear: Enter into a sympathetic and understanding relationship with people to show them what Christ can mean to them in their lives. Such only comes by developing a positive appreciation of others' lives; gaining a perspective of their concepts, culture, circumstances and conflicts; and maintaining an ongoing personal involvement with them.

The story is told about Dwight L. Moody's favorite painting. It was a picture of a raging storm, with gigantic waves pounding against the rocks of the shore. In the midst of that dangerous surf was a man who had discovered a handhold in one of the edges of the rock. It had become his salvation. Yet, according to Moody, what made the painting most endearing was that the remaining hand of the man had reached out to another man in the water to provide the same security and safety he had discovered.

As I considered the painting, another thought occurred. The rescuer had not climbed up on the rock where the waves could not reach him. He was still in the water, being pounded as much as the man he was rescuing. His greatest value was being in the water. Could it be that in today's church, we look out from "within the rock," waiting for others to reach our shore, rather than our reaching out from "within the storm," being there with them and for them?

Another key element of Paul's ministry philosophy was his total reliance on the power of the Holy Spirit to accomplish the task (i.e., to make the Gentiles obedient). This was accomplished through "mighty signs and wonders" (v. 19). This phrase is used throughout the Old Testament, in particular, during the exodus of Israel out of Egypt and in the wilderness (Exodus 7:3; 11:9, 10; Deuteronomy 4:34; 6:22; 7:19; 11:3; 26:8; 29:3; 34:11; Nehemiah 9:10; Psalm 78:43; 135:9; Jeremiah 32:20, 21; Isaiah 8:18; 20:3; Daniel 4:2, 3; 6:27). It is also used throughout the Acts of the Apostles, regarding the ministry of the early church.

Seldom was the word *signs* used without the accompanying word *wonders.* A sign (*semeion*) was evidence of God's authority and presence in a place or the exercise of His power in a particular circumstance. *Wonders* (*terata*, from which we get our word *terror*) referred to the effect such evidences had on those who were the recipients. Whereas the signs and wonders of the Exodus were extremely visible and those of the New Testament expressed themselves through the miraculous, there is no indication of a continuous hype of emotion or the spectacular. In the Gentiles' case, the goal was again obedience to the faith (Romans 1:5; 16:26).

A Christian experience that omits the possibility of God's supernatural intervention, literally overwhelming our reason, is not plausible. But a Christian experience that elevates these signs as an end in themselves is not pleasing to God. Neither is it profitable to those who revel in such. True manifestations of the supernatural will always result in the following ways:

- A yielding of control in our personal life and ministry patterns
- Greater expectancy and faith that God will do what He has promised
- Repentance and a stronger sense of God's presence and power
- Unusual joy and celebration that gives rise to a positive attitude
- Greater sensitivity to people's needs

All of this will ultimately culminate in an increase in believers sharing their faith and evangelism.

One pastor said, "In renewal nothing new is created; that which is old and tired is refreshed and invigorated with a fresh touch from heaven. This renewal is a party where people are falling back in love with Jesus, a rekindling of intimacy with Christ."

Above all, the principal reason the Holy Spirit manifests Himself through signs and wonders will always be to glorify Christ and to change us into the image of our holy, life-giving Lord. Whatever results from this present renewal must lead us to the Cross, Christ's sacrifice for us, the power of His resurrection and the fact that we are justified and made acceptable to Him, based on His blood alone. His *charismata* (gifting) *of* us will ever be determined credible by His character *in* us and *through* us to others.

According to Paul, his greatest aim was "to preach the gospel, not where Christ was named, lest I should build on another man's foundation" (v. 20). He had just written one of the most amazing reports published in the Bible. From Paul's own ministry alone, the gospel had swept from Jerusalem all the way up to Illyricum. According to Dunn, Illyricum was that area across from Italy that stretched down the northeast coast of the Adriatic to Macedonia (coinciding roughly with modern Yugoslavia and Albania).[2] It was the most dangerous northern fringe of the eastern empire.

In verse 23, Paul states there is no longer anywhere he could go in that entire region, because every part of that region had been touched with the gospel. When we remember the travel and communications of that day, we have to be amazed that even in such rural and unsophisticated conditions, the gospel had spread with such rapidity and results.

Paul had literally acted in accordance with the promise of Isaiah 52:15. The prophet had predicted that Christ should be preached to the Gentiles, and to those who had never heard of His name. Paul had set that as his purpose and his plan. And there seemed to be two conditions in his strategy.

First, Paul understood his apostolic ministry to be that of a missionary nature. Hodge's interpretation of verse 20 is: "I have been desirous of not preaching where Christ was before known, but in such a way as to accomplish the prediction that those who had not heard should understand."[3]

Second, from Luke's account in the Acts of the Apostles, it appears that Paul focused his attention on cities or major centers of trade, so that converts in the city could be the couriers to the rural areas. An excellent example of this was the church in Colossae, probably founded by those converted in Ephesus, and served by such individuals as Philemon, Tychicus, Epaphras and Onesimus (yes, the thief saved in prison under Paul's influence).

"Whenever I Journey to Spain" (vv. 22-24)

By this time, Paul is nearing the age of 60. It should be a time when he begins to slow the pace. Yet, as someone said, "You may take the missionary out of the field, but you can never take the field out of the missionary."

Having saturated his previous area of assignment, Paul now sets his sights on Spain and, I believe, the rest of Europe. In doing so, he plans to pass through Rome. Several reasons are stated:

1. He had longed to visit them for many years (1:11; 15:23).
2. He wanted to have fruit among them (1:13).
3. He wanted to be benefitted with them by mutual faith (v. 12).
4. He wanted to be helped by them, most likely with material and funds (15:24).

"But Now... to Jerusalem" (vv. 25-29)

At this point in this study, my time line for completion was interrupted by unforeseen personal circumstances.

Also at this time, I was asked to travel on assignment to Athens, Greece, to do a film project, as well as to conduct an intensive course on the Book of Romans while I was there. Imagine trying to teach Greeks the intricacy of Paul's phenomenal Greek vocabulary. My students were already far ahead of me!

While there, my host, friend and outstanding Greek Christian leader, George Patsaouras, invited me to visit the ancient city of Corinth. It was like a dream come true! I would have a firsthand view of what the apostle Paul was looking at as he wrote to the believers in Rome. When the day ended, it had been one of the most marvelous days of my life!

As I stood among the ruins of this city, which dates back as far as the Neolithic period, and was later the home of the cult who worshiped Aphrodite, I tried to put myself in Paul's sandals. I looked back over my shoulder to the towering Acrocorinth, which rises 1,500 feet above the city and has a temple dedicated to the city's deity, and remembered Paul's statement to the city's 10,000 inhabitants: "He who glories, let him glory in the Lord!" (1 Corinthians 1:31). Walking across what was once the *agora*—the market place—I was reminded of Paul's words to "eat whatever is sold in the meat market [*agora*] . . . for 'the earth is the Lord's, and all its fullness'" (10:25, 26).

Standing before the *Bema* and the *Rostrum*, I remembered Luke's account of Paul standing before Gallio in Acts 18:12-17. Hearing the water still flowing at the fountain of Pirene, which had been the center of prostitution and hedonistic worship, the admonition of Paul for Christians to "clean up their act" became very relevant. Then rising above it all is the temple of Apollo, built in the sixth century B.C., representing the spiritual darkness and mythology into which the apostle was bringing the truth and light of the gospel. Finally, seeing inscriptions to a certain Erastus (most likely the one found in Acts 19:22; Romans 16:23; and 2 Timothy 4:20), as well as the inscription which reads "Synagogue of the Hebrews," brought to reality the witness of faithful men and women living pure lives in a perverse society.

What stirred my heart the most was looking out over inlet of the Aegean Sea, 388 feet below the city. As Paul stood on the Lechaeum road in the center of the city, looking northeast toward the sea, his heart was filled with two conflicting emotions—his strong desire to visit Rome, but his sincere duty to do so by way of Jerusalem. For some it might seem it was the long way around, but history reveals that it actually was his shortest way to Rome after all, even though it took him five years to do so. Verses 25-32 are probably some of the most intimate and personal portions ever written by Paul regarding his personal values and ministry.

In verses 25-29, six words catch the attention: *minister* (vv. 25, 27), *pleased* (vv. 26, 27), *debtors* (v. 27), *duty* (v. 27), *fruit* (v. 28) and *fullness* (v. 29). In each of these words, there is a wealth of meaning. There is also a progression that reveals the process through which ministry flows.

Minister is from the Greek word for "deacon, a server." In Romans 12:1, Paul calls our service reasonable or rational. In verse 7, he implies that it is practical—relevant. Ministry is described as tangible—real. It is what James describes:

> If a brother or sister is naked and destitute of daily food, and one of you says to them, "Depart in peace, be warmed and filled," but you do not give them the things which are needed for the body, what does it profit? Thus also faith by itself, if it does not have works, is dead. But someone will say, "You have faith, and I have works." Show me your faith without your works, and I will show you my faith by my works (2:15-18).

To Paul, ministry is not an ethereal musing on spiritual concepts on a Sunday morning, but it is down-to-earth help the rest of the week. It will be discovered by using our eyes—reasonable. It will be defined by our mind—rational. And it will be directed by our hands—relevant. It will be lived out by our feet, filling that lack experienced by the recipient.

The tangible in this case seems to have been an offering received from the Gentile congregations in Macedonia and Achaia to be given to the saints in Jerusalem who were poor. This isn't the first time that such an offering had been taken. According to Acts 11:27-30 and 12:25, Paul and Barnabas had enlisted similar assistance for the believers in Jerusalem, during a time of famine that had stricken the Holy City.

There was also a deeper tangibility along with the offering. *Pleasing* denotes the idea that the donors were happy to give. I especially like the phrase in Romans 15:27, "It pleased them *indeed*." Their willingness to assist was more than delight—it was a delight that ended "in a deed."

Paul uses the word *koinonia,* translated "contribution." Dunn explains:

> For Paul it denotes particularly common participation in or sharing of something (1 Corinthians 10:16, the blood and

> body of Christ; 2 Corinthians 13:13, 14 and Philippians 2:1, the Holy Spirit; 1:5, the gospel; 3:10, Christ's sufferings; Philemon 6, faith). Here and in 2 Corinthians 8:4 and 9:13, it is used in the extended sense of "expression of what is shared," in reference to the collection.[4]

What motivated their contributions was their mutual sharing of the grace and graciousness of God. It was the spiritually natural thing to do. This was the corporate expression of the early church when they "had all things in common" (Acts 2:44).

The same progression is delineated in Paul's use of the word *debtor.* In Romans 1:14, Paul says that because he had been the recipient of the gospel, he was now a debtor to the world. In 8:12, 13, Paul says that because he had been the recipient of the Holy Spirit and all things that pertain to life and godliness, he was now a debtor to live by the power of the Spirit. Now, in 15:27, because the Gentile churches had been the recipients of the gospel (and the Holy Spirit) through the Jewish brothers and sisters in Jerusalem (their mother church), they were now debtors to share their material abundance. There was no excuse to think or do otherwise.

Duty is different from being a debtor. It implies an obligation. It adds the "ought" to our service, adding moral expectation. We can be in debt but not fulfill our obligation. Not so with our *koinonia* in Christ.

Fruit has the concept of harvest. When we have the "harvest" of the Holy Spirit at work in our lives (Galatians 5), that fruit will be authenticated (*sealed*, Romans 15:28) by our actions. Newell writes: "Confession of Christ that does not result in ministering to others, is not an obedient confession."[5]

Talk to people who have had fruitful lives, and without fail you will discover that their conviction was confirmed by a commitment to others. Their obedience resulted in what Paul calls the "fullness of the blessing of the gospel of Christ" (v. 29). *Fullness* carries the idea of being multicolored like a light shining through a prism; *blessing* speaks of a unique response God gives to those who obey. Not only will the burden of the Jewish need be lifted off the apostle's heart and mind, but there will be a fresh dynamic of fulfillment and faith (often called "anointing") that will rest upon his shoulders.

Not long ago, one of my sons, who had recently accepted a senior pastorate, asked me how to get started in his new assignment. My answer wasn't very spiritual: "What do you do when you have an itch?" His reply, "Scratch it!" I sounded like the Lord, "Go and do likewise!"

"Strive With Me" (vv. 30-33)

Have you ever watched a western movie where the robbers enter the city, rob the bank and then make their escape? The sheriff then deputizes those standing around to form a posse. Of course, they never catch the bandit until the hero arrives to save the day.

Paul now deputizes the believers in Rome to form a "prayer posse." It is an appeal (*beg/beseech*, also used in Romans 12:1) as well as an impartation of authority. Both the appeal and the authorization are backed by their relationship in Christ (their position) and the love of the Holy Spirit they have experienced toward each other, though they had yet to meet in person.

Of course, the apostle had never seen *Blazing Saddles* on the screen, but he had seen the GWF—the Greek Wrestling Federation—in person. He asks the Roman brothers and sisters to strive together with him in prayer. He describes the intense agony or effort the wrestlers in the Greek games put forth in their competitions and asks them to do the same in their praying for his trip.

He provides three requests so that they might pray intelligently and specifically. First, he asks that they pray for his safety—to be protected from those fanatical Jews who would adamantly oppose the gospel. These could very well include those Pharisees with whom he had served—his old cronies may have become his thorn in the flesh everywhere he went. Undoubtedly Paul understood the danger that might lie in wait for him, but he took every "prayer precaution" to deliver him from it. From the recollections of Luke in the Book of Acts, though those in Jerusalem tried to take Paul's life, because of the Romans' prayers, he was spared and in the end he arrived in Rome.

Second, he asks the Romans to pray for the believers in Jerusalem. Surprisingly, it is not that their need would be met, but that the gift from the Gentile brothers and sisters would be welcomed. Because of the existing schism between the Jewish and Gentile sectors of the church, in particular Paul's preaching of grace, he still might be seen with suspicion. At least in part, their prayers were fruitful; Acts 21:17-25 informs us that Paul was received by James and his fellow elders. Of interest, however, is the fact that these brothers did express some concerns about the members' reaction. Also after Paul was arrested, there seems to be little effort to get him out of prison.

Third, he asks the Romans to pray that he might come to them with joy. I'm not sure if Paul had any inkling of what "with joy" might incur. Imprisonment, delay of justice, defamation of character and shipwrecks would be enough to make anyone ask for a refund from the local tour company. But the Romans had prayed and according to Acts 28:30, 31, "Then Paul dwelt two whole years in his own rented house, and received all who came to him, preaching the kingdom of God and teaching the things which concern the Lord Jesus Christ with all confidence, no one forbidding him."

One thing about prayer: The results will look nothing like you expect them to. But they will surpass anything you had hoped them to be. It's our role to pray; it's God's role to perform.

Finally, it is not without intention that Paul, the Jew, pronounced a Jewish benediction over the Gentile church. He not only does this in Romans 15:33, but also again in 16:20; 2 Corinthians 13:11; Philippians 4:9; 1 Thessalonians 5:23; 2 Thessalonians 3:16; and Hebrews 13:20. Throughout this portion of his letter, Paul reminded everyone that his calling as a minister of Jesus Christ was to make an "offering of the Gentiles" (15:16) acceptable to God, deliver "their offering" acceptable to Jerusalem (v. 27), and to use the Roman's future "offering" (v. 24) for acceptable service in Europe, the Lord willing.

For the apostle, could the above have any connection with his *proving* what was that "good and acceptable and perfect [complete] will of God" (Romans 12:2) for his life?

How are we proving ours?

LESSONS ANYONE?

1. Paul clearly outlined his personal mission statement. In one sentence, what is your personal mission statement—that purpose for which God has called you? How are you proceeding to fulfill it?

2. Reviewing D.L. Moody's favorite painting, how many lessons can be derived? Discuss them with a friend.

3. Are signs and wonders for today? Do you see the supernatural aspect of the gospel at work in your life? In your church? Explain.

4. In your opinion, why did Paul and the Gentile church feel such a debt or duty toward the "mother church" in Jerusalem? What messages do you think such generosity sent to the Jewish saints? How about their response?

Chapter 28

No "Weakest Link"

Romans 16:1-16

You either love it or hate it; there is no middle ground! What I'm talking about is NBC's answer to the money quiz shows on prime-time television. What makes *Weakest Link* unique is the hostess, Anne Robinson, who makes quick and often snide remarks to the contestants. She admits, "I'm no Regis!" Her comments range from "Who fell off the tree of knowledge?" to "Who has mistaken life for a box of chocolates?" Making things tense is necessary for the contestants to form alliances, as each strives to remain standing at the end of the game.

Whatever your opinion, the show reveals three of the major characteristics of today's society: competition, criticism and conspiracy. By the way, these same three elements have made stars out of even more extreme programs, such as the *Survivor* series. The survivor of the fittest and the fiercest gets the prize. Unfortunately, such a mind-set also makes its way into the church, the Christian home and even the ministry.

In direct contrast to the spirit of the age, the Bible says:

> Since this is the kind of life we have chosen, the life of the Spirit, let us make sure that we do not just hold it as an idea in our heads or a sentiment in our hearts, but work out its implications in every detail of our lives. That means we will not compare ourselves with each other as if one of us were better and another worse. We have far more interesting things to do with our lives. Each of us is an original. Live creatively, friends. If someone falls into sin, forgivingly restore him, saving your critical comments for yourself. You might be needing forgiveness before the day's out. Stoop down and reach out to those who are oppressed. Share their burdens, and so complete Christ's law (Galatians 5:25—6:2, *TM*).

Living in the Spirit requires joyful cooperation, not competition; creative encouragement, not criticism; and unqualified commitment, not conspiracy.

The apostle Paul also had a few other things to say about the weakest link: "Christ is God's ultimate miracle and wisdom all wrapped up in one. Human wisdom is so tinny, so impotent, next to the seeming absurdity of God. Human strength can't begin to compete with God's 'weakness'" (1 Corinthians 1:24, 25, *TM*). And for those who feel like the weakest link, Paul testifies, "I quit focusing on the handicap and began appreciating the gift. It was a case of Christ's strength moving in on my weakness. Now I take limitations in stride, and with good cheer, these limitations that cut me down to size—abuse, accidents, opposition, bad breaks. I just let Christ take over! And so the weaker I get, the stronger I become" (2 Corinthians 12:9, 10, *TM*). Living in the Spirit focuses upon God's bountiful supply, not on our limited resources.

As he brings his letter to the Roman believers to a conclusion, Paul is quick to remember the difference between one who is an achiever and one who truly achieves. The achiever follows the pattern of the age, forgetting from whence he came and those who have helped him get there. One who truly achieves never forgets where he started and the people whom God placed in his life to allow him to arrive where he is today.

Paul's conclusion is simple: There is no one who is considered the weakest link in Christ's family. He sends greetings to 27 brothers and sisters, including two who are not named, who are active in the church at Rome. There are at least three congregations noted, and possibly as many as five. But before we meet these people, I wish to call attention to the words Paul uses to describe them.

- There are the filial terms: *sister* (v. 1); *beloved* (vv. 5, 8, 9, 12); *countrymen* (vv. 7, 11); *mother* (v. 13); *brethren* (v. 14); *household* (vv. 10, 11).

- There are the companion terms: *fellow workers* (vv. 3, 9); *fellow prisoners* (v. 7); *firstfruits* (v. 5); *helper* (v. 2); *servant* (v. 1).

- Paul is grateful for those who *risked their necks* (vv. 3, 4); *labored much for us* (v. 6); *labored in the Lord* or *labored much in the Lord* (v. 12); *are of note among the apostles*—believers even before Paul (v. 7).

- Nine of these names are women and no distinction is given between their ministry functions and those of the men.
- They seem to appear in all generations and with no regard to social class or status.
- Both Jews and Gentiles are intermingled, without reference to their ethnicity.
- They all appear to be looked upon with the same appreciation. There is no ministry identified as more important.

Paul commends to the Romans the lady *Phoebe*. She was a servant, a deaconess, in the church at Cenchrea, a port toward the east from Corinth. Most likely, she met Paul when he visited there (Acts 18:18). Whether or not she held the title of deacon, in the apostle's opinion she most definitely functioned as one. Her role was both sanctioned and openly recognized throughout the body of Christ.

There also appears to be a protocol regarding mutual recognition of church leaders, through the cultural practice of sending letters of commendation as an introduction of the individual's credibility and calling.

Next, the apostle greets *Priscilla* and *Aquila*. This couple is mentioned in Acts 18:2 as part of the Jewish community who had to leave Rome as a result of the edict of Claudius in A.D. 49. They stayed in Ephesus and even traveled with Paul when he sailed for Syria (18:18) before returning to Rome. They are also mentioned in verse 26 as the mentors of Apollos, the golden-tongued lad who so vigorously showed that Jesus was the Messiah. We are not sure just when it was that this couple "risked their own necks" for the apostle, but reading Paul's unique style of ministry, it could have been any day of the week!

Paul also greets the churches among the Gentiles. Could it have been that Priscilla and Aquila were leading a messianic congregation? There does seem to be a distinction between the church in their house and those of the Gentiles.

Epaenetus was deeply loved by Paul. What distinguished him was that he was a "firstfruit" of the converts in Asia (Romans 16:5). Not only had he turned to Christ, but he also led others. He had been a participant in the harvest.

Mary is only mentioned because she "labored much" (v. 6). There had been toil, striving and struggle in her faithfulness. According to Dunn, "Mary is picked out first for such commendation, confirming that women played a significant part in the emerging roles of leadership within the infant Christian communities."[1] Before we belittle her role in the church, how many of us would have worked to such a degree that our names would have appeared in this divinely inspired hall of honor? To have her name included in the Bible makes her special.

Andronicus and *Junia* were a Jewish couple who were incarcerated with Paul on one of his seven imprisonments. Regarding the high esteem of this couple, Leon Morris writes:

> It is fairly clear from the New Testament that there was a wider circle of apostles than the Twelve, and it would seem that this couple belonged to that wider circle. Some find an argument from this that we should understand the second name as masculine, holding that a woman could not be an apostle, but we should bear in

mind Chrysostom's comment: "Oh! How great is the devotion of this woman, that she should be even counted worthy of the appellation of an apostle."[2]

Morris also quotes Cranfield, who makes the following comments:

> That Paul should not only include a woman among the apostles but actually describe her, together with Andronicus, as outstanding among them, is highly significant evidence (along with the importance he accords in this chapter to Phoebe, Priscilla, Mary, Tryphoena, Tryphosa, Persis, the mother of Rufus, Julia and the sister of Nereus) of the falsity of the widespread and stubbornly notion that Paul had a low view of women and something to which the Church as a whole has not yet paid sufficient attention.[3]

Seeing that they had become believers in Christ before Paul, could it be that they had been some of those Jews from Rome who were present at the Day of Pentecost who were saved (see Acts 2:10)? Could it be that they were the "apostles" who took the gospel back to Rome and were active in the planting of the church in that empirical city? If so, and seeing what took place in Rome later, maybe it was this couple who literally changed the course of world and church history through their faithfulness.

Amplias is a common name, often linked with the emperor's household. Some commentators connect this name with an inscription in one of the earliest catacombs. It stated that Amplias was a very prominent member of the early church through whom the gospel had penetrated into the great Roman household. If true, then this beloved brother of Paul had opportunities and fruit that only eternity will reveal.

Urbanus and *Stachys* have been connected also with the imperial household. They are referred to as "fellow worker" and "beloved," showing the importance of relationship with those who serve alongside us.

Apelles had been "approved in Christ" (v. 10). According to most scholars, this most likely refers to the fact that Apelles had undergone a serious testing—maybe even political or personal persecution—that had resulted in an unusual maturity of character and leadership.

The "household of Aristobulus" was well known in Rome. Historians write that Aristobulus was the grandson of Herod the Great who ended his days in Rome as a private citizen. He was a friend of the Emperor Claudius. At his death, his slaves had been passed to the emperor. If confirmed, then we begin to see that Amplias may have had even greater fruitfulness in the high households of the Roman empire. It could also be one of the reasons that Nero came to despise the Christian community with such a passion. Could the burning of Rome be connected with the burning of a man's passion against God and his predecessor?

Herodion is definitely a Jew and, as his name implies, part of the followers or descendants of Herod. He was deeply appreciated by the apostle.

Narcissus was a wealthy and powerful freedman who had been prominent under Claudius but put to death early in Nero's reign. His slaves would have been passed to the emperor. According to Leon Morris, Narcissus was not of the character of a believer, so it is interesting that even from that heathen household came those who were in the Lord.

The names *Tryphena* and *Tryphosa* conjure up some interesting thoughts. Meaning "delicate" and "dainty" respectively, we wonder if these were twins, nicknames or descriptions of their size (either big or small). Whatever, they labored for the Lord and that's what counts!

From the tense of the verb, *Persis* was a lady who was either elderly or sickness had impaired her ability for service. Paul never forgot those who had given their all for Christ, nor would he let the world forget them.

Rufus ("Red" for short) was a common name for a slave. Morris sheds some light on who this might have been:

> We read in Mark's Gospel of a man called Simon who was the father of Alexander and Rufus (15:21). Now it is usually agreed that Gospel was written with Rome very much in mind, and evidently the point of mentioning Simon was that he was the father of two people well known in the Roman church. It is not improbable that this is the man Paul greets. He was a choice believer.[4]

Note that Paul greets Rufus' mother as well. Could he have been acquainted with the family in Jerusalem? Whoever she was, Paul felt he was part of her extended love.

Asyncritus, Phlegon, Hermas, Patrobas and *Hermes* were leaders in their local church. There is no record as to who they are or what they did. But God knows, and they are only representative of millions of believers never recognized here on earth. Great will be their reward in heaven!

Philologus ("full of words") was either a male secretary or he talked all the time. His wife, *Julia,* served with him.

Nereus was most likely a slave who had been declared free by Nero, and *Olympas* was a part of the leadership team that met in the home of Philologus and Julia.

Finally, Paul says, "Greet one another with a holy kiss" (v. 16). If you ever visit this part of the world, get ready to be kissed, first on one cheek and then the other. It is the standard form of greeting and today practiced even between those of the opposite sex. According to Dunn, it formed part of the introduction to the common meal—the Lord's Supper.[5] This gives us reason to believe that Paul expected this letter to be read orally in the regular gatherings for worship.

At his passing, Reverend Robert McGaffin was nearly 92 years of age. For many years, he and his wife of nearly 67 years, Helen, faithfully ministered for the Lord. He was born in Idaho, and when he was 4 years old, he moved by covered wagon to Alberta, Canada. Bob began to learn to play the violin as a lad. Bob and Helen began pastoring Foursquare churches in many different towns across central Canada, finally accepting a pastorate in a suburb of Vancouver, British Columbia. None of their congregations were large, nor did the McGaffins ever receive great remuneration for their faithfulness.

Today, Helen lives in Vancouver, where their son, Barry, pastors the Kingsway Foursquare Church and serves as the director of missions for the Foursquare Gospel Church in Canada. One of their daughters, Jan, serves with her husband, Rob Buzza, who is the president of the Pacific Life Bible College, in Surrey, British Columbia. Their oldest daughter, Jackie, was a Foursquare pastor's wife for many years.

Before his death, if you were to visit their humble home, you'd find Bob in a motorized chair, suffering with a debilitating illness. Yet, he would be writing poetry and blessing pastors and believers across North America and around the world.

Many years ago, one young pastor was just beginning his ministry. He knew very little about how to shepherd his flock. Most Thursday evenings, however, you'd find that young man and his wife visiting Bob and Helen McGaffin at their home on Sperling Avenue in Burnaby, British Columbia, receiving instruction, love and, of course, baked goods. On many occasions it saved them from mistakes and lifted their hearts out of depression. Having heard Bob play one final tune on his violin, they'd climb in the car and drive back to their congregation refreshed and full of hope.

That young man was me, and I will always be grateful.

If the McGaffins had lived in Rome during the time of the writing of this letter, the apostle Paul would have written, "Greet Bob and Helen for me, for they have labored faithfully and refreshed my life."

How important it is to live with the mind of the Spirit, rather than being controlled and defeated by the mentality of the age. We must focus on the destiny Christ designed for us to be in Him, rather than on the lies we hear from the accuser of the brethren. We do not simply survive, we are more than conquerors!

LESSONS ANYONE?

1. If Paul included you on his list of coworkers, what words would he use to describe you? After you've ended your course on earth, how do you want people to remember you?

2. Out of Paul's list, choose one person, and briefly share why that person seemed to stand out. Then consider your present service to theirs. Did it have to do with function, background or surroundings? Explain.

3. Name at least one "unsung hero" in your life, and explain how the person influenced you.

4. List at least five people who have special meaning in your service to Christ today. Why not write them and express your appreciation?

Chapter 29

A Few Final Words

Romans 16:17-27

At the end of any letter, the final paragraph will contain a few quick items the author wishes to convey briefly. New thoughts suddenly come to mind, as well as the reinforcement of a key item that had been covered previously. In Paul's case, they take the form of a warning, a few salutations and a final blessing.

The Warning (vv. 17-20)

There is much discussion as to why Paul becomes so abrupt in inserting this warning. There is also much speculation as to whom Paul is referring. Would the warning be to those who were bringing syncretism into the congregations? Knowing that the letter would be read by others than the Roman believers, could it have been the Gnostics or other cults that had been forming? Or was it a group that was still within the Roman church itself? There is no specific indications from the author.

Leaving the controversy to the scholars, I find it plausible that he would include the warning. Throughout the entire letter, Paul's goal has been to bring both the Jewish and Gentile factions into unity. He had made the following statements:

- Both groups were equally sinful and guilty before God (chs. 1-3).
- Both groups were justified through the blood of Jesus and have Abraham as their father (chs. 3-4).
- Both groups rejoiced in the process, led by the Holy Spirit, that will lead them through the love of God to be conformed to Christ's image (chs. 5-8);
- Both groups have seen God's mercy in the past, are experiencing it now, and will rejoice in it in the future (chs. 9-11).
- Both groups are called to think soberly, exhibit the fruit of the Spirit in Christian virtue, living without shame, but with great hope before others within the church, before others outside the church, even before government authorities (chs. 12-13).
- Both groups, therefore, if they think they are the strong in faith, should bear the burden of their weaker brothers and sisters in the church (chs. 14-15).
- Both groups in Rome are already living examples of how this unity can impact an entire empire—even a hostile one (ch. 16, the first half).

Therefore, when we allow ourselves to "make Romans simple," it is no surprise that Paul would throw in a few last words to again caution the believers about others who would try to divide their loyalties or lifestyles.

Though much had been accomplished, there still seemed to be enough debate and division going on that Paul begins with a strong appeal, rather than a command. His appeal is to look carefully, examine critically, mark clearly, and avoid completely anyone who would cause "divisions and offenses" (v. 17) within the church body. Throughout his writings, Paul had to confront dissension and sectarianism (see 1 Corinthians 3:3; Galatians 5:20). Invariably, these led to offensive words and behavior, causing others to stumble in their faith or even fall into sin.

There will be those who claim to have new insights into the kingdom of God. They will blatantly or seductively detract from the balance and constancy of Biblical truth. They will claim to be prophets of the Lord, and may even attract large followings. But according to Paul, the source of their "apostleship" is not the lordship of Christ, but the animalistic lusts of their own private interests. Their words are carefully honed and will draw attention away from the true content of the gospel. They will speak well, but their lives will not confirm the validity of their vocabulary. They will captivate and capture those who are unwary.

Paul commends the Romans for their pliable teachability. Such an openness and simplicity, however, could be a blessing or a danger. His desire for them is that they be "wise in what is good, and simple concerning evil" (v. 19). One of the early-church fathers translated Paul's intention in this way: "Be too good to deceive, too wise to be deceived."[1]

Paul then returns to the ultimate source of the problem—Satan himself. It is significant that Paul began with Genesis 3 at the beginning of this letter (1:20-25). Now he ends the letter with the same chapter. The God who has restored a marvelous destiny and relationship of peace among all men will crush Satan. Our sovereign God will have the final say. Our future rests in the "acceptor of the brethren," (Christ) rather than in the inflammatory words of the "accuser of the brethren" (Satan).

This is proevangelism language. In the same way that Eve would crush the head of the serpent, by faith and faithfulness the Roman believers will stand in the end. There is no question about this being a strongly prophetic statement about their future. While the Roman authorities drove the believers to the catacombs, today those same believers are remembered in the names of our children. The church still stands while the earthly kingdom has crumbled. Truth and integrity always win in the end. You can stake your life on it!

The Salutations (vv. 21-24)

As you read the men who were with Paul in Corinth when he wrote this letter, any idea that Paul was a loner is demolished. The more we understand the role of the apostle, as in the case of Paul, the more we recognize that the leader always draws men and women to serve as a team around him. True apostleship is marked by the raising up of others with like vision and like attitudes.

Take Timothy, for example. He is mentioned everywhere in the Epistles: Acts 16:1-3; 1 Corinthians 16:10; 2 Corinthians 1:1, 19; 1 Thessalonians 3:2; 1 Timothy 1:2;

and Hebrews 13:23. When he became the pastor of the church in Ephesus, Paul wrote entire letters of encouragement to him. True apostles have more interest in the future of others than in their own fame.

Other members of the team included Lucius (see Acts 13:1), Jason (probably the same person as in 17:5-9) and Sosipater (could be a derivative of Sopater in 20:4). Paul calls them his “kinsmen” (KJV). They were his brothers nationally and spiritually.

Behind every good writer there is a better editor! Tertius was the *amanuensis* Paul used to copy from a manuscript or from dictation this very letter. More than a simple secretarial role, it involves the intricacies of word choice, placement and the communication skills to make the message simple, orderly and effective. Personally, other than the Holy Spirit, Tertius is probably the forgotten genius behind Paul’s letters. And he was probably as inspired as the apostle himself.

Gaius was the Corinthian gentleman whom Paul baptized (1 Corinthians 1:14) and called Titius Justus in Acts 18:7 (*NIV*). Paul stayed in his home. The church in Corinth met in Gaius’ house, or he habitually provided hospitality for the local believers and traveling Christians like Paul.

Erastus traveled with Paul at times (Acts 19:22) and resided in Corinth (2 Timothy 4:20). It appears he was the first treasurer, and later the director of public works, for the city of Corinth. Quartus is mentioned as a brother. In Paul’s thinking, being a brother was just as important as being a fellow worker, minister or apostle.

Whereas at the end of chapter 15 Paul sent a Jewish blessing of *shalom,* he now sends the Greek blessing of *charis*—grace.

The Doxology (vv. 25-27)

When something has been said and written that cannot be improved, why try? In his short commentary on *Romans, Verse by Verse*, William R. Newell in 1938 wrote:

> We will find the Greek construction of the great doxology of verses 25 to 27, involved and difficult, unless we place ourselves in the position of Paul himself. He has been writing with the hand of the Spirit upon him, those stupendous truths which we find in this great, fundamental Epistle: the glory, holiness, and righteousness, of the infinite, eternal God; the awful guilt and helplessness of man; the story of the astonishing intervention of a Grace that not only pardoned and justified, but made believing sinners partakers of Christ of the very glory of God Himself; the absolute consistency of all this with God's promises to His earthly nation, Israel; the openness of all Heaven now to all nations, and that on the simplest possible condition—FAITH ALONE! And the Apostle has God in view as the Giver, Christ in view as the means, and the saints in view as the receivers of this mighty bounty!
>
> Therefore this great passage becomes both a doxology, and a commendation with a doxology, of praise to this great God, and a commendation of the saints unto Him. Paul thus commended the saints in Ephesus (Acts 20:32): "And now, brethren, I commend you to God, and to the Word of His grace." Therefore, if we must seek for grammatical regularity (which we do not need to do in such an overwhelming passage as this!) We may read: "Now I commend you to Him that is able to establish you . . . to the only wise God, through Jesus Christ: to whom be the glory unto the ages!"[2]

Paul praises God for His wisdom of grace in sending Jesus. As part of the fulfillment of his goal stated in Romans 15:9, the apostle also offers the Roman believers unto God, that He might establish them. The *New English Bible* states it this way: "To him who has the power to make your standing sure." If God has provided all that this letter has included, then He is fully capable of rendering them firm and constant.

Three times in this doxology the word *kata* (*according*) is used. This short word gives us insight as to why God will "establish" them.

It will be according to Paul's gospel and the preaching of Jesus Christ. Paul is not differentiating between a gospel he has concocted and that of Jesus. He is saying that his gospel is the same as what others have preached to the church in Rome. The good news is capable of keeping them secure, no matter what befalls them. It is similar to what Jude wrote: "Now to Him who is able to keep you from stumbling, and to present you faultless before the presence of His glory with exceeding joy, to God our Savior who alone is wise, be glory and majesty, dominion and power, both now and forever. Amen" (vv. 24, 25).

Paul is confident that God is able to keep them because of the power of the gospel. It is the "power of God to salvation for everyone who believes" (Romans 1:16). It never caused Paul to be ashamed, and it will never cause the believers in Rome to be embarrassed.

It will be according to the revelation of the mystery that has now been revealed to all nations. To the believers in Colossae, Paul explained it this way: "To them God willed to make known what are the riches of the glory of this mystery among the Gentiles: which is Christ in you, the hope of glory" (1:27).

God is able to keep them because of the provision of Christ. The plan of God to redeem man had been obscure and incomprehensible, totally unknown and undiscoverable by human reason. It had not only been planned before the foundation of time, but the world had to be prepared for it through the prophetic scriptures in the Old Testament. Then, through the Cross, God's righteous way of making man righteous was provided in full! The only way man could be redeemed was by the wise, voluntary, free and loving desire of God. God's plan was not to bring them to this point and then have them fail in their faith.

It will be according to the commandment from God that those in Rome would become obedient to the faith. To the church at Ephesus, Paul had written: "You were sealed with the Holy Spirit of promise, who is the guarantee of our inheritance until the redemption of the purchased possession, to the praise of His glory" (Ephesians 1:13, 14).

God is able to keep them because of the promised process that the Holy Spirit had begun in their lives. When the Spirit would complete His work in their lives, they would be obedient to the faith. Paul's letter had begun with the goal of obedience, and now the lives of those to whom he wrote would be full of obedience. The process does work.

Think of it. The future of the Roman believers *and ours* is fully dependent on the entire *Godhead*. With the Father, the Son and the Holy Spirit on our side, we can do no other than succeed and give Him praise for our destiny!

OH YES, AND WE ARE ONLY BEGINNING!

SOME FINAL LESSONS?

1. How important are motives behind our ministry? How are these motives usually expressed, both positively and negatively? How should the church respond?

2. What does it mean to you when Paul writes, "God will crush Satan under your feet"? In whom does the authority rest?

3. Are you presently mentoring (discipling) other people through your life and service? Whom are you personally raising up to follow in your footsteps?

4. Having now finished this study of the letter to the Romans, what are the major lessons you have gained? How has the study changed your perceptions, conduct and service?

Endnotes

Chapter 3

[1]James D.G. Dunn, *Word Biblical Commentary*, vols. 38A and 38B (Dallas: Word, 1988) 22.

[2]Leon Morris, *Quoted in the Epistle to the Romans* (Grand Rapids: Eerdmans, 1998) 60.

[3]Morris, 66.

[4]Dunn, 39.

Chapter 4

[1]Ernst Kaseman, *Commentary on Romans* (Grand Rapids: Eerdmans, reprinted 1990) 35.

[2]James D.G. Dunn, *Word Biblical Commentary*, vols. 38A and 38B (Dallas: Word, 1988) 54-55.

[3]C.E.B. Cranfield, *Romans—A Shorter Commentary* (Grand Rapids: Eerdmans, reprinted 1987) 29.

[4]William S. Plumer, *Commentary on Romans*. (New York, 1870; reprinted in Grand Rapids: Kregal, 1993) 64.

[5]Plumer, 79.

[6]Dunn, 66.

Chapter 5

[1]Charles Hodge, *Commentary on the Epistle to the Romans* (Philadelphia, 1864; reprinted in Grand Rapids: Eerdmans, 1951) 58

[2]William Barclay, *The Letter to the Romans* (Philadelphia: Westminster, 1957) 35.

[3]Hodge, 53.

[4]William S. Plumer, *Commentary on Romans*. (New York, 1870; reprinted in Grand Rapids: Kregal, 1993) 98.

Chapter 6

[1]2 Apoc. Bar. 48:22-24 (quoted by James Dunn, p. 110).

[2]Ernst Kaseman, *Commentary on Romans* (Grand Rapids: Eerdmans, reprinted 1990) 70.

[3]James D.G. Dunn, *Word Biblical Commentary*, vols. 38A and 38B (Dallas:Word, 1988) 138-9.

[4]William S. Plumer, *Commentary on Romans*. (New York, 1870; reprinted in Grand Rapids: Kregal, 1993) 113.

Chapter 7

[1]James D.G. Dunn, *Word Biblical Commentary*, vols. 38A and 38B (Dallas:Word, 1988) 148-9.

Chapter 8

[1]Martin Luther, *Commentary on the Epistle to the Romans*, trans. J. Theodore Mueller (Grand Rapids: Kregal, 1976) Introduction.

[2]James D.G. Dunn, *Word Biblical Commentary*, vols. 38A and 38B (Dallas:Word, 1988) 172.

Chapter 9

[1]William S. Plumer, *Commentary on Romans*. (New York, 1870; reprinted in Grand Rapids: Kregal, 1993)159.

[2]John Calvin, *Commentaries on the Epistle of Paul to the Romans*, trans. John Owen (Grand Rapids: Eerdmans, 1947) 105.

Chapter 10

[1]William S. Plumer, *Commentary on Romans*. (New York, 1870; reprinted in Grand Rapids: Kregal, 1993) 196.

[2]Ernst Kaseman, *Commentary on Romans* (Grand Rapids: Eerdmans, reprinted 1990) 134.

[3]Kaseman, 136.

Chapter 12

[1]R.C.H. Lenski, *The Interpretation of St Paul's Epistle to the Romans* (Minneapolis, n.d.) 751, 752.

[2]Leon Morris, *Quoted in the Epistle to the Romans* (Grand Rapids: Eerdmans, 1998) 246-247.

[3]James D.G. Dunn, *Word Biblical Commentary*, vols. 38A and 38B (Dallas:Word, 1988) 317.

[4]William S. Plumer, *Commentary on Romans*. (New York, 1870; reprinted in Grand Rapids: Kregal, 1993) 287.

Chapter 13

[1]Leon Morris, *Quoted in the Epistle to the Romans* (Grand Rapids: Eerdmans, 1998) 261.

[2]William S. Plumer, *Commentary on Romans*. (New York, 1870; reprinted in Grand Rapids: Kregal, 1993) 293.

[3]Morris, 304.

[4]Ernst Kaseman, *Commentary on Romans* (Grand Rapids: Eerdmans, reprinted 1990) 184.

Chapter 14

[1]William Barclay, *The Letter to the Romans* (Philadelphia: Westminster, 1957) 94.

[2]R.C.H. Lenski, *The Interpretation of St Paul's Epistle to the Romans* (Minneapolis, n.d.) 447.

[3]Leon Morris, *Quoted in the Epistle to the Romans* (Grand Rapids: Eerdmans, 1998) 270.

[4]William S. Plumer, *Commentary on Romans*. (New York, 1870; reprinted in Grand Rapids: Kregal, 1993) 315.

Chapter 17

[1]James D.G. Dunn, *Word Biblical Commentary*, vols. 38A and 38B (Dallas:Word, 1988) 454.

[2]Dunn, 470.

[3]Dunn, 471.

[4]Mattie Joseph Thaddeus Stepanek, *Heartsongs*, VSP Books/Hyperion, New York, 2001, p. 23. Reprinted with permission.

Chapter 18

[1]Leon Morris, *Quoted in the Epistle to the Romans* (Grand Rapids: Eerdmans, 1998) 331.

[2]James D.G. Dunn, *Word Biblical Commentary*, vols. 38A and 38B (Dallas:Word, 1988) 481.

Chapter 19

[1]Used with permission from Dr. Tom Wymore.

[2]Ernst Kaseman, *Commentary on Romans* (Grand Rapids: Eerdmans, reprinted 1990) 258.

[3]James D.G. Dunn, *Word Biblical Commentary*, vols. 38A and 38B (Dallas:Word, 1988) 562.

[4]F.F. Bruce, *The Letter of Paul to the Romans* (Grand Rapids: Eerdmans, reprinted 1987) 190.

[5]Haldane, on Romans 9:19

Chapter 21

[1]Charles R. Eerdmans, *The Epistle of Paul to the Romans* (Philadelphia: Westminister, 1929) 114.

[2]C.K. Barrett, *The Epistle to the Romans* (New York: Harper and Row, 1957) 218.

[3]Hodge, commenting on Romans 11.

[4]James D.G. Dunn, *Word Biblical Commentary*, vols. 38A and 38B (Dallas:Word, 1988) 681.

Chapter 22

[1]Sam Shoemaker, quoted in Hughes, 214.

[2]James D.G. Dunn, *Word Biblical Commentary*, vols. 38A and 38B (Dallas:Word, 1988) 711.

Chapter 23

[1]Emerton, quoted in Hill class notes on Romans 9—16.

[2]Leon Morris, *Quoted in the Epistle to the Romans* (Grand Rapids: Eerdmans, 1998) 453.

[3]Leon Morris, *Quoted in the Epistle to the Romans* (Grand Rapids: Eerdmans, 1998) 453.

Chapter 24

[1]James D.G. Dunn, *Word Biblical Commentary*, vols. 38A and 38B (Dallas:Word, 1988) 765.

[2]Leon Morris, *Quoted in the Epistle to the Romans* (Grand Rapids: Eerdmans, 1998) 467-8.

[3]Morris, 472.

Chapter 25

[1]W.H. Griffith Thomas, *St. Paul's Epistle to the Romans* (Grand Rapids: Kregal, 1996) 371.

[2]James D.G. Dunn, *Word Biblical Commentary*, vols. 38A and 38B (Dallas:Word, 1988) 806.

[3]Thomas, 370.

[4]William Barclay, *The Letter to the Romans* (Philadelphia: Westminster, 1957) 193.

[5]F.F. Bruce, *The Letter of Paul to the Romans* (Grand Rapids: Eerdmans, reprinted 1987) 231.

[6]Dunn, 831.

[7]Barclay, 197.

[8]Bruce, 241.

[9]Bruce, 241.

Chapter 26

[1]Leon Morris, *Quoted in the Epistle to the Romans* (Grand Rapids: Eerdmans, 1998) 505.

[2]Gordon D. Fee, *God's Empowering Presence* (Peabody, MA: Hendrickson, 1994) 622.

[3]Fee, 622, 623.

Chapter 27

[1]Gordon D. Fee, *God's Empowering Presence* (Peabody, MA: Hendrickson, 1994) 626, 627.

[2]James D.G. Dunn, *Word Biblical Commentary*, vols. 38A and 38B (Dallas:Word, 1988) 864.

[3]Charles Hodge, *Commentary on the Epistle to the Romans* (Philadelphia, 1864; reprinted in Grand Rapids: Eerdmans, 1951) 441.

[4]Dunn, 875.

[5]William R. Newell, *Romans—Verse by Verse* (Chicago: Moody, 1938) 545.

Chapter 28

[1] James D.G. Dunn, *Word Biblical Commentary*, vols. 38A and 38B (Dallas:Word, 1988) 894.

[2]Leon Morris, *Quoted in the Epistle to the Romans* (Grand Rapids: Eerdmans, 1998) 534.

[3] Morris, 534.

[4] Morris, 536.

[5] Dunn, 899.

Chapter 29

[1]Charles Hodge, *Commentary on the Epistle to the Romans* (Philadelphia, 1864; reprinted in Grand Rapids: Eerdmans, 1951) 451.

[2]William R. Newell, *Romans—Verse by Verse* (Chicago: Moody, 1938) 565-566.